The Rise and Fall of State Socialism

The Rise and Fall of State Socialism

Industrial Society and the Socialist State

David Lane

Polity Press

First published in 1996 by Polity Press in association with Blackwell Publishers Ltd.

2 4 6 8 10 9 7 5 3 1

Editorial office:
Polity Press
65 Bridge Street
Cambridge CB2 1UR, UK

Marketing and production:
Blackwell Publishers Ltd
108 Cowley Road
Oxford OX4 1JF, UK

Blackwell Publishers Inc.
238 Main Street
Cambridge, MA 02142, USA

HX
40
.L248
1996

ISBN 0-7456-0742-X
ISBN 0-7456-0743-8 (pbk)

A CIP catalogue record for this book is available from the British Library and the Library of Congress.

Typeset in 11 on 12 pt Bembo
by Best-set Typesetter Ltd., Hong Kong
Printed and bound in Great Britain by Hartnolls Limited, Bodmin, Cornwall

This book is printed on acid-free paper.

Contents

Maps, Figures, Tables and Illustrative Boxes

Maps

Figures

Tables

Illustrative boxes

Acknowledgements

I am indebted to Joe Berliner, Anthony Giddens, John Thompson and an anonymous reviewer for comments which have greatly improved this book.

David Lane
Cambridge, November 1995

1

Introduction

The October Revolution of 1917 gave rise to a model of social, political and economic organization in the form of Soviet Russia which was borrowed extensively by a wide range of self-styled 'communist countries' ranging from China to Cuba. The Soviet order provided a challenge to capitalism: in October 1961, Nikita Khrushchev, head of the Communist Party of the Soviet Union, claimed that in conditions of 'the crisis of world capitalism' the period of 'full-scale communist construction' had begun. By 1980, self-defined Marxist-Leninist states accounted for a third of the world's population and claimed 40 per cent of its industrial production. In Russia, Mongolia, China, Cuba, Yugoslavia, Albania, Vietnam, Laos and Kampuchea the communists had fought their way to power and had defended it at great cost: in the USSR alone, over 20 million people perished following the German invasion in the Second World War. State socialism appeared a solid, well-founded system, it was a beacon to many radicals in the industrialized countries and it gave hope to the oppressed in the Third World.

In the West, the claims of such communists were opposed. Rather than achieving equality and liberation, they were declared to have created a tyranny. In defence of private property, the market in economy and polity and individual freedom, the West pursued Cold War. The two superpowers, the USA and USSR, and their respective military blocs, NATO and the Warsaw Pact, stood in principled confrontation for over 45 years. In June 1981, Ronald Reagan, President of the United States of America, in a speech to the British Parliament, called for a 'crusade for freedom' against the communists, whose leaders he berated as 'the focus of evil in the modern world'. This signalled a move from 'containment' of communism to a more aggressive policy. As Richard Pipes put it, the choice was 'Reform or go to war.'[1]

In February 1986 Gorbachev launched his programme, perestroika, for the reform. Its consequences were catastrophic for the communist system.

With breathtaking speed, by the end of 1989, a major shift in political power had taken place in Eastern Europe. Following the institution of free competitive elections, an anti-communist president was installed in Poland and non-communist governments came to power in the East European countries. The Berlin Wall, a symbol of a divided Europe, was destroyed and the German Democratic Republic was absorbed into the Federal Republic. In December 1989, at the Malta summit, Gorbachev informed the American President George Bush, 'We don't consider you an enemy any more.' By December 1991 the world's first communist state, the USSR, was dismembered into 15 sovereign states: the Communist Party was declared to be illegal and its property sequestrated. The critical mass of the communist world evaporated: the former European communist countries moved to adopt market economies and they aspired to, and are attempting to create, the forms and processes of the capitalist world. In 1996, in China, Vietnam, Cuba and North Korea the communists rule but, particularly in the first two, marketization and creeping capitalism erode and undermine the traditional communist system.

These events have led to a major reappraisal of the possibility of socialism as a systemic alternative to capitalism and of the feasibility of revolution as a strategy of change. Whereas at the beginning of the twentieth century the sociological and political interpretation of socialist revolutionary practice was optimistic – at least from supporters on the left – at its end, pessimism is absolute. Some have cast doubt on whether the events of October did constitute a revolution and others have denied its socialist character. The very nature of the socialist project is clouded in doubt. In the late twentieth century, moreover, the history of the communist revolution has been shrouded in uncertainty, scepticism and rejection. The costs of revolution have been evaluated in terms of Stalinist oppression and political coercion, the arbitrary rule of the Cultural Revolution in China and political corruption. In Eastern Europe popular discontent was widespread as internal economic growth declined and the large 'socialist intelligentsia' sought greater independence. Socialism as a creed, as an aspiration, as well as a system of political rule – an alternative to capitalism – has been in retreat. How its decline may be reversed, whether it may be revived and renewed as we enter the twenty-first century, is not the primary concern of this book.

Revolution and Socialism

At the outset it may be useful to define what one means by revolution in general and socialist revolution in particular. Socialist revolutions, following that of the Russian October Revolution, are characterized as mass revolutions. By definition, such revolutions have a high mass participation, they have a long duration involving fundamental changes in the structure of political authority and the social system, and they involve mass violence.[2]

Modern mass revolution is a social, political and economic process which Theda Skocpol has defined as follows:

> Changes in social systems of societies give rise to grievances, social disorientation, or new class or group interests and potentials for collective mobilization. Then there develops a purposive, mass-based movement – coalescing with the aid of ideology and organization – that consciously undertakes to overthrow the existing government and perhaps the entire social order. Finally, the revolutionary movement fights it out with the authorities or dominant class and, if it wins, undertakes to establish its own authority and program.[3]

This definition, however, falls short of one other vital component of revolution: the major social, political and economic changes which follow after the insurgents have taken power.[4] The analysis of revolution has concentrated on two major areas. First, the dynamics of the political capture of power: study of the events immediately preceding the uprising, the actual process of political insurrection and the ideology and organization of the rebels. Second, research has sought to uncover the underlying conditions and motive forces which explain the success of the insurgents' political activity and the failure of the incumbents in power. Also, study has examined the other side of the coin: factors which promote political stability and prevent successful insurgency. It is a less developed area of study with which this book is concerned: the happenings which follow the seizure of political power – the extent to which the revolutionaries' social, political and economic policies have been put into effect, which is here considered as part of the revolutionary process.

It is precisely the aftermath of the October Revolution – with respect to the countries that set out with the goal of creating a communist society and have since failed – which is now of great importance. The character of these societies is not determined by the intentions or theories of the insurgents who led them but by their accomplishments. To what extent did they succeed in building socialism, or have we really witnessed an alternative form of industrialization? If the former, then the collapse of the state socialist regimes at the end of the 1980s may modify significantly our view of revolution. If they indeed were a new socialist order, then mass revolutions may be reversed. Was their fall a consequence of inherent weaknesses or was it contingent on external factors? An important implication is that if their collapse was predicated on popular rejection, then it follows that people who have experienced 'socialism' did not want it. This in turn poses the question as to whether their return (or aspiration to return) to some form of capitalism signals the 'end of history' – in the sense that the liberal-democratic capitalist societies of the West represent the ideal of human aspiration.

The objective of this book is to set in perspective the socialist project which began with the Russian Revolution of October 1917 and culminated with the dissolution of the USSR in December 1991. This quest is not conceived in terms simply of the history of the Soviet Union – though the USSR plays the major role in this book because the history of state socialism was dependent on it. It takes into account the expansion of communism to Eastern Europe after the Second World War and the rise of communism in the Third World – in China and Cuba. Finally, we explore the causes for the decline from the 1960s and the final collapse of European state socialism in 1989–91. I distinguish between four phases in the evolution of communist states: the seizure of power; control and development; reform; and finally collapse and transition to post-communist capitalism. The book is not concerned with the post-communist period.

State Socialism

The nature of the socialist project itself is the concern of the next chapter, where different concepts of socialism (social-democratic and Marxist) are discussed and Lenin's theory of revolution is outlined. That chapter provides an introduction to the various dimensions of the socialist and social-democratic movement. It is not claimed that this is a comprehensive history of socialism in all its variations and movements. 'Socialism' is an ambiguous term. In its most general sense it refers to an array of ideas and policies, the most important of which are equality, a positive role of government as a distributive agency (particularly in the provision of welfare) and the absence of political domination over the individual; public or social ownership is usually (not always) considered to be a necessary condition to achieve the socialist objective. Socialism, in a Marxist sense, is the first stage of communist society. The latter is a classless society, based on social harmony, in which the state has withered away and people receive 'according to their need'. Socialism emanates out of capitalism through the struggle of the ascendant class, the proletariat, over the ruling capitalist class; it is a transitory stage, characterized by the domination of public ownership of the means of production, by the hegemony of a workers' state in which people receive income according to their work – there is no rent or interest.

The main focus in this book is to discuss the features of 'state socialism'. I consider how Marxism-Leninism became a revolutionary strategy legitimating communist revolution in backward countries. Leninism is regarded as a synthesis of voluntaristic leadership and the uneven development of capitalism. What then is state socialism? It is a society distinguished by a state-owned, more or less centrally administered economy, controlled by a dominant communist party which seeks, on the basis of Marxism-Leninism and through the agency of the state, to mobilize the population to reach a classless society. State socialism then is an important component of the socialist movement and tradition. As a political movement, it is contended, state socialism occupies the space between the beginning of capitalism and its mature form. In the absence of a successful proletarian uprising in the West – a major legitimating factor for the Bolshevik insurrection – state socialist societies insulated themselves from the world capitalist system and pursued fairly successfully a policy of modernization and industrial development. In following chapters, I consider different phases in the evolution of communist states.[5]

In chapters 3 to 5, brief descriptions are made of the experience of various countries in different phases of their development. A select number of countries is considered in a holistic way to show the interaction of cultural, political and institutional factors. All the societies experienced, in different ways, similar processes: state political and economic control, industrialization and development. Each study considers how Almond and Powell's 'challenges of modernization' (identity, legitimacy, penetration, participation and distribution)[6] were fulfilled or failed.

In chapter 3, I outline the consequences of the seizure of power in Russia. Revolution was followed by civil war and terror, then by the mobilization of the population to build an industrial society which led to economic growth, a full-employment economy and relatively low income differentials in the context of comprehensive state control. The state itself assumed a forceful directing role. Coercion was a consequence, it is contended, of the continuation of internal war, of the traditional lack of control over Russian rulers and of the external threat. State socialism arose as an answer to Russian conditions and provided a form of industrialism which was an alternative to capitalism and concurrently a counterculture to it. Its distinctive features included public/state ownership rather than private, an ideological emphasis on equality rather than freedom, an economy organized on a plan, control and direction from the centre rather than through a market, and a collectivist and public form of personal integration rather than an individualist one. It is maintained that Marxism-Leninism gave rise to an 'ethic of communism' similar in character to Weber's protestant ethic of capitalism. State socialism, as it evolved between the two world wars, was a coherent alternative to the capitalist form of industrialization. In Almond's terms, Soviet socialism was a successful strategy of modernization.

Chapter 4 considers the spread of state socialism into Poland, China and Cuba. In Poland, communism was compromised from the very beginning by its association with the USSR, the strong opposition of the traditional intelligentsia and the Catholic Church; consequently the communists were unable to 'penetrate society'. The position of the communist rulers was exacerbated by problems of economic management which led to a political legitimacy crisis. Whereas in Poland, communism was instigated from outside, under the influence of the Red Army, in China the communists had fought a protracted civil war in which they made a national as well as a social revolution. They secured a base among the peasants and established a popular political identity. The leadership of Mao anticipated the degeneration of communist political leadership and provided a leftist critique of Soviet communism culminating in the Great Cultural Revolution. Policy in China also had the goal of achieving modernity. Revolution was characterized not only by the rhetoric of idealism and equalitarianism but also by corruption and, during the Great Leap Forward, by famine. In both Poland and China, nationalism provided a focus of identity, but in different ways: in the former it was an alternative to communism which was associated with a traditionally imperialist Russia, whereas in the latter a national liberation movement was concurrently a communist revolutionary movement. In Cuba, Castro led a national liberation movement which, in a Marxist sense, was originally bourgeois in orientation. This was gradually transformed into a Marxist-Leninist one. The Communist Party had not been at the fore of political activity, whereas the charismatic leadership of Castro and the army have played important roles. External forces, particularly hostility to (and by) the United States government precipitated Cuba into the communist bloc.

Until the collapse of Poland, in all three countries there had been little movement towards greater public political participation: power was kept at the top. In all three, national identity, in different ways, was an important integrating force and source of solidarity. Distribution and varying degrees of legitimacy were secured by economic growth. In all three, negative features of state socialism appeared: disproportion between the aspirations of many groups and their fulfilment, deficiencies in the quality of participation available to the new middle classes, decline in the rate of economic growth leading to shortages of commodities – in general the claims of ideology were not being met by the outputs of the communist governments. These inadequacies of state socialism were not generated from outside but were an integral part of the system itself, and they promoted movements for political and economic reform.

Reform and the subsequent denouement of socialism is considered from four perspectives, each covered by a single chapter: first, in terms of attempts to improve the economy within the framework of state socialism; second, in terms of the chronology and precipitants of regime collapse; third, from the point of view of metatheories of state socialism which seek to explain what holds the regime together and, by the same token, what pulls it apart; and finally, I suggest a systemic approach to integration and division.

In chapter 5, I consider movements for reform and policies for the introduction of the market. I outline attempts to adapt the model of state socialism as it had been set up in the USSR under Stalin; here are examined the cases of Yugoslavia, Czechoslovakia, China and finally the USSR itself under Gorbachev. An assumption of market socialism is that a sufficient condition of a socialist society is public ownership of productive assets; in such a context, it is contended, markets may function without the negative consequences found under capitalism. This idea was adapted in different ways by the state socialist regimes.

The first example is the case of Yugoslavia which, after the Second World War, advocated decentralization of administration, elements of a market economy, non-alignment in foreign affairs, and a policy of workers' control. These policies legitimated the regime following exclusion from the Cominform.[7] They also provided the basis for the revival of ethno-national politics which later became a form of internal anticommunism. Linkages with the world economy, it is argued, weakened the state sector in its redistributive objectives. Czechoslovakia is the second case, and here reforms went much further in 1968 than in any other country. The conception of 'market socialism' advocated by the reform leadership entailed the move to the market in economic policy, political pluralism in the polity and an effective 'move to the West' in international affairs. The reform failed for political reasons – the leadership of other East European state socialist societies would not let it happen and they invaded and occupied the country. The third model is China. There economic reform entailed the introduction of markets and a considerable opening up of the country to the world economy without any significant reform of the political system. This has undoubtedly been a great success economically, and economic growth has cushioned the government from criticism. A relatively small intelligentsia and urban business class have given the reform movement a narrow political base. Furthermore, the political elites in China have not undermined their own position by attributing their past mistakes to the Communist Party and the institutions of communist power (as was the case in the condemnation of 'Stalinism' in the USSR), and the revolutionary cohort of leaders remains in control. However, I contend that the growth of the market undermines the system of state socialism: it weakens the distributive role of the state and strengthens the position of the ascendant acquisitive class.

Fourthly, in the USSR, the decline in economic growth and productivity under Brezhnev led to proposals to reform the 'economic mechanism', but they were neither radical – nor implemented. Under Gorbachev, a comprehensive reform policy was introduced under perestroika. Its objective was to bring the socialist countries back into the world economic and political arena. In order to achieve economic reform, Gorbachev pursued concurrently a radical political reform: this undermined the legitimating ideology of Marxism-Leninism, the hegemony of the Communist Party and the system of central planning. He shifted the centre of political power to the Soviets (parliaments) in the republics; he legitimated an extension of private property and moved gradually to advocate market forces. In the terminal period of the USSR, Gorbachev switched to a radical conception of market socialism: he introduced the market and destroyed the political framework of planning and party control which maintained the state socialist infrastructure. His economic reforms failed – output declined, strikes and foreign debt increased – and this amplified the voices for change. The relative decline in productivity impacted on distribution and in turn weakened legitimacy. The attempt to find a 'Third Way' between capitalism and state socialism had failed. It is contended that the forces generated by a market economy, both internally and externally, undermined the institutions and values established to maintain a socialist state.

The Fall

In part II, we appraise the disintegration of state socialism and the period of transition. A chronology of the precipitants and sequence of collapse in Eastern Europe and the USSR is outlined in chapter 6. While communism collapsed first in Eastern Europe, the policy of perestroika in the USSR was crucial to the fates of these states: *glasnost*, democratization, pluralism – all had implications abroad. Notably, governing communist parties had to rule by consent. Perestroika, therefore, reduced the costs to insurgents of internal dissent, and consequently the communists were defeated in open political competition by nationalist and anti-communist forces. In the USSR, with the failure of perestroika, anti-communist movements assumed a national and regional character. Decisive counter-elites, encouraged by the success of the Eastern European states, established their own power and the USSR collapsed in December 1991. In all cases, when confronted with insurgent opposition, the incumbent elites abdicated.

We then turn to the consider the dynamics of state socialism. In chapter 7, theories of its structure and process are considered: here we go back to the historical experience of state socialism to examine and criticize theories of totalitarianism, critical Marxism and industrial society from the standpoint of its collapse. Totalitarianism emphasizes total control by the state and exploitation of the masses. While recent writers acknowledge the decline of terror and the weakening of ideological indoctrination, theorists of this sort cannot handle the rise of internal political division, the destabilizing effect of dissent and the abdication of political power by the ruling elite. Critical Marxist theories point to the role of global capitalism with which the 'state capitalist' countries had to compete, the instability of the ruling political class, which had no legitimate rights over property, and the veto power of the working class, which minimized the extraction of surplus. The fall of communism, it is contended by such theorists, is a consequence of a faction of the ruling class seeking to legitimate capitalist power through privatization. Writers on industrial society also have stressed the international dimensions of the industrializing process. From this viewpoint, the political order of state socialism was not qualitatively different from Western capitalism: both systems shared similar patterns of inequality and stratification, domination and exploitation. However, the fusion of polity and economy, a distinguishing feature of state socialism, linked stress in the economy to the polity. While these theoretical approaches pointed to latent insufficiencies, none can explain how, or when, state socialism would collapse. In the mid-1980s the system appeared to be firmly set as an alternative form of social organization to capitalism; there was no reason to suppose that internal reform would not be able to ameliorate systemic incompatibilities and it was generally agreed that political control was powerful enough to maintain cohesion.

In chapter 8, a multicausal systemic analysis is made of the fall of state socialism. Revolution occurs when there is a combination of a breakdown in the functioning of key processes of society and the appearance of potential insurgents with a collective vision of an alternative regime; incumbent elites also lose their nerve to rule. Five major crises are identified: in the economy, deficiencies in resource management; in society, the decay of sentiments of loyalty and solidarity; in the political system, a negative balance between political support and opposition; in the sphere of values, a lack of legitimacy; and, finally, incompatibilities in relations with actors in the external environment. I contend that in the process of modernization, state socialist societies move from the fusion of politics and economics to a more pluralist structure. Long-term maturation of the social structure and the growth of an educated professional class with a more 'market' orientation gave rise to a pattern of demands which the traditional polity was not designed to meet: there was a latent weakening of the loyalty/solidarity support system. This was exacerbated by inadequate economic growth and falling productivity. With the development of the productive forces, the social structure was shaped by an educated, urban middle class with greater levels of expectations. The political support system of the bureaucratic class, based on the working class, became a diminishing resource. The new professional classes had not only a demographic density but also a moral one.

In rejecting Marxist class approaches, outlined in chapter 7, I suggest that two competing forms of class system coexisted under state socialism: one was linked to the possession of intellectual assets and the other to the administrative system of political controls, the *nomenklatura*. The former, defined as an acquisition class, played a. major role in the collapse of state socialism. This class was often legitimated on a national basis, which gave the insurgents a political identity. The attempt by the reform leadership to create a new form of identity, through widening political participation, undermined the party's penetration of society and had profoundly destabilizing effects. Gorbachev's political reforms exacerbated not only the system of economic management but seriously weakened the legitimacy of the hitherto dominant ideology of Marxism-Leninism and the Communist Party. The reforms 'from the top', from the Gorbachev political leadership, amplified by the critique of the 'reform intelligentsia', undermined the confidence of the political class. The inadequacies of the bureaucratic system, its moral degeneration, led to public lack of confidence. The communists were voted out of power.

These structural features are set in a global context: exclusion from the world economy and the costs of Cold War were a price the political leadership was no longer prepared to pay. However, the core Western powers were able to dictate economically and politically the terms on which the communist societies could join the world community. A policy of entente with the West led to major changes in relations with Eastern Europe, involving greater independence there. Repercussions followed in the USSR. Latent insurgents had more potentially to gain than they had potentially to lose and they were backed by powerful Western states intent on undermining the communist order. I contend that in the absence of an indigenous bourgeois class, a motivating factor in the evolution of Western parliamentary regimes, its role was taken by external Western interests. The backing of the metropolitan capitalist countries for radical reform was crucial. The reformers under Gorbachev were dependent for support on external powers intent on bringing down the political order of state socialism. The interaction of these systemic and conjunctural factors led to the fall.

In the final chapter, the deconstruction of state socialism is assessed and its successes and failures appraised. It is claimed that while Marxism retains vitality, Bolshevism succeeded only as a mobilizing strategy. The Bolsheviks secured the adoption of some socialist values – they destroyed the power of private capital, they showed that advanced societies could be organized without an economic market, and state socialism provided comprehensive welfare outputs. But the system failed to sustain itself as a socialist enterprise and the lack of public confidence, shown by adverse electoral fortunes in 1989 to 1991, was a severe setback to the socialist project. I argue, nevertheless, that the universalistic goals of socialism are not invalidated by the collapse of state socialism.

Part I

The World of the Comrades

2

The Socialist Project

The 'socialist project', widely conceived, has been one of the major movements and aspirations of the late nineteenth and twentieth centuries. It is also an ambiguous term when analysed in a comparative and historical perspective. It encompasses a wide range of movements, ideologies, aspirations and political practices. One might distinguish between three different usages of the terms 'socialism' and the 'socialist project': first, as a value and belief system, a set of ideological or theoretical suppositions concerning social change and a future type of society, as a counterculture to capitalism; second, as a political movement or movements; third, as a post-revolutionary phenomenon, a systemic social, political and economic system under Marxist-Leninist governments – which is the topic of this book.[1]

Like the social sciences themselves, many of the assumptions of the socialist movement may be seen as expressions of the Enlightenment. This was a period in the eighteenth century when traditional authority was questioned, when it was thought that prejudice, custom and habit created conditions for the enslavement of human beings. Reason was claimed to be a major guiding principle for human action. Its application to political and economic life, it was believed, would liberate human beings from the tyranny of religion, superstition and ignorance. A critical assumption made was that people could shape a world after their own image.

This was a view held not just by socialists but by progressive liberal thinkers. Yet the aspirations of the emerging social sciences and socialism differed considerably. The social sciences, particularly economics and later sociology, sought to explain and devise methods for imposing order on the emerging forms of capitalism, industrialism, urbanism and the market. The dominant trends in the emerging social sciences accepted the boundaries of bourgeois capitalist society, with its insistence on individualism, liberty, representative democracy, the sanctity of private property, the competitiveness of the market and the impersonal forces or 'invisible hand', as Adam Smith put it, that guided it. Auguste Comte, one of the founding fathers of sociology, sought to construct a theory of urban-industrial society and to initiate scientifically determined reforms to consolidate the processes set in train by the French Revolution. An assumption such thinkers made was that reason should guide human affairs through democratic procedures, governed by altruistic argument through which people would come to a consensus about the way society should be governed.

Socialists have also accepted many of the goals of the Enlightenment. They believe in reason, in human control of societal development. They have always been critical, however, of liberal democracy, which they have considered to be the expression of bourgeois ways of thinking and doing, and as incapable of leading to human liberation. Socialism, in its various viewpoints, arose in conjunction with liberal-democratic tendencies striving for democratic rights such as freedom of association and speech, but it expressed a protest, as well as an ideology, which sought to reform or transcend bourgeois society. Engels defined 'modern socialism' as a 'direct product' of class antagonisms between 'proprietors and non-proprietors' and of the 'anarchy existing in production' under competitive capitalism.[2] This definition encapsulates the duality in the socialist project: on the one hand, the irreconcilable contradictions of classes and, on the other, the chaos, waste, irrationality and inequality generated by capitalism.

Here it is important to distinguish between a 'hard' and a 'soft' version of socialism. The first version opposes individualism, the market and competition and, in contrast, advocates community and fraternity, equality, and a democracy grounded on public and social ownership giving rise to a classless society. Socialism is a way of life informed by rationality, and society is based on planning and collective action. Even within the paradigm of 'hard' socialism, however, the emphasis and balance between these ideological axes have varied considerably between different socialist thinkers and movements. A key value is to deny the right to private property as repudiating humankind's essential sociability. Self-interest and competition, it is further asserted, are alien to progress: they divide human beings and do not lead to the efficient use of resources. Property linked to the market and competition is the essence of exploitation and conflict and the basis of a class society. Socialists emphasize cooperation and democratic control through which equality or equalitarianism may be achieved. While differing over means, on one thing such socialists are agreed: only under 'socialism' can the aspiration for the 'good society' be achieved. Capitalism cannot be reformed; it has to be transcended.

The socialist movement, at least as it evolved in the nineteenth and early twentieth centuries, had the character of a counterculture standing in opposition to the major forms of power and privilege of capitalist industrial society. Socialists were 'comrades' in a struggle against the ruling class and oppression.

The second or 'soft' version of socialism (often called social democracy)[3] is fuelled by two major critiques of bourgeois society: first, a protest against the injustice, inequality and poverty which exist in a world of political domination, social privilege and great wealth; second an objection to the inefficiency, destructiveness, waste and incompetence generated by capitalism. This outlook accepts the parameters of capitalist society – parliamentary democracy, private ownership – and seeks amelioration through reform. In a nutshell, this movement strives to redress the uncertainty and the distributive and relational inequality of capitalism by democratic reforms.

The relative appeal of these critiques defines the political strategy of different groups in the socialist movement, differing according to whether socialism is considered primarily as a revolutionary movement transcending capitalism and bringing about a new social order (such as in the various movements for revolutionary communism, like Marxism-Leninism) or as a political movement for reform within capitalism, ensuring greater efficiency and equality (such as in the traditional form of social democracy embodied in the British Labour Party).

Socialist Movements

What gives socialism as a doctrine and as a political movement its heterogeneity is the diverse range of its values and the means advocated to achieve them. In the twentieth century and on a world scale, three major political groupings may be distinguished, each claiming to be 'socialist': Marxism-Leninism ('hard' socialism); reformism (social democracy – 'soft' socialism); and populist socialism (a mixture of both).

Socialism has developed not only as a critique of capitalism but also of urban industrial society. The socialist ideal was born in Europe in countries in transition from traditional societies to modern ones. In this sense, aspects of socialism were focused backwards on what was thought to have been a communal, cooperative and fraternal way of life which had to be recreated. Populist (or Narodnik) socialism, which arose in late nineteenth-century Russia, is a prime example of the third tendency. It was a movement essentially in opposition to industrialization, urbanism and individualism, and sought to reestablish roots in a traditional agrarian collectivist society. The Narodniks emphasized the unity of the people, or the *narod*. Unlike Marxism and Leninism, which are focused on teleological goals (that is, some state of perfection in the future), it was reactionary, often espousing a supposed past ideal state in which the peasant had an exemplary relationship with nature. Populists envisaged the creation of a rural type of civilization based on peasant communes, either with communal or with individual ownership of the land. They were also anti-industrial, and visualized the development of small-scale handicrafts. Since the modernizing developments they opposed came from the West, the Narodniks were often anti-Western and sought solutions to social and political problems from their own heritage. Such movements were often revolutionary in character and hence they adopted, in the late nineteenth century, the name 'socialist revolutionary'. Their adherents believed that modern forms of oppression (of which capitalism is only one) can only be transcended by a major political upheaval necessitating violence, and assassinations of leading figures (in Russia, the Tsar and leading ministers) were part of their political strategy.[4] Lenin regarded populism as an ideology of the petty producers, especially the peasantry, who were being undermined by capitalism but who could benefit from the dissolution of feudalism – they were revolutionary, but not socialist.[5] In seeking a society based on the village commune, they were also reactionary: in Lenin's view, the liberation of people could only take place through the development of capitalism out of which would come communism.

Socialism as a movement based on reform, on the other hand, rejects insurrectionist approaches. It has two major tendencies – Fabianism and revisionism – which are closely linked as socialist philosophies. The Fabian movement in Britain and its political expression, the Labour Party, were particularly critical of the inefficiency of capitalism epitomized by the absurd waste generated by competition. The Fabians were also opposed to individualism, private ownership of the means of production and the market. They stressed collective ownership and control through the state, organized nationally and locally. State management, through publicly controlled monopolies, on the one hand, and municipal government, on the other, were major tenets of their philosophy. Collective activity was to replace competition, and equality of opportunity was the social objective. Political action was contemplated through reform and the democratic ballot box: it was parliamentary rather than revolutionary in character. As Sidney Webb put it in *Fabian Essays*: 'No philosopher now looks for anything but the gradual evolution of the new order from the old, without break of continuity or abrupt change of the entire social tissue at any point during the process.'[6] This tendency, which has informed the spirit of the British Labour Party, was not exclusively based on the manual working class because, to win in the parliamentary struggle, it had to attract middle-class support. With the development of the Labour Party, the goal of public ownership of the means of production has gradually been eclipsed by policies seeking greater distributive equality through the welfare state and equality of opportunity.[7] However, the belief in public ownership and a collectivist state orientation has many parallels among the 'hard' socialists, discussed below.

Whereas the Fabians, like Anglo-Saxon socialists generally, were not influenced by Marx,[8] even as a reaction to him, this was not the case for Eduard Bernstein and what has been called the revisionist stream of evolutionary socialism.[9] The social-democratic parties of Germany and Austria were Marxist parties and at least until 1914 considered themselves to be revolutionary. However, their leaders increasingly supported democratic forms of change through existing political procedures and institutions, and they concurrently backed piecemeal reforms under capitalism as ends rather than as a means of revolutionary change. Such revisionists stress the extent to which capitalism may improve the condition of the working classes, albeit in conditions of uncertainty and insecurity. Like the Fabians, they believed that bourgeois society was democratic and provided a means for change through parliamentary institutions. Capitalism could be modified and made to benefit all. The parliamentary political struggle comes at the fore of this movement. Critics of this strategy (writers such as Robert Michels) argued that the parties became transformed and lost their socialist vision. Their leaders, it was contended, became dependent on popular votes, bourgeoisified and cut off from their supporters. Hence the social-democratic parties lost their revolutionary edge and became absorbed into bourgeois democratic culture. Marx castigated the 'socialistic bourgeoisie' as seeking 'all the advantages of modern social conditions without the struggles and dangers necessary therefrom. They desire the existing state of society minus its revolutionary and disintegrating elements. They wish for a bourgeoisie without a proletariat.'[10]

These trends – to work within the capitalist system and to reject the class struggle – which were apparent even at the end of the nineteenth century, have accelerated.[11] In Western Europe since the end of the Second World War there has been a significant shift in the centre of gravity of the socialist movement, which has effectively been incorporated into the bourgeois political system. In 1959, at its Bad Godesberg conference, the German Social-Democratic Party accepted a mixed economy and became a people's rather than a working-class party. In Britain the Labour Party's leadership in the mid-1990s has disavowed even the symbolic attachment to public ownership[12] and in practice is a party of piecemeal reform almost indistinguishable from its rivals. Even the French and Italian communist parties from the mid-1970s have distanced themselves from the revolutionary tradition and moved towards social-democratic tactics and policies. Whereas the major social-democratic parties often included a 'hard' socialist bloc, aspiring to some form of public ownership as a principle, by the mid-1990s democratization, a vague commitment to 'social cooperation' and issue politics are the main thrust of social democracy. Social-democratic parties operate not as countercultures, but as subcultures, accepting the major values of capitalism and its democratic forms but seeking changes in priorities. The socialist movement no longer has a collective consciousness linking 'comrades' struggling to build a new Jerusalem – however distant in the past this may have been.

Socialism, as it developed before the Second World War, was a movement linked to a protest against industrialism, urbanism and capitalism. As societies have industrialized and people have adjusted to a 'modern' way of life, its appeal (particularly of the 'hard' variety) has declined. Advanced capitalism has included a gradual extension of citizenship and civil rights to all members of the community through the expansion of the franchise; it also includes more home ownership, greater accessibility of education, the provision of widespread social and health services and the bourgeoisification of a consumer society. The United States never had a significant socialist movement: it also never had a peasant population, nor an autocratic feudal ruling class – it was bourgeois from the start.[13] Its politics have been over issues rather than over class. National and ethnic (and latterly gender) identities have provided a focus for social consciousness not only in relations with other people but also in the assertion of political claims to resources through the state.

The completion of the transition from an agricultural and rural society to an industrial and urban one has been accompanied by a shift in social organization from Gemeinschaft (community) to Gesellschaft (association). This is paralleled politically by a movement from collective politics to a focus on interests. The socialist movement has become transformed into democratic parties made up of a diverse set of disparate interests ranging from traditional, economistic trade unions to ethnic, gender and environmental groups. The motive for political action has moved from class consciousness to demands for justice, equality of opportunity and greater individual identity and dignity. The abolition of private property is disavowed and loses its place even in the rhetoric of socialism. Co-operative undertakings, the welfare state, redistributive policies and municipal ventures become the major quests and strategies of socialist parties. Its one-time critical mass, encapsulated in the 'world of the comrades' in opposition to capitalism, has been displaced by a diverse set of interests lacking a common consciousness, let alone a revolutionary one. Social character is defined not in terms of class relations but in a social identity based on religion, ethnic origin, generational or gender affiliation or sexual orientation and inclination.[14] 'Postmodern' social thought denies that reason leads to human emancipation; rather – in its socialist form – it leads to repressive institutions and to totalitarianism.[15] Socialism is rejected as a flawed project of modernity. As an alternative form of economic, political and social organization to capitalism and its state formation, it has become marginalized and discredited – both intellectually and as a political movement.

This book is not primarily concerned with such developments in the socialist movement under capitalism but has as its subject the rise, consolidation and decline of Marxist-Leninist states. The decline of the socialist project, described above, had an impact on the state socialist societies. Gorbachev, for instance, was advised by Felippe Gonzales, the leader of the revisionist Spanish Socialist Party. Conversely, the denouement of state socialism in the late 1980s was an important contributor to the weakening of the socialist project in the West.

Despite its decline as a mobilizing ideology in industrialized countries, Marxism has remained the dominant theory of critique of capitalism.[16] Leninism commands attention as a novel form of revolutionary strategy and organization on which communist states, at least ostensibly, were modelled. As a backdrop to the discussions which follow, we consider here the ideas associated with Marx and Lenin which shaped state socialism; later in the book we discuss the changes that have taken place in ideology and political practice.

Shaping State Socialism: Marxism

We noted above that socialism developed in response to industrialism, urbanism and capitalism. Marxism above all is a critique of capitalism and a prognosis of its collapse leading through revolution to communism (of which socialism is the first stage).[17] What then is communism? Many Marxists see communism simply as the 'negation of capitalism', and claim that the proletariat would 'remake society' and concurrently 'remake itself'. These assertions are vague and unclear. Marxism may be analysed into three major components: a theory of history, an analysis of capitalism as a mode of production, and a prescription of communism.

For Marxists, capitalism is but one of five modes of production (primitive communism, slave, feudal, capitalist and communist).[18] All modes of production may be analysed in terms of the forces of production, and the relations of production which constitute the 'basis' on which the 'superstructure' is dependent.

The *forces of production* are defined by two criteria: the means of production – the tools and technology characteristic of a mode of production; and the labour process – the way that tools are used in production. In other words, a mode of production is characterized by the kinds of tools which are used and the productive ways that work is organized and controlled using these tools. The *relations of production* are defined by the ownership of the tools and the products of production. The dominant class is always the one that owns the means of production. A *mode of production* then is a distinct ensemble of forces of production and relations of production. Marx summed this up in a memorable sentence in the *Poverty of Philosophy*: 'The hand-mill gives rise to society with a feudal lord, the steam-mill to society with the industrial capitalist.'

The institutions of the superstructure are functionally linked to the basis: for instance, under capitalism a system of education and scientific research, a nuclear family, a market mechanism of exchange of goods and a state apparatus all operate to replicate the class relations of capitalism. The state, as an institution, does not function as a neutral political arbiter between interests and groups; its role is to maintain and to reproduce the domination of the ruling class, who are the owners of the means of production together with other intimately associated strata, such as state officials and members of the judiciary. It secures the legitimacy of private property, and provides an economic and political framework in which capitalism can thrive. Here Marx was influenced by Adam Smith, who recognized that 'civil government, so far as it is instituted for the security of property, is in reality instituted for the defence of the rich against the poor, or of those who have some property against those who have none at all.'[19]

Social classes arise from social relations generated by the labour process and relations to the means of production. Under capitalism, the capitalist owns the means of production and employs labour to produce goods and services for profit, which in turn are utilized for further investment (capital formation) or for income. In essence, the interests of capitalists and employees are antagonistic because of the need of capitalists to make profit, which they can do only by exploiting labour. (Marx believed that rises in productivity were limited.) The ongoing treadmill of competition compels capitalists to invest, and to cut costs by driving down wages while attempting to extract a greater amount of surplus from their employees.

On the basis of the assumptions made above, Marxists argue that social change must be revolutionary. The working class and capitalist class have antagonistic interests and reform is only possible so long as it does not undermine the capitalist system and the interests of its ruling class. As the ruling class is unlikely to relinquish its ownership of property, on which its power and privilege rest, the ascendant class through class struggle must undermine and replace it and establish its own power. Only after the overthrow of the capitalist class can liberation be assured under a new mode of production, communism. The working class then becomes the universal class and thus the socioeconomic basis for contradictions, particularly those expressed in class struggle, disappears. Communism arises as a classless society.

In the view of Marx and Engels, the process of social change is not voluntaristic: the history of humankind is characterized by a progression from a lower, less complex to a more advanced type of society. Marxists share with the intellectuals of the Enlightenment a belief in progress: that with the progression of society from feudalism to capitalism there is amelioration in the human condition. Hence capitalism is progressive because it enhances the productive capacity of people through the accumulation of industrial capital; it liberates the peasant from bondage to the land; it gives rise to parliamentary types of democracy and to the concept of human rights. These developments, it is contended, have been necessary primarily to secure for the bourgeoisie its class rights over feudal class interests. Moreover, when such rights to ownership are challenged, democracy and human rights are exposed as limited to the bourgeoisie.

On a world scale, the evolution of societies, orthodox Marxists assert, must follow the pattern of progression outlined above. Any given country may skip a stage and copy the existing advanced forms of another: hence it is possible for a society at the tribal stage to move directly to capitalism without experiencing the feudal stage – but only if capitalism has already been established elsewhere. Marx and Engels were confident that a revolutionary transformation could come about only when one stage had reached its zenith and the ruling class, by pursuing its class interest, prevented the further development of the productive forces. As Marx asserted in the *Preface to a Contribution to the Critique of Political Economy* (1859), 'No social order ever disappears before all the productive forces for which there is room in it have been developed.' Hence no one country can create communism out of feudalism; communism would develop out of, and supersede, the contradictions of the capitalist mode of production. What then would be the character of the communist mode of production?

While Marx and Engels refused to draw up a blueprint of a communist society, we may make a number of inferences from their work concerning their vision. The communist economy would be characterized by production that was highly capital intensive and by a highly skilled workforce.[20] As Marx put it, in the *Economic and Philosophical Manuscripts* (Third Manuscript), 'Communism [is] the positive abolition of private property, and thus of human self-alienation, and therefore the real reappropriation of human essence by and for man. Communism [is] the complete and conscious return of man, conserving all the riches of

previous development for man as a social, i.e. human being. . . . It is the
genuine solution of the antagonism between man and nature and between
man and man.'[21]

Under communism, the production and distribution of goods would
be rational and would be for 'use' rather than 'exchange', and achieved
through planning. The market, as a mechanism for the realization of
exchange value (that is for profit), would not exist. As Engels expressed
it in 'Socialism: Utopian and Scientific': 'the social anarchy of production
gives place to a social regulation of production upon a definite plan,
according to the needs of the community and of each individual.'[22]
Politically, communism is a classless society – all economically active
persons in the population participate in labour. The state as an instrument
of class rule 'withers away' and is replaced by the administration of things.
Democracy, harmony and cooperation replace conflict and oppression. In
the social sphere, distribution is according to need; the liberation of
dependent strata (for example, women, oppressed nations and ethnic
groups) is assured. Under these conditions, unfettered by the ownership
of the means of production by a ruling class, it was claimed that all people
would secure freedom and human rights.

In the *Critique of the Gotha Programme*, Marx distinguished between a
lower and higher stage of communism. The former is usually described as
socialism, a transitionary stage in which exchange through the medium of
money continues, while in the latter (communism) people give according
to their ability and receive according to their needs. The state also
continues under socialism, not only as an agency of administration but
also to defend the revolutionary gains of the working class.

Dialectics of change

Marx and Engels wrote little on the process of revolutionary transformation. They assumed that the working class would develop revolutionary
consciousness and in the process would be transformed from being a class
'in itself' to one 'for itself'. This lacuna in Marx's writings concerning the
transition from capitalism to communism has given rise to two different
interpretations of historical materialism.

According to the first, primacy in historical evolution is given to the
'forces of production'. Revolution from this viewpoint is a continuous
and spontaneous process of development. In this case, the growth of the
productive forces is assured by the propensity of human beings to be
innovative: mastery of the environment follows from the application of
human intelligence and skills. Rationality prevails in politics. When the

relations of production are perceived as a 'fetter' on the advancement of the productive forces,[23] reason leads to class action to bring about a new mode of production. The process of production is crucial here: the work process is the site where surplus is extracted and class consciousness on the part of the ascendant class (the working class under capitalism) develops. The labour process is the location for the creation of consciousness, which is manifested through labour unions and parties. Thus the assumption here is that a spontaneous coming together of revolutionary forces brings about change. A rational person (or a group of persons acting jointly) perceives the class antagonisms of capitalism, and political action is undertaken to replace the bourgeois order with a communist one.

The problem with this position is that human history has witnessed societies which for centuries have been arrested in their development, and others have regressed. Examples of the former are feudal China and Tsarist Russia, and of the latter, parts of Europe after the Roman Empire. Under conditions of modern capitalism, the work process becomes a site, not of conscious class struggle, but of integration of management and employees. In order to facilitate the competitiveness of any given enterprise, labour and management have had to come to a compromise and learn to work together. While the capitalist class reproduces as a 'class in itself and for itself', the ascendant class does not mature as a class 'for itself'. It does not become the political power necessary to propel the movement from one mode of production to another. Collective revolutionary action is only rational for the potential insurgents if the potential benefits are greater than the potential costs: in practice, the capitalist state and other forces of the ruling class are so strong, and the penalties for defeat so great, that combining to overthrow the system is not a rational choice. If the individual workers only had their 'chains' to lose, then the potential benefits would surely be positive; under advanced capitalism, however, the worker has much to forfeit – job, house and possessions, as well as the possibility for advancement for their offspring. Rather than a logic of collective action stemming from the process of production, rationality for the individual induces either inaction or improvement of existing conditions within the structure of capitalism. This is the rationality of social democracy or the 'weak' form of socialism we described above.

Shaping State Socialism: Lenin and Revolution

This gives rise to the second interpretation of the Marxist theory of the dialectics of change, one giving primacy to the 'relations of production'.

This approach stresses the ways in which domination is maintained by a ruling class over the reproduction of the relations of production and the way in which revolution may be fostered. Revolutionary change, it is asserted, is voluntarist: it requires political organization and leadership of the ascendant class. Without leadership articulating the political interest of the ascendant class, there is no advancement and no progression to a new mode of production. Hence societies may stagnate and be unable to break out of a given mode of production. Marxists adopting this line of strategy claim that a 'technological determinism' characterizes the approach (discussed above) stressing the primacy of the productive forces and the spontaneous evolution of political consciousness. The leadership and organization of insurgent forces, they argue, must play the primary role in the process of revolutionary social change. Lenin and then Mao have been the major theorists of revolutionary agency of the twentieth century. Whether this has been a legitimate extension of Marxism has remained a bone of contention among Marxists. Anti-Leninists have always argued that this strategy was opportunistic and unjustifiable in Marxist terms; it is a point we shall return to later.

Lenin's concern was revolution in Russia. Before him, all Marxists in nineteenth-century Europe regarded Russia as a country emerging from feudalism. Even if contemporary Marxists pay little attention to the progression between modes of production, in the late nineteenth century this was not the case. It was universally believed that Russia could not carry out a socialist revolution until capitalist society had been built. The orthodox view, underpinned by the idea of the development of the productive forces, was that socialist revolution would come in the advanced countries of the West. Lenin and the Bolsheviks (the latter were a faction of the Russian Social-Democratic Labour Party led by Lenin) had a different interpretation, which legitimated a seizure of power by the communists and was later used to declare the Soviet Union to be the world's first socialist country. Lenin added two dimensions to Marxist theory: first, a theory of imperialism, and second, the concept of a vanguard communist party.[24] These concepts explain why in Lenin's view the spontaneity theory of working-class revolt, described above, would not happen and why a party of a 'new type' had to be formed to lead the working class.

Marx and Engels had pointed out that capitalism could not be contained in a few industrial countries; it would spread as a world system of political economy. 'The bourgeoisie, by the rapid improvement of all instruments of production, by the immensely facilitated means of communication, draws all, even the most barbarian, nations into civilization . . . It compels all nations, on pain of extinction, to adopt the bourgeois mode of production; it compels them to introduce what it calls civilization into their midst, i.e., to become bourgeois themselves. In one word, it creates a world after its own image.'[25] By virtue of its need to make surplus product, it has to expand into new markets and thus all countries are drawn into its net. The peripheral countries are exploited by the magnates of capital in the metropolitan ones.[26]

War between countries is an outcome of this economic structure: the foreign policy of nation-states becomes the expression of the interests of their internal bourgeois classes. A repercussion of the supremacy of some countries in the capitalist system is that the working class of the metropolitan countries may become privileged at the expense of the labouring class in the peripheral countries; and here they identify with their own governments in their military contests with foreign adversaries. There is then an economic component to the character of national identity which divides the ascendant class, the working class. This explains the tendency to conformism on the part of the Western working class, which has more to gain from a compromise with their own bourgeoisie than from joining the international proletariat. It also explains the nationalism which characterizes twentieth-century capitalism: it is an ideology legitimating a form of social identity which unites people on the basis of language and history.

Uneven development in Russia and the bourgeois revolution

Lenin, moreover, saw implications of these developments which had not been anticipated by Marx. He pointed to the parallel and uneven development of capitalism.[27] The economic and political contradictions are greatest in societies undergoing capitalist development, for these do not have the stability afforded by the capitalist superstructure. While economic development disrupted the traditional economy and created a working class, the internal bourgeois political formation was weak. Foreign capitalists replaced those of an indigenous kind, and therefore the 'foreign base' of the bourgeoisie was vulnerable. Moreover, Lenin contended, the strata whose role in bourgeois society was to legitimate it ideologically (the 'liberal intelligentsia') had not been nurtured in Russia by capitalism.

The country had no writers legitimating capitalism such as Adam Smith, John Locke or Max Weber, and its intelligentsia was revolutionary and hostile to the autocracy – Pushkin and Dostoevsky had both spent time in captivity under the Tsars and Lenin's own brother was executed for revolutionary activity. Opposition to urbanization and capitalism (identified with 'the West') was strong. A critical mass of the intelligent-sia, it was concluded, was inclined to Narodism (revolutionary populism) and Marxism.

While the internal bourgeoisie was moribund, the working class in nineteenth-century Russia, argued Lenin, was a dynamic force. The number of factory and mining workers had increased from 800,000 in 1861–70 to some 2.5 million in 1913.[28] With the inclusion of workers in service industries, agricultural labourers and those in handicrafts this figure is doubled. Also, the numbers employed in very large factories (of over 500 employees) came to over half of the industrial labour force, compared to only a third in the USA.[29] Lenin, following Trotsky on this point,[30] argued that this facilitated the spread of class organization and the rise of class consciousness of the proletariat.

The dominant political formation of such countries consisted of the traditional political class (the autocracy), which became dependent on foreign capitalists (and metropolitan capitalist states). Western forms of parliamentary democracy, which brought organizations of the working class into bourgeois politics and blunted its class consciousness (particularly in the predator metropolitan countries), had not arisen here. Oppressive regimes coerced the working class: in the absence of parliamentary parties, the workers had no legal institutions to represent their interest; often workers' associations had been set up by the internal security forces. Economic exploitation of the working class was enormous and their political consciousness – at least as far as Lenin and his associates were concerned – was advanced. For Lenin, these circumstances called for a reformulation of the traditional Marxist theory of revolution: first with respect to the bourgeois revolution, and second to the communist.

Lenin argued that the theory of uneven development, briefly outlined above, entailed that under certain conditions of feudalism the bourgeoisie would not carry out its historic role as an ascendant class. Moreover, and perhaps paradoxically, under conditions when the bourgeoisie was weak and the working class was strong, the latter would play a hegemonic part in bringing about the *capitalist* revolution. Capitalism would not occur spontaneously as a consequence of the development of production relations.

In the 1905 Revolution in Russia, Lenin's strategy envisaged that the working class (led by the Bolsheviks) would take the lead in the revolutionary struggle against the feudal autocracy and its dependent strata in the state bureaucracy. In doing so, the proletariat would have to form an alliance with all potential revolutionary groups and classes. In his view, the petty bourgeoisie (lawyers, teachers, parts of the government bureaucracy, liberal writers) and the ascendant capitalist forces in the countryside (the growing class of aspiring smallholder capitalist farmers) supported a bourgeois revolution: but, as they lacked class organization and leadership, they could not make one. Under imperialism, the major capitalist institutions (industry and banking) were either foreign owned or under the control of the Russian state and hence they would not take a revolutionary role either. As the foreign bourgeoisie was under the patronage of the autocracy, it would not be a rational strategy for it to foment revolution. Therefore, it would be the role of the working class, under the leadership of the party, to bring about the bourgeois revolution.

In 1905, moreover, Lenin was adamant that a socialist revolution (in the sense of the working class taking power) could *not* be achieved. In his pamphlet, 'Two Tactics of Social Democracy in the Democratic Revolution', Lenin pointed out that 'only a revolutionary dictatorship relying on the overwhelming majority of the people can be at all durable . . . The proletariat, however, at present constitutes a minority of the population in Russia . . . it would be harmful to it if any illusions were entertained on this score . . . The objective logic of historical development confronts [the masses] at the present time, not with the task of making a socialist revolution, but with the task of making a democratic revolution.'[31]

The impending revolution would be bourgeois, facilitating the development of capitalism and making it 'possible for the bourgeoisie to rule as a class'.[32] The role for the working class was to destroy the autocratic order and secure a firm place in the coming capitalist one. Lenin wanted the working class to have full rights (of speech and association) in the bourgeois republic. In this way it would be in a stronger position to defend its own interests and prepare to launch an attack on capitalism.

The Mensheviks (a faction of the Russian Social-Democratic Labour Party) adopted a more deterministic and traditional interpretation of historical materialism. They stressed the role of the productive forces, believing that until these had reached a high level of capitalist development, and until the working class was a large proportion of the population, the historic mission of socialism could not be achieved. For them the task of social democracy was to disrupt the autocracy by supporting and even inciting revolt, but not to participate in the bourgeois revolution. The main responsibility of the social-democratic party, the agent of socialist revolution, was to prepare for the time when the working class, organized in trade unions, would be a legitimate opposition to capital; then their chance would come. The Mensheviks were very much cast in the mould of the traditional European social-democratic parties, like the German SPD.

Both these positions were challenged in the 1905 Revolution by two other Marxists, Parvus and Trotsky, who coined the theory of 'permanent revolution'. Accepting much of Lenin's argument about the facts of Russian development, they reasoned that, once under way, a bourgeois revolution led by the working class would not stop at the bourgeois stage but would 'grow over' into the socialist stage. This would be a spontaneous development.

> In a country economically backward, the proletariat can take power earlier than in countries where capitalism is advanced . . . The Russian Revolution produces conditions in which power may . . . pass into the hands of the proletariat before the politicians of bourgeois liberalism have had the chance to show their statesmanlike genius to the full.[33]

As Parvus put it in 1904: 'The world process of capitalist development brings about a political upheaval in Russia. In turn this will affect political developments in all capitalist countries . . . The Russian proletariat will assume the role of the vanguard of the social revolution.'[34] Hence they argued that a proletarian dictatorship, supported by the poor peasants, could be set up in a country which was technically just entering the capitalist mode of production. It is important to note here that the revolution was conceived on a world scale. These conclusions constituted a major break in Marxist thinking concerning the progression from capitalism to communism: the communist revolution could begin in a country emerging from feudalism.

Imperialism, the party and communist revolution

Between 1905 and 1917 Lenin's views were to become more radical. Whereas Marx and Engels assumed that communism would arise in the most advanced forms of capitalism, Lenin argued that *revolution* (though not the move to communism) could occur *first* in the countries on the periphery of capitalism. Like Parvus and Trotsky, his contribution to Marxist strategy moved the focus of revolutionary struggle from the industrialized capitalist countries of Western Europe and the USA to Russia, and legitimated revolutions in economically backward countries.

Imperialism sanctioned revolutionary activity in countries that were undergoing development and were subject to capitalist penetration and exploitation. For Lenin, imperialism was the highest stage of capitalism: it was 'that stage of development in which domination of monopoly and finance capital has taken shape; in which the export of capital has acquired pronounced importance; in which the division of the world by international trusts has begun; and in which the partition of all territory of the earth by the greatest capitalist countries has been completed.'[35] It represents a linkage between state formations and the international capitalist class.

In Lenin's view the first strike would take place at the weakest link of the capitalist chain. Marx and Engels in the preface to the 1882 (Russian) edition of the *Communist Manifesto* had mentioned such a possibility. When discussing the Russian *obshchina* (village community), they noted that the Russian revolution could become 'the signal' for the revolution in the West.[36] For Lenin, a revolution in Russia would not stop there; world capitalism would no longer be able to contain itself, as it was dependent for survival on the extraction of surplus product from the dependent countries. When such exploitation of the periphery ceased, the contradictions of capitalism in the advanced countries would intensify and lead to its internal collapse. The system would crash and the Western working class would no longer have any stake in the preservation of capitalism.

The revolution, however, in Lenin's view would not result from the spontaneous activity of the working class in the peripheral countries. Here he differed from Trotsky. He emphasized the importance of political leadership in his pamphlet, 'What is to be Done?', originally published in December 1902. Social-democratic parties in the states of Western Europe were built on a mass trade union membership and sought political power through the ballot box. In Russia, however, right up to February 1917, the bourgeoisie, the working class and the peasantry were effectively excluded from participation in the Tsarist political system. The Duma was a representative rather than an effective legislative body. Under the despotic conditions of autocracy and in the absence of rights to free association and combination (assured in many bourgeois societies by civil rights, particularly the vote), a new form of organization of the working class was required.

A party of 'a new type' was necessary to lead the working class under conditions of Tsarist autocracy. This party, which later became the Communist Party (to distinguish it from reformist social democracy), was the instrument for interpreting and acting on the laws of historical materialism. The party's role was to lead the working class in its revolutionary struggle. In distinction from the reformist social-democratic parties of Germany and England, the Bolsheviks advocated the formation of a party of Marxists intent on transforming capitalism through revolution. The party had to be 'an organization of revolutionaries which must consist first and foremost of people whose profession is that of a revolutionary'.[37] A fundamental objective of the Marxist party was to bring political consciousness to the working class.

It was Lenin's conviction that the working class (particularly in the advanced European countries) would not autonomously develop a socialist consciousness – for the ideological apparatus together with the privileges of metropolitan capitalism would corrupt it. As Lenin put it: 'Class political consciousness can be brought to the workers *only from the outside*. That is, only from outside the economic struggle, from outside the sphere of relations between workers and employees.'[38] 'False consciousness' would lead the working class to accept the amelioration of conditions within capitalism, rather than to adopt a revolutionary stance. Reformist social-democratic parties were part of this 'false consciousness'. Hence, the party epitomized political praxis: it united Marxism as the ideology of the working class with the agency of political struggle.

Lenin reiterated that revolution could not be achieved through piece-meal reformist policies because the interests of bourgeoisie and proletariat were irreconcilable. Force would be necessary initially to achieve power and later to consolidate it. Hence a centralized Marxist political party (known as the Bolsheviks[39] from 1903) was founded under Lenin to lead the working class. Lenin was thereafter subjected to criticism from traditional socialists and Marxist opponents as adventurist, with ideas not in keeping with Marx's view that 'the emancipation of the working class must be the act of the working class itself.'[40]

1917: The Bolshevik Insurrection

Following the February Revolution of 1917 (when the Tsar abdicated and power was effectively shared by the Provisional Government and the Soviets of Workers' and Soldiers' Deputies) Lenin effectively adopted the line taken by Trotsky and Parvus during the 1905 Revolution. The carnage and the dislocation of capitalism caused by the Great War was a major factor, Lenin believed, which had changed the potential for a socialist revolution. In *Letters on Tactics* (1917), he declared: 'The bourgeois revolution [of February] is completed,' and he believed that it could pass rapidly into a socialist one. There would be a 'telescoping' of development: a movement from pre-capitalist to socialist society, with the revolutionary forces led by the working class. Furthermore, a socialist revolution in Russia would disrupt the international order of world capitalism both economically and politically, and would lead to its collapse in the advanced states.

In Lenin's *April Theses* (1917), he made it clear that 'Russia . . . is *passing* from the first stage of the revolution – which, owing to the insufficient class consciousness and organization of the proletariat, placed power in the hands of the bourgeoisie – to its *second* stage, which must place power in the hands of the proletariat and the poorest sections of the peasants.'[41] He went on to advocate:

Not a parliamentary republic . . . but a republic of Soviets of Workers', Agricultural Labourers' and Peasants' Deputies throughout the country, from top to bottom.
Abolition of the police, the army and the bureaucracy.
The salaries of all officials, all of whom are elected and displaceable at any time, not to exceed the average wage of a competent worker. . . .
Confiscation of all landed estates.
Nationalisation of all lands in the country . . .
The immediate amalgamation of all banks in the country into a single national bank, and the institution of control over it by the Soviet of Workers' Deputies. . . .
Change of the Party's name [to the Communist Party].[42]

In April he pronounced: 'Any day may come the crash of European imperialism. The Russian Revolution, which you have carried out, has laid the foundation for it and opened a new epoch. Long live the world-wide socialist revolution!' In the summer of 1917 he declared, 'We stand on the threshold of a world-wide proletarian revolution . . . If we come out now, we shall have on our side all proletarian Europe.'[43] Lenin here, by invoking the potential support of the West (in the form of the proletariat), heightened the potential prospect of success of the insurrection and so strengthened the commitment of his followers to rebel. These then were the assumptions made by Lenin when he returned to Russia from Switzerland in 1917.

Between April and October, the Bolsheviks prepared to seize power. On 25 October 1917[44] the Bolsheviks through the Petrograd Soviet's Military Revolutionary Committee toppled the Provisional Government. They declared a 'Provisional Workers' and Peasants' Government' with Lenin at its head. Subsequently, they consolidated their position and declared the 'dictatorship of the proletariat'. The revolution had the character of a mass revolution. The Tsarist political and economic institutions were destroyed and replaced (at least at the top) by new people and by Bolshevik institutions: the hegemony of the Bolshevik Party, state-owned property, central control of the economy. The nascent formations of bourgeois society (parties and associations) were abolished and replaced by collectivities supporting the new political order. Lenin, however, made it clear that it was 'not our *immediate* task to "introduce" socialism, but only to bring social production and the distribution of products at once under the *control* of the Soviets of Workers' Deputies'.[45] The revolution was to be the prelude to the socialist revolution on a European scale.

Leninism, which provided the theoretical legitimation for Bolshevik-type revolutions, and later for the mobilization policies of state socialism, may be summarized as a synthesis of the two approaches to Marxist revolution defined earlier. First, the development of the productive forces of capitalism on a global basis created the objective conditions for a bourgeois revolution in Russia in the early twentieth century: the forces of production then were ripe for a revolution. Second, in Marxist terms the formal ascendant class, the indigenous bourgeoisie in Russia, was weak. The impetus to revolutionary change fell to the leadership of the working class, which would provide the energy for an uprising. Lenin had devised the strategic weapon of class struggle for the proletariat: the Marxist party 'of a new type'. The political implications of these two propositions led Lenin to two conclusions. Under the conditions of world capitalism, a bourgeois revolution led by the working class in the periphery of capitalism could not be contained within the parameters of capitalism. The contradictions of capitalism would lead to its collapse and – initially under the leadership of the Bolsheviks – to the formation of a communist society. The October Revolution was meant to be a spark to set off the conflagration of world capitalism. Lenin stressed the role of conscious political actors and political leadership. Spontaneously, the development of the productive forces of capitalism would not lead to its collapse. Political action could only be carried out by the organization of the working class through the party.

As far as revolutionary strategy is concerned, the Bolshevik movement proved to be a successful vehicle for the seizure of power in Russia. It mobilized the peasant army uprooted by war, the discontented urban masses – including significant sections of the proletariat – and the disgruntled intelligentsia into a revolutionary force under its leadership. It was not, however, the classic Marxist revolution of the working class. It was rather a revolution in a society under transition from feudalism to capitalism precipitated by collapse consequent on war.[46]

Marx and Lenin recognized that, as capitalism matured, there was a strong tendency for traditional social democracy to integrate the working class into capitalism and thereupon to become reformist. Lenin's perception of capitalism reaching an imperialist stage, when the mantle of revolutionary action was thrown to the emerging proletariat in developing countries, was a brilliant insight. For him capitalism in its imperialist stage was 'moribund'. In the last sentence of the 1920 introduction to 'Imperialism', Lenin wrote, 'Imperialism is the eve of social revolution of the proletariat. This has been confirmed in 1917 on a world-wide scale.'

The October Revolution was a success in terms of political leadership. Lenin devised the tactics for a successful insurrection and he formulated a legitimating ideology for the seizure of power. But it was an outcome of a faulty analysis of capitalism. Imperialism truly led to its globalization: but it was not 'moribund'. It held immense possibilities for the development of the world's productive forces and for the inclusion of the working class into its fold. October did not precipitate a socialist revolution in Europe.

Lenin helped to create the conditions: but the leadership of the Western working class was not prepared to move for revolution.

Viewed in a less charitable light, Lenin drove the train of Russian history into West European socialism. In this way, his critics argue, he subverted the socialist idea; he sacrificed the self-emancipation of the working class for the success of the October insurrection. Subsequently, Russian and Soviet history, it is contended, are evidence of the denial of working-class autonomy; the Russian system of Tsarist autocracy was replaced by Stalinist tyranny. Nevertheless, Soviet Russia, as it was later called, had cut free from the world capitalist system and had to make its own way as a revolutionary power. In the next chapters we shall discuss how the revolution was consolidated and how it spread. Its final collapse in 1991 may have its roots in the faulty assumptions which legitimated the October revolution.

3
State Socialism: The Soviet Model

The Impact of Revolution

In the introduction, revolution was defined not only as a major political break from the previous sociopolitical order, but as a set of measures carried out by the new incumbents in power. In post-revolutionary Russia, the revolutionary process was not one of 'putting socialism into practice'. Lenin's initial vision was to assert political control. His prognosis of the legitimation of a Bolshevik seizure of power in Russia leading to a socialist revolution was based not only on the weakness and incompetence of the Russian bourgeoisie but also on a belief that a socialist revolution in the advanced countries of the West was latent and would be precipitated by a workers' uprising in Russia.

This crucial consequential contingency, however, did not happen, and the absence of any effective working-class power in the advanced countries of the West has bedevilled the communist movement ever since. In addition to being confronted by the metropolitan capitalist powers, the communists in Soviet Russia were challenged by all the accumulated problems of an autocratic order and by civil war. The party not only had to organize their supporters for revolution, but later – which was not the intention of Lenin in 1917 – to 'build socialism'. In this chapter we consider the formation of state socialism in Russia, which later became a model for other societies.[1] We shall see that the cultural heritage of Russia, already apparent in Lenin's theory of the party, had a major impact on Bolshevik policies. 'Socialism' became defined in terms of Russian cultural and economic conditions.

The Bolshevik leadership was badly equipped theoretically to rule and transform autocratic Russia. The party's major task had been to organize the working class to seize and maintain political power; it lacked a vision of what socialism should be or how it should be constructed.

Bolshevism itself was a collection of orientations rather than a set of preconceived policies.[2] It was influenced and even corrupted by non-Marxist ideas and suppositions. Russia's pre-revolutionary intelligentsia (Leninist and Populist alike) had authoritarian elements, taken, for instance, from Tkachev's ideas of a conspiratorial, centrally led political party.[3]

An important element was the social and political backwardness of Tsarist Russia. There were critical limits on the ability of the Soviet leaders to effect their policies. These stemmed from the immense land mass, the inhospitable climate and the scarcity of economic resources. The country was at an early stage of capitalist development. Its political and social structure was not bourgeois. The productive forces were at a relatively low level of development, very much below that of the European capitalist states. In 1913, for instance, the output of Russian large-scale industry was only 6.9 per cent of American gross industrial output. The Bolshevik leaders were confronted with relatively autonomous social forces which defied control. The large traditional peasant population was a 'heavy millstone' and 'made the Bolsheviks adjust their policies on every issue'.[4] The mores of the peasant family continued and the new incumbents of power proved incapable of penetrating the family structure. Under the Tsars, there was no division between state and society: religion had no autonomous sphere of operation and the Orthodox Church, sanctioned by the Tsars, asserted a monopoly over religious organization. A 'protestant ethic' as a spirit of capitalism could not develop autonomously in Russia as part of religious faith. There was no right to combination – political parties were illegal, as were trade unions, and workers' associations operated under government auspices. The weakness of civil society inherited from Tsarism also perpetuated a parochial political culture which was not appropriate for the introduction of a socialist democratic order. The social base on which the Soviet regime developed was largely composed of poorly educated people and a large number of illiterates infused with superstition. As late as 1937, only 43 per cent of adults (aged over 15) were self-defined as non-believers and in the census of that year 42 per cent professed allegiance to the Orthodox Church.[5] The difficulties of communication were compounded by the low level of literacy and the poor infrastructure in the form of roads and telephone links. Russia, economically, politically, ideologically and culturally, was unready for socialist revolution.

Moreover, many factors impelled by the revolution itself created disruption. Revolutions are consequences of polities being unable or unwilling to change gradually under conditions of stability. The post-revolutionary years were ones like those following the French Revolution – internal war, oppression and the exercise of terror. The immediate

impact of revolution was civil war, in which the West intervened unsuc-
cessfully against the Bolsheviks. At its end, in 1920, famine confronted
Russia. The period from 1920 until 1929 was one of political consolidation in which the institutions and processes of Soviet power were being
put in place. The years 1928 to 1940 were an era of internal transformation 'from above'.

The emigration of many of the intellectual and business classes led
to an upward mobility of the masses which ensured loyalty, but by the
same token such people lacked confidence in their new positions. They
were uneducated and poorly trained. These structural factors worked
against 'putting socialism into practice'. The revolutionaries who had
seized power were not without support, but from the very beginning
they were a minority. The Bolsheviks received 9 million votes – some
25 per cent of those cast – in elections to the Constituent Assembly
in November 1917. There was, as Lenin had noted, a critical mass
of support for the new political order. As John Maynard Keynes put
it after his visit in 1925: 'Leninism derives its power not from the
multitude but from a small minority of enthusiastic converts, whose zeal
and intolerance make each one the equal in strength of a hundred
indifferentists.'[6]

Could a socialist society be built in such an environment? This is the
crux of the Marxist dilemma as it has remained after the Russian Revolution in the analysis of states of the Soviet type. Have they succeeded in
moving to a stage qualitatively higher than capitalism; and if not, what
type of society are they?

The answer to these questions depends to some extent on the frame of
reference adopted. Supporters of traditional Soviet Marxism (a term
coined under the leadership of Lenin and Stalin), including the leaders of
its client states when they were in power, emphasized the success of
directed economic and social development. Western 'progressive' intellectuals, such as the Webbs,[7] hailed the Soviet Union as a 'new civilization'. Critics, however, cast doubt not only on the efficiency of the
system, but also on the enormous costs – social and human – of communist development. John Maynard Keynes came to different conclusions
than the Webbs and echoes many of the criticisms made since. He wrote:
'Red Russia holds too much which is detestable . . . I am not ready for a
creed which does not care how much it destroys the liberty and security
of daily life, which uses deliberately the weapons of persecution, destruction and international strife.'[8] But critic and supporter alike regarded the
USSR (and later countries which were to follow it) as being qualitatively
different from capitalism. The profit motive and the market had been
abolished and replaced by planning; the values of collectivism and equality

had superseded those of individualism and freedom. As Keynes rather quaintly put it:

> The effect of these social changes has been . . . to make a real change in the predominant attitude towards money and will probably make a far greater change when a new generation has grown up which has known nothing else. . . . money-making and money-accumulation cannot enter into the life-calculations of a rational man who accepts the Soviet rule in the way in which they enter ours. A Society of which this is even partially true is a tremendous innovation.[9]

Supporters of Soviet Marxism argued that rationality in human affairs could be achieved through direct human intervention in the form of conscious political guidance and control by the Communist Party. Its early achievements included the full employment of productive forces (particularly labour), relatively equalitarian income distribution, a universal welfare state and the provision of social security. The formation of a 'classless' society was on the agenda. These views underestimated not only the problems of the construction of socialism but also the traditional and non-socialist aspects of developments which were taking place.

Pessimism about the nature of the Soviet model of socialism and its internal political processes had been expressed from the time of the Kronstadt rebellion (1921), when the sailors there revolted against 'communists and commissars'. Its critics have focused mainly on the political and economic inadequacies of the regime of Stalinism: the use of brutal coercion, arbitrary rule, the absence of democratic and property rights, the lack of consumer sovereignty and the failure of the administered economy to operate as efficiently as the capitalist market economies of the West.

These stances may be summarized under three major interpretations of state socialism. The first considers the Russian October Revolution to have created conditions for the creation of a socialist society. This is the subject of this chapter. We discuss here the structural forms and policies pursued, which were later followed by other state socialist societies (examined in chapter 4). The second are Marxist critiques denying that these societies had moved to a socialist formation. Third is a critique of the impossibility of the Soviet experiment itself – from those who believe that the Marxist paradigm of society is seriously faulty. These critical theories will be considered in part II below (chapter 7) after we have outlined the way in which state socialism developed. Unlike favourably disposed writers, such as the Webbs, and critics, such as Keynes, we are able to analyse developments in a comprehensive way following the collapse of state socialism, and to assess it retrospectively.

Building State Socialism: The Early Stages

Faced with the backwardness inherited from the Tsars, the aftermath of the First World War and the destruction of the Civil War, the Bolsheviks became 'modernizers'. Marxism, which had arisen as a critique of bourgeois society, became transformed into Marxism-Leninism, an ideology of development which provided an intellectual rationale for the policy undertaken under Stalin. As an ideology of development, it had four components:

1 An advocacy of the need to copy advanced forms of production processes and methods from the advanced capitalist countries.
2 A theory of imperialism which condemned the political hegemony of the predator capitalist states over the societies in the periphery, such as Soviet Russia and other dependent states.
3 An organizational theory of centralized decision-making with a strong centre controlled by the communist apparatus.
4 A subject role for the masses in public affairs and an assumption that the masses had to be mobilized for the development of social and productive forces.[10]

Priority was given to organizing resources to build the economic basis of communism. Soviet 'socialism' was almost synonymous with the development of the industrial base, the growth of the forces of production. This involved copying the advanced forms of industrial production known in the West, particularly the United States – the most advanced capitalist country – and it included the adoption not only of its technology but also of its organization and management of labour, such as Taylorism.[11]

But the institutions of Soviet society in which industrialization was carried out were quite different from those of Western capitalism: there was complete public ownership of the means of production; the state directed economic surplus for developmental investment; the outflow of profits which occurred when states were dependent on core capitalist states was prevented. This meant administrative direction and control instead of the market mechanism.

Comprehensive central planning was adopted. Distribution and production were controlled by central planning bodies. The market and its institutions, such as independent banks, as well as monetary indicators such as the rate of interest, were abolished. Demand operating through the market played little role in the determination of prices and investment. The economy was supply dominated. The market system was abolished and replaced by a centrally organized and government-controlled economy: this has become known as a 'command economy'. The government concentrated resources on rapid industrialization – rather analogous to Western governments under a war economy. The rate of capital investment was high: it favoured heavy industry rather than light, and producer rather than consumer goods. There was little investment in agriculture. Not everything was subject to central command, however. Money continued as a means of exchange and a store of wealth. Employees were paid money wages, which they used to purchase goods and services. Even after the collectivization of agriculture, the peasants were allowed to keep a few animals and small plots of land, the produce of which could be legally traded on the collective farm market. Thus the market continued in an attenuated form and is sometimes called a 'proto-market'.

In agriculture, Soviet socialism failed to achieve a voluntary movement to industrialized and large-scale industrial type farming. The October Revolution resulted in land reform (nationalization of land by the government abolished the large estates) and an equalization of holdings. This gave rise to a large number of peasant farmers with less capital per unit than before the revolution. State farms (that is large-scale agricultural units under state management), favoured by Lenin, were few in number. On the contrary, in the place of the pre-revolutionary large estates there was a reversion to small-scale peasant agriculture.

Collectivization of agriculture began in 1929. This involved a brutal administrative process in which peasants were dispossessed of most of their stock and of rights over most of the land they had previously farmed. By 1937, 235,000 collective farms had replaced the 26 million productive household units of peasants existing in 1929. Cooperative production of agriculture was organized: peasants were put under the control of collective farm chairpersons who, as agents of the central planners, controlled the product mix and, most important of all, the surplus produce.

The political leadership considered that such a course of action in agriculture was necessary for two principal reasons. First, it enabled resources to be channelled to the towns to feed the newly mobilized working class – surplus derived from agriculture rose from 20 per cent in 1913–14 to 36 per cent in 1939. Second, the policy crushed any potential counter-revolutionary groups in the countryside. It established urban economic and political power over the village.

On a comparative basis, growth of Soviet agriculture compared favourably with Japan and the USA at similar growth periods. According to Western estimates cited by Wilber,[12] Soviet total agricultural growth rates averaged 2.2 per cent between 1928 and 1961, and per capita growth rose 1.1 per cent; comparable figures for the USA (1870 and 1900) were 3.3

per cent and 1.2 per cent, and for Japan (1861–65 to 1891–95) 2.0 per cent and 0.8 per cent.

The surplus population moved from the countryside to the towns and the urban population increased at a phenomenal rate: the non-agricultural workforce increased from 10 million to 45 million between 1926 and 1955 – a similar rate of growth in the USA (between 1880 and 1930) took twice as long. The urban population rose from 28.1 million in 1929 to 63.1 million in 1940, from 19 per cent to 33 per cent of the population.

The economic effects of Soviet developmental policy were positive and compared favourably with capitalist type economies. Western estimates for annual rates of economic growth for the period 1928–40 range from 8.8 per cent (Nutter) to 13.6 per cent (Seton); for the more backward areas the figures were 9.2 per cent (Nutter) to 14.1 per cent (Hodgman). Figures for Western economies in similar periods of economic development were 5.6 per cent for the USA in 1839–69; 6.2 per cent for Japan in the period 1905–9 to 1930–4; 7.2 per cent for India in 1952–62.[13] Estimates by Gerschenkron show that output of Soviet large-scale industry increased at an annual rate of between 15 and 17 per cent between 1928 and 1938; Soviet industrial output as a ratio of American rose, being 6.9 per cent in 1913, 27.3 per cent in 1932, 45.1 per cent in 1938.[14] Consequently, the defence capacity of the Soviet Union was greatly enhanced and the armed forces had an economic base on which to fight the Second World War.

The Bolsheviks pursued a policy of cultural revolution and social development. The objective here was to introduce comprehensive mass social services and to capture the minds of the people. In place of the stratified system of education inherited from Tsarist Russia, comprehensive and polytechnical education was introduced with a common syllabus for all pupils. Mass literacy campaigns were instigated. In 1926 the Soviet authorities claimed that 51.1 per cent of the population aged over nine years was literate, and by 1939 the figure reached 81.2 per cent.[15] This figure probably errs on the side of charity: according to the census of 1937, of 98 million people aged over nine, 37.3 million (38 per cent) were illiterate.[16] Even by 1959 the census showed that by far the largest group of the population had received only an incomplete secondary education.

Such developments were not restricted to the Russian Republic (RSFSR) but were also paralleled in the other republics. Educational achievements broken down by republic are shown on table 3.1 (data are shown for later periods for comparison). These data show the higher levels of tertiary education in the European areas of the country. The strata of upper professionals are to be found in the capital cities of the

Table 3.1 Educational levels of the population in the USSR, RSFSR, Latvia, Ukraine, Tadzhikistan and Uzbekistan, 1959, 1970 and 1979 (per 1,000 of the population aged 10 and above)

	1959	*1970*	*1979*
RSFSR			
All higher	35	57	86
Full gen. secondary	58	108	188
Latvia			
All higher	39	67	95
Full gen. secondary	75	119	187
Ukraine			
All higher	31	52	78
Full gen. secondary	64	139	225
Tadzhikistan			
All higher	24	41	61
Full gen. secondary	48	112	220
Uzbekistan			
All higher	30	52	74
Full gen. secondary	67	141	275
USSR			
All higher	34	55	83
Full gen. secondary	61	119	207

Source: Census data, *Chislennost' i sostav naseleniya SSSR* (Moscow: 1984), pp. 26–41.

European areas. But the differences are not as marked as one might have expected. Indeed, the figures for full general secondary education give both Tadzhikistan and Uzbekistan higher ratios than the USSR as a whole. The main reason for this is that the Central Asian republics do not have the large number of older people who had inadequate facilities before 1959. There was a significant raising and equalization of educational levels throughout the USSR.

Free rudimentary health and welfare services were spread comprehensively over the whole country. However, compared to other countries at similar levels of development, spectacular advances were made in the field of public provision. The number of physicians per thousand of the population rose from 0.17 in 1913 to 0.74 in 1940 and 1.97 in 1961; in India in 1956 the ratio was 0.17, in Japan in 1959–60 it was 1.09 and in the USA in 1961 it was 1.28.[17]

Political mobilization was achieved through exposure to the mass media, which was dominated by political values. Propaganda sought to organize loyalties around an image of a supranational USSR – though its values were highly infused with Russian culture. Traditional titles and honorific awards were abolished. They were replaced with orders and medals bestowing social and political recognition on servants of the Soviet state: the Order of Lenin, Hero of Socialist Labour (Double Hero for persistent socialist endeavour). To reward women who had many births (that is, excelled in reproducing the means of production), the title of Heroine of Socialist Motherhood was awarded. 'Socialist' ceremonies of marriage and initiation into the working class were instituted.[18] Public holidays celebrated things socialist and Soviet anniversaries replaced religious ones: the October Revolution and May Day. In the 1920s a new calendar was introduced (counting the years from 1917), and during the first Five Year Plan the names of days were also dropped and were replaced by numbers. The objective here was to create a climate of expectancy and change in which people could be mobilized into Soviet society. In the early days after the revolution, to combat religious superstition, anti-Christmas and anti-Easter campaigns were introduced – though these faded away in the 1930s. A characteristic feature of the communist countries was the atheistic values sponsored by the communist leaders; especially in the earlier years of their power, they took an uncompromising stance on religion and its associated superstitions. The objective here was to destroy old values and to create new forms of symbolic legitimacy for the socialist state.

The absence of a market, the tradition of an autocratic and large state bureaucracy and the internal and external consequences of internal war led to the growth of the administrative system, including the army and the security organs. A monolithic state structure (with a single political party and no division of powers) came to characterize state socialism – though significant administrative divisions, coinciding with national and ethnic divisions, were set up. Soviet administration was 'national in form and socialist in content'. Such divisions strengthened national identity and were to have important consequences later in the break-up of the USSR. Legitimated by Lenin's emphasis on the party as the expression of the interests of the working class, the state became dominant and the forces of civil society – weak though they were – were suppressed. In the interwar period, terror was utilized 'not as a tool of social *change*, but as a method of rule and *governance*'.[19]

In the early years following 1917, other more ostensibly 'socialist' measures were taken by the government. In addition to the seizure of the landed property of the aristocracy, the personal possessions of the rich were expropriated. An attempt was made to enhance the status of manual labour. Initially, the pay of political commissars in Soviet Russia was reduced to the level of that of the average manual worker and there was an assumption that wage levelling was an intrinsic part of socialism. Income differentials became much narrower. However, this did not bring the equal distribution of services and commodities: they were disbursed according to the contribution to society of workers and employees – allocation was 'according to work'.

In the immediate aftermath of revolution, three notable objectives were achieved in the Soviet Union (and later in the other countries that followed its path). First, wage differentials, even when payment in kind was included, were narrower than in market economies and favoured manual workers. Physicians received the average skilled worker's wage, for example. There was a remarkable long-term equalization of income – to the advantage of manual labour and to the disadvantage of non-manuals. Figure 3.1 shows the trend from 1932 to 1986: the average pay for manual workers is shown as an index of 100 against which the ratios for office workers and non-manual technical employees are shown. Money wages, of course, were not the only determinant of income but they were the most important. Absolutely and relatively compared to

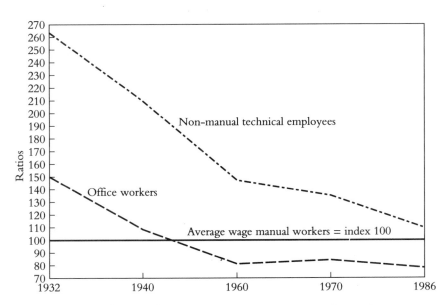

Figure 3.1 Index of wage differentials between manual workers, office workers and non-manual technical employees in the USSR, 1932–1986

similar occupational statuses in the West, the technical employees and professionals (not shown on the graph) were very much worse off in the USSR and other state socialist societies. In comparison to capitalist countries, the prestige of skilled manual groups rose, and that of unskilled non-manuals declined. For instance, the standard international index of prestige for clerks was 43.4 whereas for the Soviet Union (data for 1969) it was only 29.4; for miners the USSR scored 54.1 and the international index was only 31.5.[20]

In later years – particularly from the mid-1970s – partly as a consequence of relative wage equality, the role of illegal and non-monetary payments became greater, particularly for commercial and industrial executives. Additionally, one must bear in mind that the professional strata generally fared better with respect to redistributive policies and payments in kind: they had better access to education and foreign travel. However, industrial workers also had privileges: access to goods sold in the enterprise, and to housing and social services financed from enterprise funds. At the end of the scale, poverty continued, especially for people who had incomplete labour records and therefore lower than average pensions, and for disabled groups; single-parent families were also in poverty. But wage ratios are still the best guide we have to relativities. They reflected the desire on the part of the political leadership to enhance the position of manual workers at the expense of the non-manuals, creating a feeling of relative deprivation on the part of the latter social stratum.

Next, as the second objective, structural unemployment was averted. Social policy had as one of its goals the maintenance of a fully employed labour force. This had the consequence of reducing considerably the amount of poverty, which, in industrial societies, is closely linked to unemployment. The advocates of state socialism pointed to the absence of a reserve army of labour, which gave the working class security of living standards. Women increasingly became an important part of the labour market. Probably the most important cause of this high level of labour utilization was the high rate of industrial development.

Third, welfare (education, health) and state benefits and subsidies (for housing and food) became significant components of the standard of living. The educational system was adapted to make it more appropriate to a socialistic system. Previous forms of stratification of education into different types of schools were abolished and a comprehensive type of polytechnic education was set up with a common syllabus for all children. Subsidies for utilities (gas, electricity, housing) were introduced: for instance, the cost of accommodation was less than 5 per cent of earned income. Medical care and education were universally available and provided from public funds. The market was substantially weakened as a distributive mechanism and replaced by administrative redistribution. We shall show below that this gave rise to considerable problems.

Moreover, distribution was according to desert, to work performance, not by need. There was an unequal distribution of commodities and services, and status differentiation characterized different social groups. Research has shown that, with some notable exceptions, the ranking of the desirability of jobs followed a similar scale to that in the capitalist West, though the income relativities did not. The exceptions were the positions of groups of manual workers (such as miners), who were ranked higher, and farmers (in practice, peasants in collective farms) who had less prestige.[21] Even though the money incomes of professional workers such as physicians, lawyers and artists were severely depressed and were not more than the wage of the average industrial manual worker, their prestige ratings remained relatively untouched.[22]

The Soviet Notion of Socialism

By 1936, the political leadership of the USSR felt able to declare that socialism, the first stage of communism, had been completed. The level of productive forces had been enhanced as a result of the five year plans. The class relations of production had been secured by the nationalization and state control of property. According to Soviet theorists, *class* relations had transcended those of capitalism: no classes based on ownership of property existed. From an economic point of view, production was not for 'exchange' but for 'use', and capital accumulation was not the consequence of a class of individuals exploiting the workforce through extracting surplus and consequent capital formation. The state was the agent of investment, and the mechanisms of planning had superseded the market. Consequently, the state exercised considerable influence over the distribution of income. The Soviet Union, from the time of the Stalin Constitution in 1936, was 'officially' a 'socialist' society.

The supporting argument advanced by Soviet ideologists for the period between 1936 and 1991 rested on four suppositions:

1 That the class relations to the means of production had been socialized following the seizure of power by the Bolsheviks and the nationalization of the means of production.
2 That state planning had replaced the bourgeois market as a method of coordination of the economy and the allocation of resources; competition between capitals had been superseded and labour had lost its character as a commodity.

3 That following the industrialization process (during the first Five Year Plan), the level of productive forces was sufficient to define the economy as being at the socialist stage (that is, the first stage of communist society).

4 That, given the hegemony of the Communist Party and its control of the major institutional systems (the state, ideology, science, education), the superstructure was socialist. The remaining incongruities (religious views, personality cults, petty crime, oppression of minorities) were 'leftovers' from previous modes of production. It was confidently believed that with the maturation of socialism, these incompatibilities would disappear.

This approach to Marxism (which is our topic here), it was claimed, vindicated Lenin's voluntaristic approach to revolution. The 'relations of production' had triumphed over the 'level of productive forces' in the sense that an ascendant class (the proletariat) had built the basis of socialism and thus legitimated the October Revolution.

Compared to an 'ideal type' of communism as a mode of production, Soviet Marxists would concede that the system was not communist. There remained a state apparatus: the party, police and 'ideological state apparatuses' operated to constrain the population. As in capitalist societies, the state's role was to defend society from external foes, and it managed resources for industrial development. Stalinism added another dimension to socialism: it became a developmental ideology; society was mobilized by the Communist Party and the advance to a communist mode of production was to be achieved through state ownership, control and coercion. During the inter-war period there is considerable evidence to show that there was a substantial amount of popular support for the Soviet regime. As Keynes had predicted, the Harvard research project on Soviet refugees (which would be likely to underestimate positive views rather than amplify them) showed that the younger and better educated were the more supportive of the regime.[23] (This was to change 25 years later,[24] when the young and highly educated were the most dissatisfied with the regime, a point we shall consider below.)

Within-system contradictions

These developmental policies were considered by the Soviet leadership to have secured the development of the economic and social infrastructure of a socialist state. Initially, these measures strengthened the solidarity of state socialist society. What then of internal conflicts of interests? Was the

Soviet system one of harmony? Advocates of the state socialist model argued that, from a Marxist point of view, there were no antagonistic contradictions because their class basis – through the nationalization of physical assets – had been abolished. However, many 'non-antagonistic' contradictions continued – particularly between manual and non-manual labour and between town and country – and antagonisms based on gender and on national and ethnic origin remained. These differences, linked to the division of labour, gave rise to variation in lifestyles, access to valued goods and services (such as education), and inequalities in political influence. It was believed that these contradictions would wither away with the maturation of the economy and the growth in productive forces.

Early in the 1970s, however, a more pessimistic outlook appeared which cast doubt on whether the system itself would be able to transcend the 'non-antagonistic contradictions' obvious in the society. It is important to grasp at this stage that the nature of the state socialist system itself generated its own incompatibilities, tensions and incongruities. Systemic changes were therefore suggested – with respect to the role of the market and to competitive elections – but not carried out until much later during the reform process.

Within the USSR and other state socialist countries following in its path the focus and frame of reference of 'contradictions' changed over time. In the early years of the regime the political leadership and its supporters were concerned with opposition from the previously incumbent ruling classes, and the mobilization of the population and development of the economy were dominant goals. With the passage of time, however, the internal and often external political threats diminished, but the bureaucratic form of administration grew.

The comprehensive economic and cultural policies were carried out by a centralized Soviet state apparatus. The political mechanism was dominant. The 'fulfilment of plans' was the major political indicator. The political market – in the sense of competing political parties through elections – was destroyed and replaced by administrative control. The extent of government activity, itself inherited from the Tsarist regime, made police control much wider than in Western liberal capitalist societies, where there is a division between polity and economy. Much of the process of the administration was bureaucratized, subject to little popular control and adopting the practices of the old Tsarist administration. A line of political offices emanating from Moscow was staffed by commissars. Observing a parallel, Roger Pethybridge quotes approvingly from De Tocqueville, who pointed out that the French Revolution changed the form of government and 'decapitated' the administration, but left the

'trunk of the administration' untouched.[25] Officials reproduced their ha-
bitual activity. The state bureaucracy, moreover, had now become a
massive economic and political institution.

The planning bodies were directed by the leaders of party and state;
with time they spawned a vast and powerful network of bureaucratic
offices concerned with economic and social institutions. The structure of
the Soviet government included the major elements of the economy and
made it one of the world's largest bureaucracies: the total number of
ministries and committees constituting the government of the USSR rose
from 18 in 1924 to 132 in 1984, and the number of people employed in
the government bureaucracies rose from 6.2 million in 1922 to 118
million in 1985. This was a gigantic bureaucratic enterprise operating at
the level of the USSR (all-union ministries) and in the republics (union
republican ministries).

Despite formal controls which were intended to make the power
holders accountable (to the Soviets and the party under traditional state
socialism), in practice bureaucratic politics entailed the accretion of political power to various elites. The Tsarist concept of state politics held sway
over democratic and participatory politics. Local government and the
ministerial system of administration had strong analogies with the Tsarist
political order. Democratic ideals were espoused by many of the leaders
of the Bolshevik revolution. The Soviets were considered to be elected
revolutionary bodies representing the working and toiling masses. Whatever the ideals of the Bolsheviks, however, in practice, control by the
leadership of the party and increasingly the state bureaucracy was dominant. The elected Constituent Assembly in 1917 had only a Bolshevik
minority and had been dissolved. After October no nationwide competitive elections took place to the Soviets, which became a tool of the
leadership and a form of audience participation.

The need for political surveillance to guard against real and imagined
oppositional forces led to the creation of a comprehensive web of police
and security services. These in turn matured into important political and
economic formations: the security forces became a law unto themselves
and they accumulated considerable economic powers from the forced
labour camps which came under their jurisdiction. An extensive system of
forced labour and punitive exile colonies was set up by the police.
Political purges, including the murder of leading Bolsheviks, were important features of Stalinist rule.[26] Oppression also became a characteristic of
Soviet society under Stalin: while the exact numbers of victims are
unknown, millions of people were moved from their homes and dubbed
enemies of the people. The system which was created under Stalin was far
from that espoused by a Marxist, or even an idealistic Bolshevik, notion
of socialism.

This oppressive system was due to a combination of factors. Political revolutions are always indicative of internal war. The political culture of Russia traditionally had not developed controls and checks over administrative rule, and the centralization of the party and its claim to political hegemony provided a legitimation of central control (though not violence). This, together with the uncompromising personality of Stalin and the people he promoted in the process of political mobilization, as well as the external threat – from ex-communists (such as Trotsky), the capitalist world and the rearmament of Germany – all contributed to the creation of a regime of oppression.

Later some of the more socialistic policies began to lead to resentment. There were manifest grievances on the part of non-manual workers who wanted greater financial recognition for skills and qualifications. Important 'status incongruencies' developed: lowly paid but highly skilled professionals such as physicians had high prestige and they felt a sense of injustice. As the world system of communications developed, comparisons were made with differentials in Western societies, where the professional classes (the 'intelligentsia') were more highly rewarded. The level of equality itself led to dissatisfaction on the part of people who thought that 'equal misery' should be replaced by equality of opportunity to become rich and participate in a consumer society like that of the West.

The Soviet Union became independent of the world economy. The nationalization of assets without compensation to their foreign owners and the belligerent attitude towards capitalism isolated the country from the capitalist world. Development was achieved through internally generated savings. This had the effect of making the Soviet Union detached from the world market and the international division of labour. While comprehensive rather than piecemeal development was achieved, the USSR and the socialist bloc became cut off from the benefits of the international capitalist division of labour and the flows of capital which came from it. By the late 1960s, the socialist countries were increasingly unable to provide the consumer type of society which characterized the advanced capitalist countries, and the more successful developing ones even of the Third World.

While Lenin's leadership of the insurrection in October 1917 was masterly, one might point to a serious deficiency in Lenin's theory. Capitalism did not turn out to be dying. World capitalism has proved to be resilient, innovative and dynamic. Rather than being a catalyst for world revolution, the events of 1917 have proved to be a cul-de-sac for socialism. This, however, was not at all obvious until the 1980s. In the pre-war period the Soviet Union had achieved considerable economic and social advances under the regime of state socialism, and the defeat of Germany in the Second World War was universally hailed as a major achievement of the Soviet order. This was not only in terms of the provision of military equipment, but also in terms of the organization, discipline and fighting capacity of the Red Army.

State Socialism and Underdevelopment

In the second chapter, I noted that the concept of socialism and the growth of the socialist movement arose in societies experiencing the early period of capitalist development. State socialism as it unfolded in Soviet Russia under Stalin can hardly be said to have fulfilled the goals of nineteenth-century utopian writers on socialism. However, as a social system, it developed a different form of organizing principles from the capitalist states of the West and these bore a certain affinity to some of the goals of socialism. All societies have to devise processes and institutions to ensure efficiency, effectiveness, control, integration and gratification. The competing organizing principles of capitalism and state socialism are shown in the box below.

In the middle column, the familiar principles of capitalism are shown. People have rights to private property and 'freedom'. The market is dominant in the economy. In the third column, state socialism is shown to have different precepts: property was in state ownership; equality rather than freedom was the motivating principle of policy; planning and admin-istration rather than the market were the main form of economic organi-zation; central control under the party (and state bureaucracy) replaced interest aggregation through democratic competition; social solidarity and personal integration were to be achieved through collectivist and public rather than pluralist and private associations; politics (rather than law) determined the application of rules; labour rather than leisure was a major

---

Organizing principles of capitalism and state socialism

Resource	Capitalism	State socialism
Property	Private	Public/state
Goals	Freedom	Equality
Efficiency	Market	Planning
Effectiveness	Democratic	Central control
Solidarity	Pluralist	Collectivist
Integration	Private	Public
Rule application	Law	Politics
Gratification	Leisure	Labour

mode in which personal gratification was to be achieved. I am not saying, of course, that 'actually existing state socialism' approximated to the goals of idealistic Marxists or utopian socialists, but I am pointing to the fact that state socialism as an organizational form of industrialism was a coherent alternative to capitalism.

'State socialism' may be considered to be a form of state and society appropriate for a transition where the bourgeoisie is weak. The origins of dictatorships and parliamentary-type democracies are closely linked to the role of the ascendant bourgeoisie. As Barrington Moore in his work on the origins of dictatorship and democracy has put it: 'No bourgeois, no democracy.'[27] Moore, of course, is concerned with modern parliamentary-type 'bourgeois democracies' – it is untrue to assert that all forms of democracy are dependent on the formation of a propertied market class. The bourgeoisie has a stake in the institutionalization of private property, on which legal rational norms are based. Furthermore, a parliamentary type of democracy is dependent on a private entrepreneurial class because its interests are furthered by a limited state and, initially at least, representative parliamentary-type institutions. These were not present in pre-1917 Russia: paradoxically, therefore, Lenin was right to point out that capitalism could be developed by the leadership of the party and state (legitimated for Lenin as the 'leadership of the working class'). The state therefore became a dominant force in the development of the productive forces; in this it carried on a tradition of the Tsars. The ideology of socialism underwent a mutation: it legitimated the creation of industrialism and a modern society. (It did not lead to state capitalism, for reasons we shall discuss in chapter 7 below.)

In a different theoretical context, Gabriel Almond has defined five challenges which have to be solved in any developing or modernizing state: identity, legitimacy, penetration, participation and distribution.[28] Identity has to do with the units to which people believe they belong, the state, social class or nation being the most important forms of identity here. For governments to rule they have to enjoy the confidence of their subjects, obedience turning might into right; ideology is the main instrument of legitimacy in modern states. Penetration is the ability of politics to cope with the complex organizational structures and forms of division of labour. Participation is a companion dimension to penetration, providing the public with involvement in and exposure to politics and decision-making. Distribution involves the ability of the polity to allocate resources between sectors, social groups and individuals; it is the 'output' aspect of government.

The Soviet Union under Stalin developed a national identity. The USSR was defined as a socialist state with strong elements of traditional vernacular identities in the republics and regions. People were able to identify either with an All-Union Soviet nationality or with a parochial national one (Russian, Ukrainian, Armenian, etc. – rather as in Britain someone can be both British and English, or just Scottish, depending on the way they feel). Class identity was less important as a mobilizing principle. Ideology promoting legitimacy was given by Marxism-Leninism: this was an admixture of Marxist class theory which defined an external class enemy (the capitalist West) and gave an ideological basis for solidarity grounded on the working class and legitimated the political leadership and its policies. Penetration was secured by the organizational means of the Communist Party, by the centralized state bureaucracy and by various centrally led organizations such as the trade unions. The mass media was pervasive and a single unambiguous message reflecting government policy and ideology was signalled to the population. Participation was ensured by the Communist Party, the Young Communist League, the Soviets (parliaments), trade unions and various 'social organizations' (such as friendship societies and sports clubs). Such participation was not of a liberal democratic kind associated with quasi-independent groups in a civil society, but consisted of controlled organizations ensuring a kind of audience participation for the masses. Distribution was secured through the state's control of consumption and the institution of welfare services on a rudimentary but fairly equitable basis.

Even though this system was not 'socialist' in an ideologically respectable form, the system of state socialism acted as a powerful tool to integrate the socially and geographically mobile population into a stable society. While the 'protestant ethic' of Calvin provided a legitimation for the formation of capitalism, the 'communist ethic' formulated by Lenin and Stalin did likewise for the advancement of industrialism under state socialism. Marxism-Leninism may be likened to a developmental ethic of communism.

While the system of state socialism had many imperfections and inadequacies, Soviet Marxists confidently claimed that the October Revolution had succeeded in transcending capitalism and had completed the building of the first stage of socialism. This view has been strongly contested by critical Marxists, who hold that exploitation and conflict of one form or another continued in Soviet-type societies and that the revolution, for one reason or another, had failed to surpass capitalism. Opponents of socialism in the West also strongly denied that Soviet power ensured human liberation; rather – as Keynes had commented – it was a form of domination. We shall consider these positions in more detail later. Whatever its class and political character, state socialism emerged from the Second World War as a viable model of state-directed development and many of its characteristic systemic features were adopted by other countries. State socialism provided a systemic alternative to capitalism. It acted as a counterculture with its own organizational forms – particularly with respect to property and the market, to Marxist-Leninist ideology and to the centralization of economic and political decision-making.

4

The Growth and Spread of Communism

In the introduction, we distinguished between four phases in the evolution of communist states: revolution, control and development, reform and collapse. In the last chapter, we considered the impact of revolution in Soviet Russia and the creation there of state socialism. In this chapter we turn to discuss the rise of world communism, to consider the ways that communist power was extended into Eastern Europe and the Third World and to appraise the policies adopted by these new governments.

The Soviet model of politics and development was inaugurated in the 1930s in the Soviet Union when the world capitalist powers were relatively autonomous and divided. Following the First World War, they initially had no strong motive or interest in defeating the newly founded Soviet republic. Allied intervention in Russia in support of the opponents of Bolshevism during its civil war indicated the Western powers' opposition to the Bolshevik seizure of power. But the stakes involved were not perceived then to be very high and Europe and America were weary of war and had problems of reconstruction at home. The Western powers vied with each other for superiority. The Germans were completely vanquished following the Treaty of Versailles, the British still presided over a declining empire. The United States was only emerging as a world power. In such conditions the Soviet republic was able to develop, to be sure with little help and assistance from abroad, and gradually it was recognized by other states diplomatically. Though Soviet Russia was viewed with suspicion by the Western powers during the inter-war period, the country was able to evolve relatively autonomously.

After the Second World War, the USSR emerged as a strong, internationally powerful state. Whatever weaknesses were latent in the Soviet form of organization, they were not manifest by the end of the Second World War. Indeed, the industrial developments of the inter-war period in the context of state planning were universally respected. At this time, state planning in a centralized, politically controlled economy was widely considered to be a success. Furthermore, the Allied victory over the Axis powers, in which the USSR played a principal role, enhanced the standing of the USSR; political security and planning, with the state having an important role, became popular in many countries. Soviet socialism now appeared in the West to be a major challenge to the supremacy of the Western states, and Soviet political forms were either exported or consciously copied by countries, accumulating into the world communist movement.[1]

State Socialism in Comparative Perspective

One might distinguish between three different initial phases through which ruling communist powers evolved:[2]

1 *Autonomous internal revolution* with a more or less popular revolutionary movement led by an explicit Marxist-Leninist party. Communists fought their way to power against internal (and sometimes external) enemies in the following countries: Russia (1917), becoming the USSR (including Tuva), Mongolia (1924), Albania (1944), Yugoslavia (1945), Republic of North Vietnam (1945), formed into the Socialist Republic of Vietnam in 1976, the People's Republic of China in 1949; the People's Democratic Republic of Laos and the People's Republic of Kampuchea were both formed in 1975.

2 *Imposition of communist rule* following conquest by a major existing communist power. Most of the Eastern European socialist states (formally termed People's Republics) fit into this category. They were set up between 1946 and 1949: Bulgaria (1946), Romania (1947), Poland (1947), Hungary (1949), German Democratic Republic (1949). The Baltic states (Estonia, Lithuania, Latvia) were incorporated into the USSR during the Second World War. The Democratic People's Republic of Korea was founded in 1948 following the partition of Korea after the Second World War.

3 *Internal political or military coups* bringing to power leaders who were initially populist or democratic and later declared themselves to be Marxist or Leninist. The Republic of Cuba in 1959 and Zimbabwe in 1980 are examples here.

There are also combinations of the above: a populist movement aided or impelled by a dominant Marxist-Leninist movement, with Czechoslovakia (1948) and Nicaragua (1979) as examples.

While the history of the Eastern European states, where communist rule was linked to the power of the Soviet Union and followed the imposition of a pro-Soviet government, shapes popular attitudes in Europe, by far the majority of countries (and certainly the largest ones) adopting Marxist-Leninist regimes had their own spontaneous revolutions. The communists fought their own way to power and have to be seen as emanating from internal political and social tensions, rather than being the consequence of exogenous forces.

By 1980, there were 16 communist states which were the core of the 'world socialist system', as it was triumphantly termed by their political leaders. It is claimed that these countries accounted for one-third of the world's population and 40 per cent of its industrial production. In 1979, however, only three of these countries were at levels approximate to the Western European capitalist states: USSR ($4,110 per capita income per annum) and two other small European societies, Czechoslovakia ($5,290) and GDR ($6,430). These states also included some of the world's poorest: Laos ($90), Vietnam ($170) and China ($260).[3]

In addition to these explicitly Marxist-Leninist states, there were a number of states of 'socialist orientation' which are distinguished by having accepted the hegemony of the USSR and some elements of Marxist-Leninist ideology. They included Afghanistan, Angola, Congo (Brazzaville), Mozambique, Ethiopia, Madagascar, the Yemen. Other states more vaguely linked to Marxism-Leninism and having an allegiance to the USSR included Nicaragua, Zimbabwe, Benin and Grenada.[4] By 1980, of the 50 independent states in Africa, seven were self-defined as Marxist-Leninist.[5] (See the map on p. 60.)

With the notable exception of the Soviet Union, and some of the East European states, the socialist bloc at the height of its power was made up of poor, Third World countries, with large peasant populations. Of the societies in which the communists came to power of their own accord, all shared socioeconomic similarities with the Russia in 1917: they were all at an early stage of industrial development and had a small, relatively undeveloped capitalist class. The Soviet Union was the second world power in terms of its military capability and economic strength. It headed the communist common market, the Council for Mutual Economic Assistance (CMEA, also known as Comecon), and the military alliance of the Warsaw Treaty Organization.

Initially after the Second World War the Western powers did not treat the Eastern European people's democracies or the People's Republic of China as hostile states. The former were under the direct tutelage of the Soviet Union, whose armies were at once a liberating and an occupying force. They gained a legitimacy from the Allies' agreement, signed at Yalta, in which 'spheres of influence' were agreed between the major parties fighting against the Germans in the war: the USSR, the USA and

Britain. The countries of the West, too, had internal differences and problems. There was animosity towards the Germans on the part of the Allies, and the British and French still had to work out their positions with regard to their colonial empires. The USA was undoubtedly the major world capitalist power, in economic, military and political terms, but until the founding of NATO in 1949 there was no institutional basis on which a major offensive could be mounted against the emerging East European bloc of communist states. The Western world was tired of war; social reconstruction was the main objective of the Western European states, most of them headed by social-democratic or reformist governments. Indigenous communist parties in Western Europe also had considerable popular backing and had sizable parliamentary parties in France and Italy. The political right was discredited by association with fascism and world war.

In this context, direct intervention in the affairs of the East European states or China was not a practical political choice. The military power of the Soviet Union and its effective occupation were the other major factors which secured the internal development of the East European states. Like the Soviet Union following 1917, they had little economic help from the capitalist powers (aid was offered under the Marshall Plan in 1948, but it was declined).

Under these conditions, the Soviet Union was able to dictate terms to the Eastern European states under its auspices. The Soviet form of polity and economy was built, sometimes with popular support – in countries such as Yugoslavia and Albania – but often in spite of reluctance or even disapproval, in countries such as Hungary and Poland. The previous political culture and institutions of the East European states influenced the structure and process of the system of state socialism which arose, but the distinctive features of the Soviet institutions became apparent in the 1950s.

The organizing principles of capitalism were disavowed by the political leadership installed in these countries, and a new type of societal organization, state socialism, modelled on developments in the USSR as discussed in the last chapter, was adopted. The 'world of the comrades' was based ideologically on a class world-view, on collective and fraternal public organizations and had the teleological goal of building communism. Property was brought under state ownership, the Communist Party was hegemonic, central planning replaced the market. Foreign policy was aligned to that of the USSR.

It is impossible to describe in detail the building of socialism, as it was called, in all of these countries. Here the various trajectories taken by three of them – Poland, China and Cuba – will be described.[6] This account is intended to give the reader some understanding of the complex

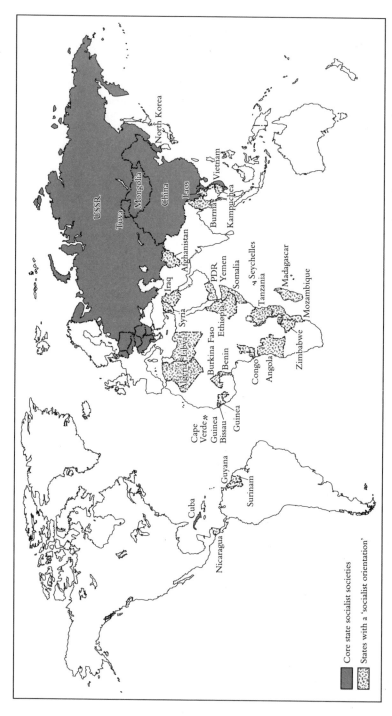

Core state socialist societies and states with a 'socialist orientation', world-wide, 1985 (data derived from Graham Smith, *Planned Development in the Socialist World* (Cambridge University Press, 1989), p. 2)

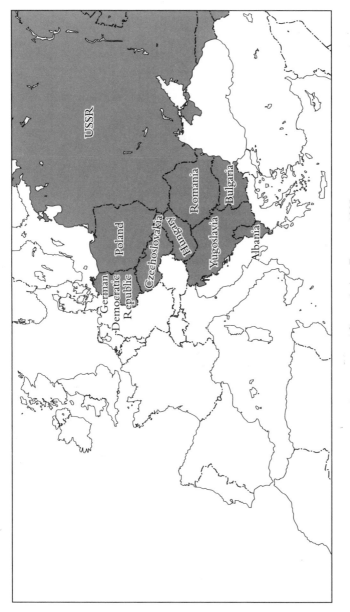

Core state socialist societies, Europe, 1985

patterns of development and the different cultural and political contexts in which communists came to, and later fell from, power. The story here is limited to the rise and development of these states. While some of the tensions are noted, the emphasis is on the 'building of socialism' as it was perceived. The reform movement is considered in the next chapter, where the story of the People's Republic of China is considered again, in addition to accounts of developments in Yugoslavia, Czechoslovakia and the USSR.

People's Republic of Poland

The Poles have the characteristic of being a strong nation but having had a weak state.[7] For many years before the Second World War, Poland did not exist as a sovereign state. It was partitioned in 1891 between powerful neighbours: Russia, Austria and Prussia. During the periods of partition the Polish nation was held together by a powerful intelligentsia and the Catholic Church. Only in 1923 was the country reconstituted as a state, and at that time over 10 million out of a population of 32 million were non-Poles. The Polish people were mainly Catholics, forming the bulk of the peasantry, the formal political elite and the intelligentsia. The business classes were predominantly composed of non-Poles, particularly Germans and Jews. Before the Second World War there was considerable animosity between these national groups. The Catholic Church had a long history as a focus for national unity, and the Polish intelligentsia was a proud bearer of national consciousness. The political culture was not of a Western, liberal-democratic, participatory type. Parliamentary institutions, introduced after the First World War, were ineffectual; and after 1926, when Pilsudski took effective control of the executive, the political system has been described as one of 'ineffectual authoritarianism'.[8] With the exception of the central industrial region after 1936, the economy stagnated between the wars. Lacking a firmly based liberal-democratic tradition, Poland had disastrous right-wing authoritarian governments before the Second World War – when in 1939 the country was invaded simultaneously by the Germans and Russians.

Following the victory of the Germans, Poland was divided, with two-thirds coming under German jurisdiction and one-third ceded to the USSR. In 1941, following the German invasion of the Soviet Union, the whole of Poland was incorporated into the Third Reich. The Second World War decimated Poland. Six million Poles were killed and the Jewish population was largely exterminated. The war had the effect of strengthening the Polish nation but once more weakening the Polish state. Afterwards, with the agreement of the victorious Allies, Poland's land area again changed – areas in the east were lost to the USSR, but areas in the west and north were gained from Germany. The regained lands were repopulated by Poles and the incumbent Germans were expelled. This process in the 1990s would be called effective 'ethnic cleansing'. The post-war population was now 98 per cent Polish and 95 per cent Catholic.

The country had a history of being strongly anti-communist and anti-Russian. The Communist Party before 1945 had been very weak. It had been declared illegal in 1919 and was further weakened when dissolved by Stalin in 1938. The party's peak pre-war membership was 12,000, 59 per cent of whom were intellectuals and only 10 per cent industrial workers.[9] The communists, following the heritage of Rosa Luxemburg, were internationalist. The working class mainly supported the Polish Socialist Party (PPS), which was highly conscious of Polish nationalism. In 1944, the Communist Party and the pro-Soviet Patriots Union had a joint membership of only 20,000.

But neither the communists nor any other Polish political party or group decided the form of polity and society after the Second World War. The major political actor was the victorious Soviet army, which liberated Poland in 1945. The internal non-communist opposition movement organized around the Home Army was not recognized by the Soviet Union and when it led the Warsaw uprising against the Nazis, the Red Army did not come to its aid. Consequently, Warsaw was taken by the Russians. A Soviet-type regime led by the communists, many of whom returned from the USSR, was inevitable and a government was formed with 16 positions out of 20 taken by the Soviet-backed Lublin Committee. There was no Western support to recognize the London-based émigré Polish government.

In the immediate post-revolutionary period, the factories of former German citizens were seized and the nationalization of firms with over 50 employees took place in 1946. As in Russia in 1917, a land reform was enacted: the land, including that in the new territories in the West, was divided up and largely worked in small plots by the Polish peasantry. This was a popular move and disarmed peasant opposition to the government. Following the Soviet pattern of industrialization, capital investment was made in heavy industry, making it by 1950 a greater contributor than agriculture to gross national product.

Much of this was due to Poland's geographical changes. The eastern territories transferred to the USSR were largely rural and agricultural. Those in the west gained from Germany included significant industrial capital. It has been estimated that industrial fixed assets per capita rose by about 50 per cent as a consequence of these changes, taken in conjunc-

tion with population loss.[10] The movement of rural population to the
towns and the increased capital stock inherited from Germany contributed greatly to the industrialization of Poland. Nevertheless, one should
not belittle the transformation over which the communist government
presided. The introduction of social services, comprehensive education
and an industrial economy enjoyed widespread support.

The fundamental relationship between state and society, however, was
one of division: the communist state was identified with the power of
Soviet Russia. This was a double liability since public sentiments were
neither positive towards communism nor sympathetic to Russia. The
ruling party lacked social support and found it increasingly difficult to
control Polish society. Though the communist government had succeeded in quelling a minor civil war in the immediate post-war period, it
failed to penetrate the countryside. Whereas in the USSR collectivization
was carried out in one fell swoop, in Poland, at the peak of the collectivization drive in 1956, only 8.6 per cent of the total cultivated area was
collectivized. Furthermore, collectivization was abandoned as a policy
in that year and made voluntary. By 1962, only 1.2 per cent of the
cultivated area was collectivized. This left an important area of private
enterprise and anti-communist sentiment in the countryside.

The Polish government was unable to command authority. Underlying
social factors severely weakened legitimacy – the traditional intelligentsia
and the Catholic Church were strongly hostile to communism. The
Church was well organized and preserved Christian values, which became
an alternative belief system to Marxism-Leninism. It successfully undermined communist attempts to use the media to create a Marxist-Leninist
outlook. The communists' strategy was to create a working class, which
they believed would provide a basis of social and political support. They
succeeded in the former but failed in the latter. By 1960, manual workers
constituted 44.2 per cent of the employed population compared to only
28.6 per cent in 1931; independent farmers had fallen from 51.1 per cent
to 27.8 per cent. Whereas in 1939 the urban population was 35.1 per
cent, by 1960 it was 48.3 per cent. The government hoped that such
demographic changes would provide a political ballast for the new regime
and it was also believed that the Church's influence would wane with
the industrialization and secularization of the population. These hopes,
however, were not to be fulfilled, for reasons we shall consider in later
chapters.

Political crises and collapse

With the destalinization which took place in the USSR following
Khrushchev's liberalization there in 1956, Poland experienced a series of

legitimacy crises. The government fell in 1956 and Wladyslaw Gomulka took over. In 1968 and 1970 there were further serious disturbances, and Gomulka was replaced by Edward Gierek.

While in the early years after the end of the Second World War, Poland had staged a remarkable recovery and experienced positive economic growth, by the late 1970s economic advance had declined (this will be discussed comparatively in chapter 5). The steep rise of international oil prices in the 1970s, coupled to the recession in Western economies, meant that the terms of trade turned against Poland and the real price of exports fell. Agricultural production also declined and Poland found itself having to import grain. These external conditions exacerbated Poland's economic problems. Over the period 1971–5 Poland's hard currency debt increased tenfold from $750 million to over $7 billion and reached $21.5 billion in 1979. By 1986, Poland's external debts came to $36,638 million dollars: this was double that of Hungary ($17,218 million) and only just below that of India ($41,088 million).[11] The long-term debt of Poland was 48.5 per cent of GNP in 1986; it was greater than that of India (15.1 per cent) or Brazil (37.6 per cent), though Poland was not in the top world debtor group (Chile at 120.1 per cent and Zambia at 240.5 per cent).[12] The repayment of interest and capital on these debts was a tremendous strain on the Polish economy.

The communist government was faced with severe internal predicaments. There was suppressed inflation, and attempts to raise the prices of basic commodities led to widespread strikes and public disturbances. It was not possible to meet the population's economic expectations, which had been engendered by successive communist governments as part of a policy to gain legitimacy through increased economic well-being. The working class required the government to provide comprehensive social services, a rising standard of living and security through permanent employment, and concurrently to reduce the uncertainty generated by inflation and shortages. Gierek tried to overcome the austerity and shortages of the Stalinist years; with the help of Western credit and imports, standards of consumption rose. When this improvement was not sustained, the legitimacy of the government further declined.

Moreover, Gierek was confronted by even more serious forms of internal dissent than his predecessors. In 1980, the government was faced by massive strikes, led by 'unofficial' trade unions. In August an important accord was made between Gierek and the strike leaders, conceding the rights of citizens to form trade unions and also the right to strike. 'Solidarity', a spontaneous trade union movement, received legal recognition in November 1980.[13]

These developments signalled not only that living conditions were unacceptable but that the forms of participation of workers under the communist state were inadequate. The official unions and party organizations had failed to articulate worker interests and rather had been instruments of the central leadership. In 1980 Solidarity claims to have involved 12 per cent of the non-agricultural labour force in its activities.[14] The movement was strongest in the shipyards of the Baltic, but later spread to cover other industrial areas of Poland, claiming to encompass more than 12 million workers (including rural ones) by December 1981.[15]

The major objectives of the working class, as expressed in the early years of Solidarity, were economic. Roman Laba shows in a study of workers' explicit demands in the years 1970, 1971 and 1980 that they were mainly economistic in orientation. Of the top ten demands made by workers, the first was pay rises in all three years, while calls for free trade unions came second in 1970 and 1971 and fourth in 1980 (placed after increases in family subsidies and non-working on Saturdays). The most political demand – the elimination of privileges of members of the apparatus – came tenth in 1970 and ninth in 1971 and 1980.[16]

While Solidarity rose first as a movement in support of workers' rights and conditions, it later developed into a political opposition led by a shipyard worker Lech Walesa. The government did not use force to suppress the movement and instead sought a pact. This not only secured the right to strike, but also concessions on censorship and a relaxation of state control over the Church, which supported the workers' demands both nationally and locally. In contrast to the workers' uprisings of 1971 and 1976, the rise of the Solidarity movement witnessed, for the first time, an alliance between the workers and the intelligentsia against the government. Intellectuals in the form of the Workers' Defence Committee (KOR) played a major role in the movement, along with the support for Solidarity coming from the Catholic Church.

The period 1981–9 was one of economic stagnation and political stalemate. As the economic situation worsened, the government was under continual threat from forces of opposition led by Solidarity and the Church. In 1980, Gierek fell from power and was replaced in September by Stanislaw Kania, who lasted until October 1981, when the prime minister/defence minister Wojciech Jaruzelski took over. In December 1981, martial law was declared by Jaruzelski and the country was ruled by a military government. In Poland the military has been another unifying factor based on Polish nationalism, unlike in the USSR, where it has played a minor political role. While the Polish state could now maintain political order, economic conditions worsened greatly: the debt in convertible currency rose rapidly, reaching $40 billion in 1988; inflation reached three figures, shortages of commodities persisted and the quality of life declined.[17]

The Soviet Union had always played a major role in Polish policy. In

1968, the invasion of Czechoslovakia by Warsaw Pact countries legitimated by the Brezhnev doctrine illustrated the limits to which the
countries of Eastern Europe could pursue their own interests. The rise of
Gorbachev and his 'new political thinking' led not only to a more liberal
and open regime in the USSR but to significant changes in Soviet foreign
policy. Gorbachev intended to concentrate on building socialism at home
and to limit support for foreign ruling communist parties and revolutionary parties (see chapter 5 below). Essentially, ruling parties had to legitimate themselves in their own countries and rule on their own merits on
the basis of popular consent. As internal democracy and civil rights
developed in the USSR, so too they were claimed by the opposition in
the Eastern European countries. This was the context in which a move to
a multiparty system and non-communist government could develop in
Poland. (These developments will be considered in chapter 6.)

The Catholic Church, which had played a leading role in opposition
to the communists, lost its political role to the new political parties.
Poland remained in the Warsaw Pact until it was dissolved in July 1991,
and maintained good relations with the Gorbachev government in the
USSR. Solidarity turned from an opposition into a government. It proved
to be an unsatisfactory body to rule the country. As an oppositional
movement combining trade union and political party it was successful in
opposing the communists. After their fall, Solidarity had to combine all
three roles: trade union, oppositional political party and government.

Communism in Poland

Communism in Poland may be seen to have had a quite different impact
compared to that of the USSR. Consider once more the challenges to be
solved in a modernizing or developing society, as suggested by Almond
and Powell.[18] The Polish nation had a strong independent identity before
the communist assumption of power. Both the Polish intelligentsia and
the Catholic Church long histories of independent identities. The
working class identified more with Catholicism and Polish nationalism
than with communism. The communists then were unable to forge an
alternative set of symbolic attachments to replace traditional Polish nationalism and the Catholic religion. Communist ideology was too dependent on a foreign Soviet Marxism to counter the ideas of Church and
the mainly anti-communist intelligentsia. The communist government set
up after the Second World War by the Soviet Union inherited a double
handicap – of little pro-communist support and association with a Soviet
regime which itself had invaded Poland in 1939 and had taken parts of
pre-war Poland. Anti-Russian popular sentiment was also particularly

strong. The Polish United Workers' Party was quite unable to secure legitimacy as a ruling party.

Economic decline also had crucial politically delegitimating effects. The fusion of economic and political aspects in the government apparatus promoted political legitimacy when the economy was working well. However, when economic growth and incomes fell, this became a responsibility of government and its legitimacy was put in doubt. In so far as planning is one of the organizing principles of state socialism, a crisis of economic management leads to a crisis of political management. The lack of identity and legitimacy were underlying weaknesses which explain why the communists failed to penetrate society. They had insufficient support to collectivize agriculture; consequently, the land reform strengthened ownership links between peasantry and private property. They were also confronted by the Western orientation of the bourgeois intelligentsia and by a Polish pope based in Rome: Pope John Paul II became a principled opponent of communism. According to a feature article in *Time* magazine, John Paul II and President Reagan in June 1982 jointly planned 'a clandestine campaign to bring down the communist empire'.[19] Exogenous factors created conditions of instability. (Foreign factors are discussed in more detail in chapter 6).

By comparison with the conditions inherited by the Soviet communists in Russia in 1917, civil society had much firmer roots in Poland. The regime failed to secure effective positive participation in the political system. The Soviet model of trade unions was not acceptable to workers who had had experience of more economistic unions before the Second World War. The government had to concede important forms of pluralism: from the very beginning of the People's Republic, there were multiple parties, greater professional independence (in films, art, philosophy, social sciences) and the Church played an independent role. Such associations provided alternative focuses for participation and, being alien to the communist system, undermined it. Solidarity became an expression of economic and political demands which destabilized the regime. Of all the revolutions which took place in Eastern Europe, Poland's was the only one in which the working class played, through strike activity, a major role as a catalyst of change. In this, too, the West supported a destabilizing role.[20]

In the Soviet model, which was adopted in Poland, there is no division between economy and polity: the government is responsible for economic and social welfare. In the early years of state socialism, redistribution of land and the creation of a welfare state enhanced legitimacy. Socialism, moreover, engenders high levels of expectations for increasing welfare. When things go well, there is a positive effect on well-being and political support. However, if there is poor economic performance, people do not blame the world market or private enterprise. The government is held responsible for economic mismanagement whatever its causes. When expectations are not fulfilled, dissatisfaction with government ensues. In Poland a large expectations gap developed between what the population expected in both material and ideal forms and what was available. In combination, all these phenomena led to a position of ungovernability. We return to outline the collapse of the communist government in 1989 in chapter 6.

People's Republic of China

The rise of communism in China is notable on many counts. In its revolutionary phase, communism arose as a movement with a rural and peasant base. In its period of development, it first copied the model of socialist modernization pioneered in the USSR, then adopted a radical course of Maoism which rejected many of the features of the model of state socialism as it had developed under Stalin. Finally, China and Hungary were the first countries explicitly to recognize the limitations of the Soviet paradigm of development and they led the movement for economic reform towards markets and participation in the capitalist world economic order.[21] In this chapter we discuss the period of revolution in China culminating in the Cultural Revolution; in chapter 5 we turn to the reform process.

The communist revolutionary movement in China arose in a country which was economically centuries behind the level even of Russia in 1917. From the time of Peter the Great (1672–1725) Russia had been copying European technology and had been in close contact with European culture; it had a prominent intelligentsia, and by 1917 modern forms of manufacturing industry and communications had already been implanted. In contrast, in 1949 China was one of the world's poorest countries. There was only a rudimentary railway system, no large-scale public works and industrial employment was on a very small scale: 'by far the greater part of the country carried on, as for the last 2,000 years, an early iron-age economy.'[22] The urban working class and bourgeoisie were extremely small and the country had a predominantly peasant population. It was among these that Mao Zedong was to organize not only a political party but an army to establish communist power in 1949.

As in the countries of Eastern Europe, the Chinese communists came to power following war and military occupation. But there was one important difference compared to the revolutionary struggle in Russia and Eastern Europe. In China the communists had fought a protracted military campaign for more than 20 years before the Chinese People's Republic was formed. Mao had formed the nucleus of a Red Army in 1928 and the Communist Party had existed since that date as a revolutionary guerrilla army with a base in the countryside built from peasants with rural support. By 1945 the Communist Party of China claimed a membership of 1,210,000.

The communists were leaders of a struggle for national liberation and had support from many of the entrepreneurs, executives and professional classes. Unlike in Poland, where communism was associated with an unpopular neighbouring foreign power (the USSR), in China socialism developed under Mao as a movement in opposition to foreign oppressors – it was a movement for national liberation. Once in control, the relations with opposing classes initially were less confrontational than in Russia after 1917. The Constitution of 1954 guaranteed the right of some individuals to private ownership of the means of production. The national bourgeoisie was recognized as part of 'the people', of the 'democratic dictatorship' based on the alliance of the 'working class, peasantry and the urban petty bourgeoisie'. The public ownership of the means of production was also implemented much more gradually than in Eastern Europe. Between 1949 and 1952 only the businesses of capitalists supporting the Kuomintang were nationalized. (The Kuomintang was the dominant party in China after 1928. Led by Chiang Kai-shek it opposed the Japanese then the communists.) Small-scale entrepreneurs were only absorbed into state ownership as 'private-state' enterprises in 1956 and the owners received compensation for their property and were encouraged to continue their work.

Economic policy

After taking power, the Chinese communists consciously copied the policies and organizational forms of the Soviet Union.[23] The slogan during the First Five Year Plan (1953–7) was: 'Learn from the Soviet Union.' Comprehensive economic development with an emphasis on heavy industry was favoured, and the Soviet Union helped financially and with personnel in the early industrialization drive. Organization, as in the Soviet Union, was centralized and management was hierarchical under branch ministries. Monetary incentives followed the pattern of the Soviet Union, people being paid 'according to their work' and labour being graded according to level of skill and type of industry. Bonus and piecework schemes were introduced in the period from 1953 to 1957. As in the USSR, the role of trade unions was to promote efficiency to implement economic plans and to administer social security services.

Social policy followed a similar course to that of Stalin's Russia: comprehensive education, mass literacy and mass health care were introduced. However, there were important differences here: the provision of social services was limited to the urban areas and to permanent workers in state industry, the peasantry being largely excluded from such provision.

Policy in agriculture also had parallels with the Soviet Union. There were three steps. First, a land reform destroyed the gentry and gave the land to the peasants, who subsequently worked it in small plots. Second, collectivization weakened the rich peasants and was then regarded as a precondition for large-scale agricultural production with intensive factory-type farming. While a considerable part of the peasantry was alienated in Russia and collectivization was a violent process, in China it was more gradual. At first, a policy of piecemeal and voluntary collectivization was envisaged. The Common Programme had stated that 'the People's government . . . shall guide the peasants step by step to organise various forms of mutual aid [and] labour and production cooperation according to the principle of free choice and mutual benefits.'[24] This did not succeed, however, as the yield of grain was low and hoarding of grain was widespread. The third step was rapid and forced collectivization. By 1956, 83 per cent of all peasant households had joined 'advanced cooperatives'.

From the mid-1950s policy radically departed from dependence on the Soviet model. This is a second phase of socialist development; it was a response to deficiencies in the Soviet model as applied to China and involves one of the earliest critiques by a communist government of the Soviet model of development. Before considering it, however, we may summarize at this point the Chinese form of socialism as it developed in the first ten years of power.

The Chinese communists effectively identified with traditional Chinese society. Unlike in the USSR and European states, a distinctive character of the Chinese revolution was the degree to which the communists integrated non-proletarian social groups into the revolutionary movement. A national liberation movement was based not only on the peasantry but also included the petty bourgeoisie. The Chinese communists succeeded in the national (and concurrently revolutionary) struggle against the Japanese and the Kuomintang and established the legitimacy of a communist state. The revolution was a popular synthesis of a national and a social revolution. Mao was able to secure a base in society so that the party and army were agents able to penetrate society. The Chinese Communist Party adopted a much deeper form of mobilization of the masses than had been possible in the Soviet Union. The concept of a mass line involving participation 'from below' was different from the Russian revolutionary process. It emphasized the fact that development and 'building communism' had a human component; it depended on people's attitudes and motivation, which could be influenced by cultural revolution. This was due to the need to secure peasant support during a guerrilla war. Participation, however, like that in the Soviet Union, had the character of audience participation, and decision-making was centralized under the leadership of the communists. In the immediate post-revolutionary period there was less stress on rewards according to work and the party recognized the need to compensate previous bourgeois groups. However, the educational and social services were limited to the towns and industry – the peasantry was largely excluded from such provision. In contrast to a situation of ungovernability, as in Poland, in China deficiencies were seen in the Soviet model from a revolutionary and socialist perspective. The Chinese communists were a confident, popular mass movement who sought their own identity as a revolutionary movement.

The rise of Maoism

In order to establish this identity, the Chinese came into conflict with the leadership of the USSR. The Chinese leaders resented the hegemony exercised by the USSR and sought a more independent line and more respect in the international communist movement. In the late 1950s, relations between the two countries were severely strained and the USSR ceased all economic and political assistance. Hence the Chinese reforms which were introduced under Mao Zedong had an international as well as a domestic component. The 'Chinese way' was an indication to the communist movement (particularly in the Third World) and to unaligned countries that China deserved recognition as a major communist world power.

The Chinese leadership under Chairman Mao then attempted a leftist critique of Soviet policy which differed in six major ways from Soviet state socialism. Firstly, planning priorities were revised. Greater attention was given to agriculture and light industry. In 1958 the policy of the Great Leap Forward envisaged very high targets in labour-intensive workshops in the countryside. They would use little capital but much labour. This was a sensible policy in a country with a great shortage of capital and a surplus of labour. The gestation period of investment was short and returns were rapid. The effect here would be to raise incomes and consumption, in contrast to the austerity of Soviet planning under Stalin, which Mao referred to as 'draining the pond to catch the fish'.[25] In its economic aspects, the policy was appropriate to utilize the small-scale, labour-intensive and primitive industry of traditional China. It signalled a move away from the introduction of the advanced technology (of the day) entailed by the Soviet model. Mao advocated the use of intermediate and 'native' technology. Decentralization and 'self-reliance' replaced dependence on foreign technology and 'learning from the Soviet Union'.

Secondly, the system of management and incentives was fundamentally reappraised. The centralized form of management under ministries was repudiated.[26] In place of one-man management, control was placed under local party committees. Political expertise rather than technical skill was advocated in management. Popular mobilization of the masses under a revolutionary party replaced the bureaucratic centralism thought to be endemic in the Soviet form of administration. This idea of the 'mass line' was something peculiar to Mao's policy. 'Building communism' was dependent on the human factor, on people's attitudes.

Thirdly, Mao was the first socialist leader to point to the contradictions derived from the structures and processes of the early socialist formation. Here he echoed the ideas regarding state capitalism which we shall consider in more detail in chapter 7. A reversion to capitalism can take place if a degenerate socialist leadership becomes a bourgeois class through its command of bureaucratic position and exploitation of the masses. He argued that this is what had occurred in the USSR under Khrushchev. The major sources of the 'new bourgeois elements' were in the party–state machine. A new capitalist class, it was conceded, could arise out of the state economy: the administrative cadres and the intelligentsia were the basis of this new exploiting class. Under Khrushchev in the Soviet Union, Mao argued, revisionism legitimated the privilege and power of this new class. To combat such degeneration, recognition had to be made of the continuation of class struggle under socialism.

Fourthly, the socialist revolution had to continue during the period of transition. Economic policy moved away from the use of material incentives to a greater emphasis on ideological imperatives and 'greater reliance was placed on the revolutionary fervour of the masses.'[27] Material incentives, it was contended, had led to the growth of individualism and egoism. In the sphere of motivation towards work, putting 'politics in command' meant 'first of all the awakening of enthusiasm', and emphasis was placed on emulation campaigns intended to develop 'collectivist attitudes and behaviour'. Honorific rather than material rewards became dominant. This policy adopted the traditional socialist opposition to prices as signals, money as incentives and markets as determinants of production and consumption. It also opposed any economic and political linkages with economies which worked on these principles. China embarked on a policy of isolation from both the major world power blocs.

Fifthly, institutional forms were introduced to fulfil these principles. In the villages 'communes' were started. Production brigades were organized which could handle the building of water works and small-scale industries. Consumption in kind accounted for 70 per cent of members' income. In the communes, food was provided collectively and was free of charge.

Finally, a Cultural Revolution was devised as a strategy which sought to implement the new revolutionary goals of the Maoist leadership. In 1964, a 'socialist education' campaign took place which was seen as part of the ideological struggle against the bourgeois outlook associated with Soviet communism. The aim here, as in the Great Proletarian Cultural Revolution which began in 1966, was to indoctrinate youth with a militant revolutionary consciousness. This was considered to be the continuation of the socialist revolution.

The Great Cultural Revolution

Schram defines the two general aims of the Cultural Revolution as 'to change the structure of power in society, and to carry out an irreversible transformation in the patterns of thought and behaviour of the Chinese people'.[28] This entailed an ideological and political campaign against hostile groups – bureaucrats and intellectuals – to prevent any tendency to drift away from socialism. Direct action was undertaken by Mao's supporters. These were located in the army and among the Red Guards – youth who were revolutionary students. A decisive shift took place in 1964 when the army became the 'dominant force in Chinese society and the arbiter of ideological orthodoxy'.[29] In 1967, 'revolutionary committees' were established composed of members of the People's Liberation Army, new revolutionary activists (the Red Guards) and party and government personnel. They were charged with supplanting the existing party and government organizations.

Revolutionary committees were instituted in industry. These abolished the old form of hierarchical management. The educational system was fundamentally changed. Elitist and specialist types of study were discontinued. Education was to be socialist and to 'serve the people'. Resources were shifted to the countryside in order to make education available to the rural masses rather than to the more privileged urban population. Learning was oriented towards vocational training. The teaching of medical auxiliaries in the form of 'barefoot doctors', it was contended, was an appropriate policy for an underdeveloped country, rather than the training of specialists in advanced medicine. A greater stress was put on communist values, on serving the people, rather than on personal achievement: education was 'a universally available prerequisite for useful participation in a modernizing economy'.[30]

Important changes took place in the role of the Communist Party. The authority of the party was replaced by the masses led by Chairman Mao. The Leninist idea of the party spreading 'consciousness' among the masses was replaced by an ideology of 'learning from the masses' – a continuation of the policy instituted during the guerrilla war. The Constitution recognized Mao as 'the great leader of the people of all nationalities in the entire country'. The Constitution adopted in 1975 declared that 'Marxism-Leninism–Mao Zedong Thought is the theoretical basis guiding the thinking of our nation.' Mao's position was unassailable and he ruled like one of the previous emperors.

The Cultural Revolution has to be interpreted in the context of the Chinese Revolution. The Chinese party did not have a significant base among the working class, unlike in Russia, where in 1917, 60 per cent of party members were manual workers. In China the communists had mass support in the countryside from peasants whose culture was parochial. The Cultural Revolution aimed to bring about a transformation of the political culture. It sought to root out traditional practices encapsulated in the campaign against the 'four olds' (ideas, culture, customs and habits). As an instrument of modernization, it must be seen in the wider perspective of achieving modernity: of inculcating initiative and mobilizing an extremely backward peasant population through collectivist pressure.

Internal and international politics must also be taken into account. Mao asserted the power of his supporters in the political class against possible contenders located in the government bureaucracy (this will be discussed further in chapter 7). In international affairs, the cultural revolution provided a political legitimation for China's leadership in its struggle with the USSR. In a Marxist sense, the emphasis was put on the relations to the means of production. Not only could the class in control create the material forces of socialism (as suggested by Stalin), but the political leadership, through its control of the relations of production, could also establish a superstructure of a socialist type.

The Chinese model had a great appeal to radicals in the West and also had influence in the Third World in the late 1960s and 1970s. It appeared as a socialist policy and, by contrast with the Eastern European countries, it was idealistic rather than technocratic. It held out hope for the elimination of the poverty, privilege and bureaucratic control which seemed endemic to both capitalism and the socialist bloc. It also had a rhetoric of equalitarianism. While it is difficult to make an accurate appraisal of the pluses and minuses of development, social indicators showed real improvements in the standards of life: life expectancy rose from 40 years in 1950 to 61 in 1970; illiteracy fell from 70–80 per cent of the population in 1950 to 55–60 in 1960.[31] But the period of the Great Leap Forward of

1958–9 was one of chaos and famine: it has been confidently estimated that 10 million people died of hunger in those years; other estimates are as high as 25 million and 40 million.[32] For the whole of the period between 1950 and 1976, estimates of deaths from famine and persecution have been put at 80 million.[33] Bands of Red Guards undoubtedly acted in an arbitrary and violent fashion, and massacres took place of people suspected of coming from the landlord or ruling classes. It is now widely held that Mao's policy was mistaken, leading to unwarranted deaths and retarding development. However, Mao has never been officially exposed in China in the way Stalin was in the USSR. The ruling communists have minimized the faults of their previous history to prevent themselves (and communist institutions) being implicated. In the preamble of the 1982 Constitution, the four Basic Principles of the state are constituted as the leading role of the Communist Party of China, adherence to the socialist road, upholding the people's democratic dictatorship and the guiding role of Marxism-Leninism and Mao Zedong Thought.

After the death of Mao, however, his policy was repudiated by the new leadership and replaced by yet another form of revision and control. China turned from being the instigator of a socialist pattern of development to a system which copied extensively from the economic practice of the advanced capitalist states: the country entered world trade and enthusiastically adopted market mechanisms. This policy will be considered in the next chapter.

Republic of Cuba

On 1 January 1959, Fidel Castro led his guerrilla army into Havana.[34] A coup d'état, rather than a communist revolution, had taken place. Most of Castro's followers had no knowledge of Marxism and were not communists. The army was an important symbol of national unity in Cuba, as in Latin America generally, and it, rather than the party, was the spirit of the uprising. Castro was very much a charismatic leader around whom gathered a nucleus of revolutionaries – wholly of middle-class and Spanish, rather than African and peasant, origin. The guerrilla movement was organized in the mountains with support coming from agricultural labourers. The only Marxist element in the leadership was that provided by Fidel's brother, Raul Castro, and the Argentinian Che Guevara. The 1953 programme of Castro differed little from that of other groups in Latin America seeking national liberation; only one reference to 'capitalism' may be found in it.

Pre-Castro Cuba had been unstable politically, with opposition being led by military and student groups. Initially, the revolutionary movement saw itself as part of the movement for national liberation from colonial oppression. It was an anti-imperialist movement and one which stressed individual freedom, to be achieved through revolution. Castro was seeking to establish a society independent from the influence and control of the United States. His guerrilla movement against the Batista dictatorship had the main objective of safeguarding the rights of the masses against a corrupt, foreign-dominated regime. The Communist Party was small and not influential. In 1958 the communists regarded Castro as 'bourgeois' and played a minor role in his guerrilla movement.[35] Castro himself had little knowledge of Marxism and he did not consider himself to be a Marxist even when he came to power. Moreover, he initially had indirect support from the United States when in 1958, during his struggle against Batista, they placed an embargo on arms for the regime. After gaining power, in the early days of his leadership, he went with moderate government ministers to the USA expecting economic help; he made anti-communist statements comparing communism to fascism, and said that American capitalism promised 'humanistic freedoms' for Cuba.[36]

Then the Castro leadership moved from pursuing a coup d'état with liberal-democratic aims to revolutionary change. Taking this route, Cuba followed a pattern of politics similar to other Latin American societies. There was a tradition of revolutionary activity with a high participation by the military. Initially, Castro filled leading positions in the government with friends and family. The new regime had Batista supporters shot and confiscated their property. The plantations owned by absentee Americans were expropriated, as was the property of other large landowners. The losses to American interests – in fruit production and tourism (casinos and sex services) – led to relations worsening with the USA, and Castro was accused of being communist.

Spurned by the Americans, Castro then turned towards allies in the communist world and to communism as an ideology. It must be borne in mind that the world context of the late 1950s was still one of great confidence in the success of communism. The USSR had claimed considerable credit in putting the first man into space and Khrushchev boasted of the USSR catching up and even outstripping the economic levels of the advanced Western states. Castro expelled anti-communists from the political leadership and banned all political parties except the communists. He adopted a Marxist-Leninist ideology. His links with the Soviet Union increased and led to more nationalization of US property; this led to a US embargo on sugar purchases which drove Castro even further into the Soviet orbit. In 1960 nationalization continued and effectively put the economy under government control.

Castro and Marxism-Leninism

But it was not until 1961 that Castro declared himself a Marxist-Leninist. He merged his own 26 July Movement with the Communist Party and from 1965 his movement adopted the title of the Communist Party of Cuba. However, the First Communist Party Congress did not take place until 1975, when a comprehensive policy was worked out. Castro met little internal dissension and no internal military threat largely because the previous political and business elite fled to Florida, whence it campaigned for the overthrow of Castro by the USA.

In the earlier period of Castro's rule, Cuba had elements of policy clearly linked to socialist norms. There was a strong emphasis on moral incentives towards work, a reduction of wage differentials and a policy of reducing the gap between town and country. Before 1970, he aspired to abolish the use of money. One of his major objectives was to create a new person: 'People aspiring to live under Communism must do what we are doing. They must emerge from underdevelopment; they must develop the forces of production . . . The problem from our point of view is that Communist consciousness must be developed at the same rate as the forces of production.'[37]

After the First Congress, the role of the Central Committee of the party became more important. The apparatus was expanded and a party control commission was set up. The secretariat was organized along the lines of traditional communist parties, with the political leadership exerting control over other administrative forms.[38] As Castro moved from being a patriotic revolutionary leader, the party provided the organizational and administrative form for the Cuban revolution.

Communism, however, arose out of needs for internal reform and for international allies. It provided an integrating ideology and a form of political organization and control. The policy of the United States to Cuba was of paramount significance. The economic boycott of Cuba and the abortive invasion (the Bay of Pigs, 1961) supported by the United States pushed Castro to find international allies. In April 1961 Cuba declared that the revolution was a socialist one and consequently identified with 'proletarian internationalism'. Thereafter, Cuba became part of Comecon and its 'Sovietization' started, with the Soviet Union providing military security.

Castro supported the armed struggle of oppressed groups struggling for independence in Latin America, and Cuban troops participated in revolutionary movements in Angola, Vietnam and Ethiopia. Though this is often said to be a consequence of Soviet influence, other factors were equally or even more important. The military is very influential in Cuban society and it continued the tradition of revolutionary struggle in Third

World countries. Castro considered himself to be a Latin Africanist as well as a Latin American.

Castro's economic policy differed significantly from that pursued by the Soviet Union. In such a small island it was impossible to have a comprehensive independent economy and it remained highly dependent on sugar exports. Cuba, moreover, adopted a policy of comparative advantage derived from the production of sugar, traded in exchange for other goods. Membership of Comecon secured markets and brought Cuba into the communist trading bloc.

Before 1970 labour policy was geared to moral incentives and equalitarianism. The harvesting of sugar was seen as a continuation of the guerrilla struggle and moral incentives were an attempt to create social solidarity through socialist commitment. The attempt failed. After 1970 monetary incentives were reinstated and used as a stimulus for efficient work. The economy was planned on a more balanced basis than in the Soviet Union during its period of industrialization. More resources were devoted to building and to light industry, providing higher levels of personal consumption.[39]

The initial stage of revolution was radical and popular; it was led by the middle classes with the support of the agricultural labourers. It was a national movement for reform and it differed from other communist revolutions by virtue of the leadership and charisma of Castro and the role of the guerrilla army. National liberation from imperialism was a major motivating force, rather than anti-capitalism or class struggle. This has given the army a symbolic role in Cuba.

A Cuban commitment to communism was adopted in the modernization and development period. Castro's anti-Americanism and anti-corruption campaigns led to considerable nationalization of property. His comprehensive state-run social policies had an affinity with state socialism. The independent development of the revolutionary movement, moreover, gave Cuban communism a different character from the Soviet: it is more participatory, allows relatively greater freedom of speech, has emphasized women's emancipation, involves an exalted role for the leader and gives a symbolic role to the army. The Cuban system displayed a high degree of solidarity. There was relatively little internal dissent (though there has been much external dissent from émigrés) and no 'reform movement' as in China and in the Eastern European countries.

The legacy of imperialism, constant vigilance against the United States and the continuation of the revolutionary ideal through foreign military expeditions sustained Castro's particular brand of state planning. Cuba, however, being the first socialist country in Latin America, has been a challenge to American hegemony which, based on the Monroe doctrine, has regarded the area to be one of American influence. Castro sought to aid revolutionary movements and in 1967 he convened the Organization of Latin American Solidarity. The United States refused to recognize Cuba, maintained a severe trade embargo and conducted subversion against the regime.[40] In an interview with Lee Lockwood in 1966, Castro said: 'The CIA maintains its activities incessantly and with all possible resources. It works systematically with all the Cubans who are now in the United States, with the relatives and friends of the counter-revolutionaries who are there, trying constantly to organize webs of information, espionage and counterrevolution. . . . Proofs of the activities of the CIA? We have millions of proofs.' This has continued right up to the present day. In public, political terms, in 1989 President Bush's conditions for a change in American policy were similar to those he enunciated for the European socialist states: 'a free Cuba, self-determination and the people deciding what they want.'[41]

Until the fall of its communist allies in Europe, despite problems in supplies caused by the US embargo, Cuba had no serious economic problems and experienced rising standards of living. As in China and the USSR, life expectancy improved, from 59 years in 1953 to 70 years in 1970; illiteracy fell from 22 per cent of the population in 1953 to 13 per cent in 1970.[42] The trade embargo forced Cuba into dependence on the Soviet Union and Comecon (of which it was a member). By 1985 the USSR accounted for 80 per cent of Cuba's total trade, and gave $5 billion annually in economic and military aid.[43]

Despite the collapse of communism in Eastern Europe and the USSR, Castro remained a fundamentalist. In 1989, Soviet pro-reform journals such as *Moscow News* and *Sputnik* were not distributed and perestroika was declared to be contrary to the principles of Marxism-Leninism. Relations with Gorbachev were strained; Hungary and Poland, engaging in reforms, were described as 'apprentices of the capitalists'.[44] Castro continued to support popular insurgents in Latin America and to denounce the USA; internally, he was not threatened with a dissident or reformist movement, though this existed outside.

Consider, finally, Cuba's solution to the five functions suggested by Almond and Powell. Identity was established by Castro as a charismatic leader, with roots in the traditional aspiration for Cuba to be a free independent state. Legitimacy was assured initially through a successful internal civil war against dictatorship and imperialism and later through the adaptation of Marxism-Leninism as an ideology of development; it was also a consequence of American foreign policy. Penetration was ensured by the state bureaucracy and party apparatus created during the Castro leadership. Participation was achieved through the army, 26 July Movement, and the Communist Party. Distribution was assured through the seizure of land and enterprises and the development of a welfare state.

'State Socialisms' Compared

I have suggested that when in power the communist movement became one of development and control. On the basis of these three studies, how may we summarize the post-revolutionary social formation? Compared to capitalism, state socialism succeeded in adopting different organizing principles of economy, polity and society: property was owned publicly; economic coordination was attained through administration and planning; political effectiveness was achieved through centralization of control; an explicit social class form of politics was declared; social integration was to be achieved through collective and public goods. In all these societies, however, aspects of the traditional and capitalist societies continued. A quasi-market was retained to distribute commodities at a retail level and employees were paid money wages according to the level and quality of their work. Inequalities of income and of living standards and aspirations persisted. Important cultural legacies remained, some of which were at odds with the new political order: the Church and intelligentsia in Poland, the army and peasant masses in China and the army and the legacy of American influence in Cuba. These traditional features of the old regimes gave each society a unique character. National liberation has also been an important mobilizing factor, with national consciousness, though in different ways, an important basis for identity and solidarity in all three countries.

Both positive and negative features of the Soviet model of development were becoming common in all the state socialist societies. The positive features may be summarized as a qualitative increase in industrialization, urbanization and the movement to a modern society; improvement of the position of women and of previously underprivileged groups, such as ethnic minorities; mobilization of peasants and workers into an industrial economy; massive upward social mobility caused by industrialization and modernization. Finally, all these states had a greater defence capacity.

Other, more negative features had become apparent as state socialism had evolved: disproportions between the aspirations and the achievements of many groups of the population, particularly the lack of real political participation for the rising educated population; the adoption of a centralized bureaucratic system unable to cope with an advanced form of economy; an economy thus unable to satisfy rising levels of material expectation on the part of the population; credibility problems as the ideology of communism (society of abundance and equality) became divorced from reality. These disproportions and the social groups which had been formed under state socialism prompted the reform movements which sought a greater role for markets in both politics and economics. The Communist Party, which in Russia was defined by Lenin as the hegemonic force, was eclipsed in different ways in all three countries. Political elites from the state administration and army, rather than a purely communist elite, fragmented the political system. In Poland the army, under Jaruzelski, had a unifying role, and in China, under Mao, it has also been a major actor in the movement for and the consolidation of communism. In both China and Cuba, personal and family networks have also been at the apex of the system of political power, and charismatic leadership has displaced party leadership. Before the collapse of Poland, in none of the societies had the political leadership devolved institutional power to the masses.

How may one explain the revolutionary developmental process of state socialism? What are the tensions and contradictions within these societies? We have discussed the ways that contradictions were perceived within the dominant ideology of Marxism-Leninism sustaining the order of state socialism. Other paradigms, however, stress different systemic contradictions. Such approaches may be analysed into three kinds. First, criticisms from within the Marxist movement itself. Such views condemn the fundamental character of the state socialist regimes and deny that they have transcended capitalism. Second is an appraisal from those who oppose Marxism as an analysis of societal development and deny the possibility of creating socialism. Third is criticism from within the state socialist societies themselves. They focus on the inadequacies, imperfections and internal contradictions which are generated by state socialism. These positions will be considered in following chapters. In the next chapter, our concern will be with the internal movements for reform which stemmed from within the communist state political elites.

Movements for Market and Political Reform

While Marxist criticism of the order of state socialism took place largely outside the countries themselves, important reappraisals of the system which arose under Stalin occurred within the Soviet Union, as well as societies modelled on it. We noted above the developments in China. Those, however, supported and extended in some ways the socialist project; here we consider the different reform strategies which questioned the relevance and the applicability of aspects of the system of state planning and party control. Such criticisms not only focused on drawbacks and inefficiencies of the economic aspects of planning, but also, when radicalized, were transformed into major political reforms. These revisions originated from within the state and party apparatus. They were led from above by a faction of the political elite to address two major problems under state socialism: the bureaucratization of the system of planning and its economic inadequacies as manifested in falling rates of growth and productivity (discussed in more detail in chapter 8 below). What all these reforms shared was a legitimation of markets and a shift away from the central planning which was a cardinal feature in the formation of state socialism.[1] They all, in one way or another, advocated a theory (or partial theory) of market socialism in opposition to central planning or a capitalist market economy.[2]

We consider the reform movement in four different settings. The first major set of revisions occurred in Yugoslavia, under Tito. Following a revolution after the Second World War, the Soviet system as it developed under Stalin was enthusiastically copied and Yugoslavia adopted the major institutional forms of the Soviet state. However, changes were enacted initially on political grounds and involved a reform which sought to resolve the contradictions inherent in the command system by emphasizing the development of new forms of socialism. Secondly, we consider the Czechoslovak reform movement of the late 1960s, which predated many of the political reforms of perestroika carried out by Gorbachev in the USSR in the late 1980s; these not only combined political and economic reforms but also sought changes in Czechoslovakia's international network. Third, we appraise the changes in China, leading, after the Cultural Revolution, to economic but not political reform. The fourth context is that of the Soviet Union under Gorbachev, where the policy of perestroika anticipated an economic and political reform; then it will be considered again as a precipitant of the collapse of state socialism in chapter 8. Before tracing the ways reform proceeded in these societies, the theory of market socialism which underpinned and preceded these developments is outlined. At the end of the chapter, I return to appraise market socialism as a strategy of reform, a 'Third Way'.

The Theory of Market Socialism

Marxists and many socialists regard 'the market' in their analysis as an intrinsic component of the capitalist mode of production. Only through its operation may surplus value be extracted from the working class; production of services and commodities is for exchange, which can only take place through the market. This approach, an intrinsic part of state socialism, defines capitalism as an organic system based on a property/class/market nexus. As we have noted earlier, state socialism not only abolished the ownership relations of capitalism by replacing private property with public property but also largely (but not completely) replaced the market by an administrative allocation of resources. The economic and political systems were fused in the planning process; through administrative allocation the party was able to define its priorities and make them stick. As the productive forces were developed, so the need for markets would decline, money would become superfluous and direct exchange of products would take place. Under socialism a different set of property, class and administrative relationships replaces the property/class/ market nexus of capitalism. The logic of this position is that if markets are adopted, they will undermine socialist society in a distributive sense, so that greater wealth will accrue to some than to others, which in turn will lead to the growth of a property-owning class. Furthermore, markets have an irrational logic, the sum of the individual preferences of individuals failing to constitute the collective good.

Not all Marxists or socialists, however, have accepted that markets *per se* are incompatible with socialism. Rather they have called for a disaggregation of the market from the capitalist context in which it is embedded. Such revisionists have argued that markets take different forms in different modes of production; their technical aspects allow them to operate in different class systems and make them appropriate instruments even under socialism. The revisionist position contends that the essence of capitalism lies in the property–class nexus. It is private property, in the sense of ownership relations of the means of physical assets, which is the defining characteristic of the class nature of capitalism. Markets are politically neutral and may (nay should) be utilized under socialism – the first stage of the communist mode of production – as long as scarcity of resources exists.

What then is a market? The economists' definition of markets focuses on the production and exchange of goods and services: 'The market mechanism is a form of economic organization in which individual consumers and business interact through markets to determine the central problems of economic organization.'[3] In this sense, markets are an economic mechanism of exchange.

Theorists as early as the 1930s had distinguished between a socialist and a capitalist market. The most influential among them here was a Polish economist, Oskar Lange. He argued that capitalist economics enabled one 'to grasp the phenomena of the everyday life of a capitalist economy'. Bourgeois economists, he pointed out, provide a 'scientific basis for rational measures to be taken in the current administration of the capitalist economy'.[4] He went on to argue that the 'institutional . . . cornerstone' of the Marxist analysis of capitalism is the division of society into two antagonistic classes; it is particularly valuable as a theory of 'economic evolution'. Bourgeois economists, however, are not concerned with this division; the concept of capitalism is irrelevant to economics, but the principles of economic theory worked out under capitalism are applicable to all exchange economies because 'the nature of the economic process in the capitalist system is not substantially different from the nature of the economic process in any type of exchange economy.'[5] In Lange's view, a 'theory of equilibrium . . . can also serve as a basis for the current administration of a socialist economy. . . . Marshallian economics offers more for the current administration of the economic system of Soviet Russia than Marxian economics does . . .'[6] These views provide the theoretical basis for the utilization of the market, and equilibrium theory in general, in a socialist economy.

Market socialism, however, is subject to many different interpretations, especially in terms of institutional practice.[7] There are two main approaches. The first is to regard it as an alternative to state socialism. According to this approach, the market would replace the institutions of state planning and the directing role of the Communist Party. The government would have a coordinating role with respect to investment and would operate in other ways as governments do under capitalism. The context would be one of public ownership of material assets.[8] The important suggestion is that the directing role of the party-state, which has economic and political drawbacks, is replaced by the market as a coordinator.

The second version is to utilize the market in the context of public ownership and central planning; to combine a market, in the sense of prices reconciling demand and supply, with central planning. The advantage, it was thought, would be a more precise economic calculation, yet one free of the disadvantages of the capitalist environment of private ownership and exploitation. Politically, given the existence of planning and party control organisms under state socialism, this position suggests a way forward from state socialism to market socialism. It is conceded that a political institution is necessary to ensure not only levels of investment but also the replication of public property.

Reformers of state socialism taking the second position argue that all industrial systems must adopt some features common to all advanced societies, such as the division of labour and markets. The absence of these has led to what a Hungarian economist, Janos Kornai, has called the 'shortage economy'.[9] Planning leads enterprises to hoard labour, as they have no need to compete and the wage fund is financed by the state. The effects of the labor shortage are the loosening of labor discipline, the deterioration of work quality and the lessening of workers' diligence. The security of employment – people rarely lost their jobs – gives rise to irresponsibility in anyone susceptible to it. Absenteeism exacerbates the shortage. Output becomes erratic and the supply of commodities and services falls short of demand. Shortage characterizes the wholesale sector. Shortage of inputs in the form of supplies, materials and services in turn leads to slackness on the job, creating 'storming' (rushing to complete orders) when they become available. The efficiency of the economy is seriously undermined. Labor productivity falls. Innovation is not encouraged. Economic growth declines. This has serious consequences for social stability and national security, for the economy is unable to meet the population's aspirations for a rising standard of living. There is no reason to suppose, reformers argue, that markets could not operate in the context of planning and welfare. The crucial element in the introduction of unregulated transactions (that is, markets) in economics and politics is that they are embedded within the context of public ownership, planning and the hegemony of the party. Market socialism of this sort implies that a sufficient condition for the maintenance of a socialist system is the abolition of private property, destroying the basis of the ruling class. The market is a politically neutral institution which can be utilized in many different property contexts. Hence the property–class nexus is the essence of socialism as well as capitalism.

Before appraising the difficulties with this approach, we turn to consider the ways and the context in which similar ideas were put into practice in the evolution of state socialism. Here we consider the manner in which the political leadership initiated reforms, and their political background.

Socialist Federal Republic of Yugoslavia

As in Russia and China, the Yugoslav communists came to power by their own efforts following a successful partisan struggle against the German occupation during the Second World War.[10] Marshal Josef Broz Tito declared his government in 1943 and his guerrilla movement had considerable support: at the end of the Second World War, the Communist Party of Yugoslavia claimed 240,000 members and nearly half a million in 1948. The area of Yugoslavia is made up of four nationalities, the Serbs making up nearly 50 per cent of the population, Croatians around a quarter, Slovenes about 10 per cent and Macedonians around 5 per cent. National differences are associated with different religious groupings, the Serbs being Orthodox, the Slovenes and Croatians, Catholic. Approximately 5 per cent of the population are Muslims and located among the Serbian and Slovene populations. Croatia and Slovenia are situated in the west of the country and are very much more developed industrially, and richer; Serbia, Macedonia and Montenegro are more rural and underdeveloped. Whereas the Croats look to the West, particularly to Austria and Germany (backed by many of them during the Second World War), the Serbs' traditional allies are the Orthodox Russians and Greeks.

Initially, following the end of the Second World War, the Yugoslavs followed the course adopted in the USSR. Property was nationalized and collectivization of agriculture took place. Changes occurred in the 1950s; workers' control was introduced and in 1951 the economy was decentralized. In 1952 the Communist Party changed its name to the League of Communists of Yugoslavia and declared that the administrative control of the party over industry had been replaced by political guidance.

Under Tito three principles were enunciated which distinguished Yugoslav communism from that which had developed in the Soviet Union: decentralization of administration, self-management and, in foreign affairs, non-alignment. The first was expedient in a country with different national traditions and communities, and the last two legitimated Yugoslavia's internal and foreign policy. The centralized state administration characteristic of the Soviet political and economic system was replaced by devolution of political controls to the locality. Rather than a centralized form of nationalized state ownership, the Yugoslav communists developed ideas of municipalization and self-governing communes. Such forms of decentralization and the greater role given (at least in theory) to the masses, it was argued, was a return to Marxism. The centralized forms of party and government administrative control of state socialism as developed in the USSR were conceived to be a 'deviation' from Marxism; workers' self-management was advocated as a more legitimate form of socialism.

Decentralization was particularly appropriate in a state with many different and potentially conflicting nationalities. However, decentralization of power and decision-making to lower bodies leads to problems of exchange between them. If administrative means are not used to allocate resources, then the market is the obvious mechanism to perform this function. The operation of the market as a form of economic coordination was revived and market mechanisms were to operate in the context of state ownership of the means of production, with state control of a very decentralized kind. More specifically, enterprises were allowed to fix prices and to trade on the market, keeping a proportion of their profits. The country also entered the world economy; the dinar was made convertible and trade was organized according to the principles of comparative advantage. This was the first practical implementation of the ideas of 'market socialism'.

In the post-Second World War period, while Yugoslavia was a much more liberal society than other countries in the Eastern bloc, there was little concern with individual or political rights and political censorship was still strong. There was no move to pluralism in the Western sense of competing political parties and policies. The hegemony of the party was retained; the Programme of the League of Yugoslav Communists adopted in 1959 endorsed class struggle and the role of the party as the 'ideological vanguard and organizer'. Political opponents were not tolerated lightly. Self-management and decentralization, though they certainly enhanced participation by the masses, took place within the framework imposed by the League of Yugoslav Communists.

These policies, moreover, were not merely inspired by considerations of economic efficiency. There were major political differences between Tito and Stalin (and his supporters in the other Eastern European countries). The Yugoslavs had been excluded in 1948 from the Cominform (the association of communist states headed by the USSR). Consequently, Yugoslavia was relatively isolated in the world community. Tito needed to distance himself and his country from Stalin to gain legitimacy in the eyes of the capitalist countries. He had no choice but to enter the international division of labour and seek political approval by the Western countries.

The focus of the reforms following the break with the Soviet Union was on the economy. The objective was to overcome the lack of incentives, to resolve the disproportions between supply and demand and to curb the 'expectations gap' presented by systemic shortages of consumer supplies through the price system mediated by the market. Concurrently, Yugoslavia was able to open a window to the advanced economies of the West. In 1961 import controls were lifted and by 1966 the country had joined the General Agreement on Tariffs and Trade (GATT). Yugoslavia was exposed to the world economy. By 1964, subsidies were withdrawn from many goods and a general price liberalization occurred. Central control over investment was also relaxed. From 1967, foreign capital could be invested up to a maximum of 49 per cent of the assets of a company.

In the late 1960s and 1970s the effects of these reforms were to import many of the characteristics of Western economies: prices doubled between 1970 and 1974 and unemployment rose from 290,000 in 1971 to 410,000 in 1974; the emigration of some million workers to Western Europe occurred during this period. Income differentials increased and inflation led to strikes. Foreign debt rose.

A free market always benefits the strong, who can compete, and penalizes the weak. The easing of central controls promoted the richer republics at the cost of the poorer. In Croatia in 1971 local nationalist sentiments were voiced both by the press and by nationalist organizations. These demanded greater devolution (particularly a greater share of foreign currency earnings) and even Croatian independence. The republic's party leadership was split on the issue. A students' strike in November forced the direct intervention of Tito (himself a Croat). On this occasion his will prevailed; the local political leadership was removed and the powers of the centre maintained. The League of Communists maintained its political monopoly and competing political parties were not allowed. The communists also attempted to maintain their political hegemony over the economy, not only through the institutions of the party but also through economic controls over major investment, the rate of interest and the money supply, but their economic power was increasingly undermined. Local self-management strengthened local elites, who legitimated their political claims on ethnic national foundations.

In 1980, Tito died. The tensions between republics and political factions were exacerbated. Gradually, the old political elites who had come to power with Tito were pushed out by younger opponents with a base in the republics.[11] Increasingly the republican elites asserted their influence and the powers of the centre waned. Political reform did not follow the path of Poland. There was no strong independent *anti-communist* movement. Rather political activity had a regional basis and was linked to local elites who were increasingly dominated by the technocratic and cultural intelligentsia and sought not only a move to the market but also to a pluralist and bourgeois polity. We shall return in chapter 6 to discuss the disintegration of Yugoslavia.

The implications for the theory of market socialism are threefold. First, a division between economy and polity may be secured, maintaining a communist state within a market economy. Second, the market itself, especially when linked to the global economy, would appear to generate its own political interests, undermining the communist state and leading eventually to political reforms. Finally, these in turn further threaten the hegemony of the communist state. A crucial factor in undermining the 'socialist market' economy are the linkages with the external (capitalist) market economy. The world economy brings with it the world division of labour; exogenous markets influence internal financial priorities, the distribution of investment and the levels of employment, and thereby limit, if not undermine, the socialist objectives of government.

Czechoslovak Socialist Republic

Czechoslovakia had copied the Soviet model in the years following the end of the Second World War. By 1953, 84 per cent of national income originated from enterprises under state ownership, and by 1959 the collectivization of agriculture was completed. Policy had been successful and the economy experienced high rates of growth. In 1960 industrial output grew by 11.9 per cent, but thereafter the rate suffered a consistent decline: in 1963, growth was negative, falling to minus 0.6 per cent. The average increase in national income between 1960 and 1965 was only 1.8 per cent. As Czechoslovakia was the most advanced industrial society of the Eastern bloc, its reformers argued that the system of central planning was at fault.

Following the relaxations of the Khrushchev period, reform of the economic planning mechanism was advocated by leading party and government officials, particularly Ota Sik, head of the Institute of Economics in the Czechoslovak Academy of Sciences. The old system, it was contended, was inefficient in the use of materials and labor. It did not direct investment to industries requiring modernization, and it was unable to determine the assortment and quality of consumer goods required.

The objective here was not just an economic reform but a thorough-going reform of the political and economic system. Overcentralization of the administration was a consequence of a command economy, of which the state apparatus (of party and government) was an integral part. This had to be weakened or dismantled to enable economic and market reforms to go to work. Athough the basis of the critique of the reform movement was economic, it had important political implications.[12]

The reforms rested on three policies: economic, political and international. First, the market was to be utilized as a mechanism to reconcile demand and supply; material incentives would play an important part in stimulating production. The objective of the reforms was to increase growth by relying on economic rather than administrative and moral stimuli. Sik argued that markets had an important place under socialism and subscribed to the Marxist 'revisionist' approach outlined above. The problems of combining factors of production and determining output needed the economic mechanism of the market. The socialist market was to determine the relationships between production, distribution, exchange and consumption.

Sik insisted that under the socialist market there could be no form of 'capitalist profit-seeking' because there is 'no private profit and no private person can appropriate the income and make a profit on the exploitation of the labour of others'.[13] The market under socialism was a mechanism which 'harmonizes group and social economic interests'. Under capitalism, the markets operate in the context of a capitalist class; under socialism, however, Sik argued that it reflected 'the general interests of the whole society'.[14] This is a clear statement of the assumptions of market socialism adumbrated earlier in this chapter: socialism as a mode of production is based on class and ownership relations, not market ones.

In practice, the proposed reforms were ambiguous and limited. Market control over capital and investment was not envisaged, at least not initially. Enterprises were to be given greater autonomy and would have to compete with other firms (including foreign ones). Prices in principle would be determined by market forces. Wages and salaries would also be dependent on the 'market position' of various groups of workers, which would lead to greater income differentiation. Managerial and technical personnel, as well as the professions, would be likely to gain as a result of these changes. Manual workers would lose the advantages they enjoyed in the allocation of income.

Central planning was to continue. The distribution between investment and consumption, between social consumption (education and social services) and personal consumption and between the major forms of capital investment and research would continue to be controlled by the government, which would also play an important role in defining the levels of credit, money supply, prices and wage policy. Some prices and regional policy would also remain within the orbit of central control. One might note ambiguities here: if competition were to bite, resulting in the failure of enterprises, how could this be squared with planners directing investment according to a national plan?

Second, economic reform, it was contended, could not be carried out if there was not a reform of the political system. Overcentralization of the administration was a consequence of a party and government command economy. The market could not work if politics intervened. Allocation of resources by plan conflicted with market forces. For example, banks would not be able to limit the credit of enterprises if party secretaries – in securing full employment – were able to tell bank managers to give credits to the enterprise. Similarly, factory managers could not widen wage differentials if party and trade union chiefs could intercede to prop up the wages of the low-paid and oppose higher salaries for executives. Efficiency would not be achieved, it was further contended, if worker lay-offs were prevented for reasons of political stability and social policy. Party control had to be weakened or dismantled to enable economic reforms to have their effect.

The Prague Spring of 1968 gave rise to a form of socialist political pluralism – and here there were major differences from Yugoslavia and China. The Prague Spring (named after the city's annual music festival) is the name given to the reforms introduced by the Communist Party in that year; it was led by Alexander Dubcek, a Slovak communist. Political pluralism was justified, it was claimed, because there were no antagonistic conflicts in socialist society. In 1960 a constitution had been adopted which declared that Czechoslovakia had completed the socialist stage of development and had entered the epoch of the construction of communism. As in the Soviet Union under Stalin, it was contended that as public property sustained socialism, there was no basis for class conflict. The Czechoslovak reformers, however, took this argument a stage further. The time had come for the party to lose its hegemonic character. After all, if there were no 'antagonistic classes' how could the party legitimate its 'leading role', there being no classes to rule over? Thus the leading role of the party was put into doubt by the reformers, some of whom advocated a multiple party system working under the guidance of the Communist Party. The political system would be the legitimate expression of interests based on the division of labour, on regional attachments and issue politics, as well as promotional associations. The political authority of the party would be necessary to aggregate these interests for the good of society as a whole. Hence the party could still be said to be hegemonic, but in quite a different way from that under traditional state socialism. Under the leadership of Alexander Dubcek, political reforms were effected: interests would be allowed – though in a single-party rather than a competing multiparty system – and the government and judiciary would have autonomy; a free press would be allowed and censorship was abolished.

Finally there were implications for foreign affairs. Czechoslovakia, it was argued, should look to the West, not only to the economic market but also by changing their allegiance and role in the Warsaw Pact. These proposals, together with the weakening of the party and its political control, ensured the downfall of the Dubcek government. On 20 August 1968 the Warsaw Pact countries invaded Czechoslovakia. They argued, under what has become known as the 'Brezhnev doctrine', that the interests of the socialist bloc were threatened by the reforms. The market would undermine the economic linkages and an orientation to the West would weaken their military capability. Dubcek was deposed and replaced by Gustav Husak, who rejected the reform programme. Censorship was reimposed, allegiance was reaffirmed to the Warsaw Pact and to Comecom, and 'normalization' replaced reform.

The experience of Czechoslovakia, it might be contended, does not invalidate the theory of market socialism. The reformers not only proposed to introduce markets but also to change the international political parameters in which they operated; this decisively ensured political intervention and the termination of the reforms. 'Market socialism' was not put into practice in Czechoslovakia.

People's Republic of China

The People's Republic of China began its market reforms much later than Yugoslavia, and in quite a different context, maintaining the political structure of state socialism concurrent with a significant move to the market. We noted in the previous chapter the political character of the Cultural Revolution, which was an attack on the elites located in the government apparatus. Unlike in Soviet Russia under Stalin, where the opposition was physically annihilated, Mao Zedong banished his enemies to physical labour in the countryside. Deng Xiaoping, for example, during the Cultural Revolution worked as a lathe operator at a tractor repair shop. They in turn resisted Maoism and were still there to provide the impetus to reform after Mao's death in 1976 and the subsequent imprisonment of the Gang of Four. (The latter, led by Jiang Qing, Mao's wife, were leading supporters of the Maoist line on the cultural revolution in China after Mao's death.)

From 1978 a new developmental strategy characterized Chinese politics. Four 'modernizations' distinguished the period after the Cultural Revolution: applied to industry, agriculture, science and technology, and the military.[15] Policy involved a depoliticization of economic management. The Maoist principle of 'politics in command' was renounced, and there was a reemphasis on material rather than ideological incentives. The command-type administrative system was maintained but decentralized. It was conceded that a degeneration of the political leadership had led to a declining rate of economic growth and to popular dissatisfaction with the standard of living. A significant shift to a socialist market economy took place, with the following features. In agriculture, effective privatization in the form of 'leasing' of land was allowed. Collective farms were split up into small family plots and were managed as family farms which were encouraged to trade on the market. Small-scale industries were encouraged in the rural sector. Profit retention was allowed in state industry, though right up to the mid-1990s there was no policy to privatize enterprises in the state sector. The banks were given a greater role in the control of finance, and an 'open door' policy was pursued with respect to world trade.[16]

The changes were reminiscent of the Yugoslav reforms. There was a shift to greater independence of economic enterprises, which could exercise more initiative over their own funds, including setting levels of investment, prices and payments to their own employees. But the state was to continue with overall macro planning. The idea was, in the words of reformer Chen Yun, to set free the market bird inside the cage of central planning. In this policy the leadership may have been influenced by the other Confucian South-East Asian economies (the four dragons – Hong Kong, South Korea, Taiwan and Singapore), which had all pursued successful economic reforms under authoritarian rule.

The state's direct productive role was maintained but significantly reduced: the non-state sector in industry, accounting for under a fifth of industrial output in 1978, rose to 45 per cent in 1990[17] (61 per cent in 1992). This increase took place in the rural sector, where quasi-private industries were set up after the decollectivization of agriculture; in 1988, for example, there were nearly 19 million rural enterprises.[18] By the late 1980s only a third of construction employment remained in the state sector, and there was a boom in rural house construction. In transportation and communication, the government maintained a monopoly. In the retail trade, by the late 1980s under 40 per cent of retail sales were transacted in the state sector.[19] From 1979, the banks were given the right to allocate and regulate credit. They became more profit orientated and monitored the activity of borrowers. In this way financial and economic criteria were to become more important in industry.

The conclusion to be drawn here is that the market was given a legitimate and important place under state socialism in China and the consequences of greater differentials between sectors of the economy and between different groups of employees were acceptable to the communist leadership. Not only was the market recognized as an internal distributive institution, but also the international market was acknowledged as beneficial. Policy encouraged foreign trade and foreign capital through loans, direct investment or joint ventures; special economic zones were set up to stimulate the investment of foreign entrepreneurs. The monopoly of foreign trade held by the Ministry of Foreign Economic Relations and Trade was broken. The yen moved towards open convertibility with foreign currency. (By 1990, the internal auction rate of the dollar approximated the black market rate.)[20] By the late 1980s more than 5,000 independent foreign trade corporations had the authority to engage in international transactions[21] and by 1988 50 per cent of foreign exchange earnings could be kept by producers. This led to production enterprises receiving higher prices for exported goods, and boosted trade.

Between 1979 and 1991, China received $80 billion in foreign capital and imported $24.6 billion in foreign technologies. By 1991, China had moved to the eleventh place in the ranking of world trading nations; whereas in 1978 exports accounted for only 4.65 per cent of Chinese GNP, by 1992 they had risen to 19.5 per cent.[22] The economic effects of these moves were positive: industrial and agricultural output increased considerably and gross domestic product in China rose at an annual rate of 8.8 per cent between 1979 and 1990.[23] The creation of Special Economic Zones encouraged foreign investment, especially from Hong Kong and expatriate Chinese. The consequence of these internal and external changes was that incomes rose and greater differentiation took place, benefiting both the richer peasants in the countryside and the skilled and technocratic personnel in the towns, whose influence increased under the reform programme.

From 1985 the government pursued a policy which liberalized banking and encouraged the formation of financial markets. White and Bowles point out that policy-makers and officials 'became increasingly absorbed into an international discourse on financial systems and financial liberalisation . . . by financial experts and international institutions such as the World Bank and International Monetary Fund, which became increasingly influential elements in the Chinese policy-making process in the mid-1980s'.[24] The banks moved towards greater financial autonomy and the financial market developed to include investment companies and insurance offices which provided the infrastructure for the financial system.

Economic reform has been successful in China. A domestic market has been introduced for agricultural and rural industrial production, for the exchange of commodities and in finance. Economic growth has increased significantly during the reform period and industrial and agricultural output has risen noticeably (see chapter 8 below). The share of the non-state sector has increased dramatically. Foreign trade has increased considerably to China's advantage. Here the country enjoyed advantages in international affairs which the Soviet Union did not. China was not seen as a rival to the West in the way the Soviet Union was; indeed the country had been regarded by the USA as a counterweight to the USSR during China's split with Khrushchev.

The lack of political reform

Reform in the economy, however, did not transform the political system. The struggle continued between the traditional political leaders – those steeped ideologically in ideas of class politics, state control and planning, as well as the chiefs of government-run industry – and the reformers. The Chinese political leadership under Deng Xiaoping supported a move to the market in the economy, privatization in agriculture and participation in the world market, but the economy has not moved to an open market economy or full-scale privatization of industrial assets.

While the government reformers allowed economic market reforms, they resisted 'radical' political reform in the sense of a pluralism of groups and political parties. In 1978–9 pressures for economic and political reform came from below, from the 'democratic movement', with some arguing that democracy was a 'fifth modernization'.[25] However, the movement was repressed by the authorities. Later, in 1986, further demands were made for a system of checks and balances, competitive elections, and the abolition of censorship in art and literature, and opposition was voiced to the doctrine of Marxism-Leninism.[26] Such views had some support among the political leadership, particularly in the figure of Hu Yaobang. But they were resolutely repudiated by the leadership under Deng Xiaoping. The hegemony of the Communist Party continued. The Tiananmen Square incident illustrates the determination of the leadership to maintain its political authority and the limits to the reform process. In June 1989, it has been estimated that as many as a million people, mainly students, marched through and participated in gatherings in the square. The anti-government demonstrators demanded democratic rights, the resignation of Den Xiaoping and political reforms. The political leadership held firm, sent in troops to clear the square and physically dispersed the demonstrators. (As many as a thousand were reported killed.) China maintained a single-party system, and the movement to pluralization and to autonomous groupings in a civil society has been blunted. Tiananmen Square, however, indicated that considerable opposition existed to communist political hegemony. This was fuelled not only by the growth of the urban intelligentsia but also by the beneficiaries of the market reforms noted above.

Incremental reform has been a successful economic policy and it has occurred independently of radical political reform. The Communist Party has preserved its monopoly of political organization. Marxist 'revisionists' who have advocated the introduction of the market in the context of state ownership and a party-led planning system would seem to be justified in their arguments that market reforms *per se* need not lead to political reform which undermines the socialist political system. Democratic reform in a Western sense has not materialized: there is no competition of political parties, and individual rights of the sort existing in a pluralist society have been resisted. How long this can continue is a matter of speculation. The growth of marketization, the rise of a technical and cultural intelligentsia, and also the increase in the business and bourgeois classes would suggest that these groups will move into the ascendancy in the future. Following the Tiananmen Square incident in 1989, 'pro-democracy' political movements were suppressed, though the growth of the private sector has continued. As Minxin Pei has cogently argued, these developments weaken the communist party–state by transferring resources away from its control.[27] The economic reforms have eroded Marxist-Leninist ideology and it is clear that a crisis of political legitimacy is likely. But while the development of the private sector leads to the creation and strengthening of the business class and the intelligentsia (which may profit from market relations), stability has been maintained by the success of the economic reforms in which people have prospered. In other words, unlike in Poland, economic well-being has fortified the political status quo.

Political factors have also been important in maintaining stability: the political class is strongly ensconced in power in China. The revolutionary generation which fought its way to power is still in control (unlike in the East European countries where a post-revolutionary generation entered politics) and it maintains a will to govern. The army is a major political power in the political class and remains in support of the traditional political leadership. Private trade has had a continuous history under the communists. The social base of political reform is also weaker than in the European states. In 1979 in China only 18.9 per cent of the population was urban (compared to 65.7 per cent in the USSR in 1986 and 61.2 per cent in Poland), 24.6 per cent of the labour force in 1979 was in the non-agricultural sector (81 per cent and 73 per cent in the USSR and Poland in 1987 and 1988 respectively). In China in 1982, only 1 per cent of the population had received higher education compared to 13.9 per cent in the USSR in 1989 and 5.7 per cent in Poland in 1981.[28] (These points are further elaborated below in chapter 8.) The growth of the private sector has developed in the countryside rather than in the towns. The peasants in China have had less to lose from the decline in government transfers than in other socialist societies, for they were not included in the social welfare benefit services. Hence the potential costs of political opposition for potential reformers outweigh the potential gains.

All these factors have led to an economic reform without formal political reform in China. Economic reform may occur without political reform if the political elites are united in policy and ideology, if they have the effective means of political control at their disposal and if they have the will to maintain boundaries. Authoritarian governments in many countries, particularly in East Asia, pursue market economic reforms in the context of dictatorial rule. The analogy, however, may not be appropriate under state socialism, for marketization gives rise to an economic class whose interests may not be secured by the traditional ones of a political class. Authoritarian capitalist governments do not challenge property relations; rather they protect them concurrently with the procurement of preferential transfers to themselves. The party in China has already conceded considerable power to the economic class; its effective control over the economy is being eroded. The dynamic of development clearly lies with the private enterprise and intellectual class. And it must be questioned as to whether the political hegemony of the party (with a Marxist-Leninist outlook) will continue when the present cohort of leaders dies. The implications of this analysis are that it will not.

Common Features of Economic Reform Movements

The reform movement in Yugoslavia, China and Czechoslovakia shared many features in common, and a wide spectrum of informed opinion, especially among planners and economists, conceded that the planning system as it had developed in the USSR had considerable failings. The points made included:

1 The scale and complexity of the economic system could not be handled efficiently under a central plan; an economic market was a mechanism which could be adopted to make the socialist system work more efficiently.
2 The planners were not altruistic; bureaucratic control was centralized and the state apparatus had uncontrollable power.
3 Bureaucracies lacked entrepreneurial drive; there was a tendency to stagnation, to reproduce the system rather than to innovate.
4 State socialism lacked incentives to increase efficiency and to raise productivity.

5 Forms of political privilege and consumption were created by the bureaucratic institutions. Reform of the economic system would not be successful without a political change.

Theorists of planning and reformers in the countries themselves began to consider the possibilities of moving to a mixed economy in which the market played an important role. Increasingly, reformers legitimated their position by assuming that the 'private property/class nexus' was the essence of capitalism, that markets could make socialism work more effectively and socialism would not be undermined if public property relations were maintained. They argued for a shift in organizational principles from a central 'state-led' economy to one in which the government provided a strong framework of financial control and basic industrial output, with an enterprise-led form of production for the market. In Czechoslovakia economic reforms were conjoined with changes in the polity involving a weakening of the hegemony of the party. In Yugoslavia and China reform was initially limited to the economy, though it weakened the role of the polity and its political class. In the former it led to the collapse of communism, and fragmentation in which *anti*-communism took a nationalist form. In the latter the effective power of the communist political class has been eroded. It maintains itself in power through political control.

Union of Soviet Socialist Republics

Whereas in the 1960s in Eastern Europe and China doubts were being expressed about the efficiency of the administrative command system, in Soviet Russia the leadership was confident that the Soviet model of development was essentially sound. In October 1961, Khrushchev introduced a new Programme of the Communist Party of the Soviet Union which was adopted by the Twenty-Second Party Congress. It reflected the optimism of the political leadership. Khrushchev claimed with confidence that the USSR and the socialist world would triumph given the cumulative 'crisis of world capitalism'. Within ten years, it was asserted, the Soviet economy would catch up and even surpass the levels of the United States. He endorsed the advantages of state ownership, central planning and Communist Party leadership based on Leninist principles. The 1961 programme marked, in its own words, the beginning of a period of 'full-scale communist construction'. This was a period of confidence, even assertiveness, on the part of the Soviet leadership. Contradictions and conflicts, to be sure, existed in Soviet society, but these were considered to be 'non-antagonistic' and could be resolved within the context of state socialism. It was contended that the 'fundamental interests of classes coincided', the major sources of conflict being between the 'emergent shoots of communism' and the 'survivals of capitalism'.

By the 1970s, targets for economic growth and labour productivity were unfulfilled. Such shortfalls led the political leadership to examine reforms of the system of economic planning. Two approaches to reform crystallized: first, the more conservative 'reform of the economic mechanism'; second, a more radical emphasis on the development of markets.[29]

Reform of the economic mechanism entailed keeping the Soviet administrative command system intact and improving the planning process: that is, devising a more accurate form of economic calculation. The following features of the economy were to remain unchallenged: the definition of economic priorities by the political leadership and their execution by the government planning agencies and ministries; central planning through Gosplan; the maintenance of a full employment economy; wage policy involving relatively modest differentials; and economic enterprises driven by the fulfilment of plans. The market would have no effect on investment, and only a limited role in determining the level of consumption.

Reforms in this context were essentially of the supply side and involved the improvement of economic management. The formation of 'production associations' bringing together numerous producers would, it was hoped, lead to economies of scale. Many of these moderate reformers considered that modern data analysis processes would enable more accurate economic calculations to be made. Policy in the 1980s, however, was piecemeal rather than comprehensive. Bonuses were introduced to stimulate the fulfilment (and overfulfilment) of contracts and to improve labour productivity. Wholesale prices were brought in line with real costs of production. Regional differentials were introduced for fuel and other commodities whose prices differed by region. Economic ministries were allowed to keep some of the earned profits. To improve labour productivity, various 'experiments' were introduced to encourage enterprises to shed labour. Methods here included the 'Shchekino experiment' in which plants were given a stable wages fund for a five-year period, and were able to allocate wages according to their economic needs.[30] Furthermore, workers were organized by 'brigades' and were able to redistribute the income given for a job according to their own preferences. It was hoped that such methods would lead to the shedding of excess labour and to higher levels of labour productivity – and the movement of such workers to places of labour shortage.

These policies, which were adopted under the leadership of Leonid Brezhnev and Alexei Kosygin, who followed Khrushchev in 1964, failed for four major reasons. First, central planning requires an enormous amount of information which is not always available and is often out of date; on the basis of that information, it also requires the simultaneous solution of extremely complicated equations to ensure that demand, output and price are equilibrated. Central planning was not able to cope with the management of a complex economy. In the 1980s, for example, the administration had to cope with 10 quadrillion (10,000,000,000,000,000) units of economic and political information per year.[31] Imbalances and distortions caused waste and incompatible relations between money and goods, and led to an unbalanced economy. Second, a supply-dominated economy has a built-in tendency to supply what the centre wants to supply, rather than what consumers would prefer. Third, the political context ensured that when reforms began to bite they did not undermine those policies guaranteed by the Soviet state, particularly full employment, a not-too-arduous work environment (for management and employees) and a welfare state. Finally, the operation of the economic system did not reflect relative scarcities, making optimum economic decision-making impossible.

In this context the more radical group of economists and critics put forward views which moved significantly in the direction of the market. Such proposals included the formation of 'market equilibrium prices', the freedom for enterprises to choose customers and suppliers, and a shift to competition and consumer sovereignty. Many economists called for the abandonment of 'administrative methods of management' in favour of the introduction of a market mechanism and the decentralization of decision-making.[32] At the time, these views were marginal and did not enjoy a great deal of support. It was widely believed that the introduction of the market was tantamount to the reintroduction of capitalism: property, planning and party control were interdependent; a shift to the market would certainly undermine the position of the political and economic elite in Russia, and possibly lead to unemployment and higher income differentials to the detriment of the working class. What I have described above as the property-class-market theory dominated the world-view of the political leadership. Under Yuri Andropov and Konstantin Chernenko, who came to power after the death of Brezhnev, reforms were introduced within the parameters of the centrally administered command economy. Measures were introduced to promote 'labour discipline', anti-corruption campaigns were launched and curbs were put on the sale and consumption of vodka. These essentially were palliatives. Gorbachev, however, was to bring in his own version of market reforms.

Perestroika: a new paradigm of state socialism?

Almost a quarter of a century after Khrushchev had boasted of his conviction that the Soviet bloc would outstrip the economic level of capitalism, on 25 February 1986, Mikhail Gorbachev presided over another version of the party programme. After praising previous achievements, as was the usual laudatory mode of party leaders, Gorbachev launched into a critique of Soviet practice. He criticized the state system and its bureaucratic nature of control. 'The forms of production relations, the system of running and managing the economy . . . took shape . . . in conditions of an extensive development. Gradually they become obsolete, they began to lose their role as incentives and here and there they turned into impediments.' He noted the contradictions between productive forces and production relations, between socialist property and the economic forms of its implementation, 'between goods and money' and between 'the combination of centralization and independence of economic organization'.

The thinking of the leadership under Gorbachev involved a movement away from administrative methods of control of the economy to greater reliance on the market, prices and competition. Ideologically, Gorbachev turned away from Marxism-Leninism. Compared to the objectives of Khrushchev's Programme of 1961, there is no mention in the revised party programme adopted in 1986 of increased public consumption, of the withering away of the state, or of the decline of money as an instrument of exchange and store of wealth. On the contrary, claims for an advance to a communist society were no longer made. Over the next five years, the organizing principles of state socialism were publicly questioned and finally discarded. In the period between 1986 and 1989, the reform policy of perestroika was born.[33] It was a venture to reconstruct the communist system as it had developed from the time of Stalin and to achieve a major recasting of the organizing principles, though not the fundamental institutions, of Soviet society. This duality between principles and institutions, with its implicit contradictions, was to prove the downfall of the last serious attempt to reconstruct the Marxist Leninist state.

Perestroika is the term used to describe the process of change. It may be translated by 'restructuring', or 'radical reform'; with the passage of time it came to mean revolutionary transition. The significance of perestroika is that it is a comprehensive policy of change. While reforms had occurred under Khrushchev, Kosygin and Brezhnev, they were piecemeal rather than systemic; they assumed that the underlying structures were essentially sound and ensured fundamental social and political harmony – they needed improvement rather than radical reform. Underlying the process of perestroika was a major theoretical reappraisal of social relations in the USSR. There emerged a critique of political power under state socialism which focused on the various forms of incompatibilities, tensions and conflicts generated in society. A redefinition took place of the nature of contradictions under socialism. Previously, as discussed in chapter 3 above, the view was that contradictions under socialism could be resolved peacefully, with mutual goodwill, through common understanding and good leadership. But it was argued by policy-orientated sociologists, such as Tatiana Zaslavskaya,[34] that contradictions within 'socialist society' do not originate from the relics left from capitalism but are created by the structure of state socialism itself, which generates group and class interests. Such interests gave rise to antagonisms between groups. These antagonisms, it was insisted, were at the heart of the malaise of Soviet society and they accounted for the deceleration of economic growth and the lack of dynamism. The political leadership under Brezhnev, it was further argued, had itself been a source of contradiction in that it perpetuated bureaucratic forms which acted as a brake on the development of the productive forces. Production relations (the system of economic management and political control) were in conflict with the potentialities of the productive forces and they lead to 'stagnation': to the retardation of economic development, to corruption, to a decline of socialist morality, and to public apathy and alienation. These views conceded many of the points made by the reformers in Yugoslavia and Czechoslovakia described above: the traditional planning mechanisms and forms of political control were obsolete in an advanced, complex industrial economy.

From state socialism to social democracy

Other leading academics and policy commentators advocated greater public involvement in societal affairs, and to secure them they called for major shifts in the organization of the communist state. Boris Kurashvili, a member of the Institute of State and Law, and Georgi Shakhnazarov, a leading political scientist, argued for political pluralism within a one-party state and for contested elections; Fedor Burlatski, an influential journalist and political commentator, went much further in urging market relations and competitive elections.[35]

From the beginning of 1988 these radical views were forcibly argued by Gorbachev and became party policy. At the February 1988 plenum of the Central Committee, Soviet society was defined by Gorbachev in terms not only of a 'plurality' of opinions but also of opposing 'interests and views'. Various vested interests and groups at the heart of the political system, it was contended, had prevented development; they were a brake or a fetter on the development of the productive forces. They were legitimated by the cult of personality under Brezhnev and administered by the apparatus of government and party. To break out of the vicious circle of complacency, decline and stagnation, the mechanisms which perpetuated them had to be replaced and those individuals and vested interests who had benefited had to be removed. Conceding (albeit unknowingly) a point made by Mao Zedong, this position involved the recognition of endemic conflict under state socialism; mechanisms had to be arranged which allowed for the articulation, aggregation and resolution of different interests. This approach came to subvert completely the guiding role of a dominant Communist Party, as it had previously been accepted by the orthodox leadership, and seriously undermined the ideology of Marxism-Leninism.

The contradictions inherent in the more complex economy and more mature society would be resolved by a modernization of the traditional structures and processes of Soviet communism. The formal monopoly of power by the Communist Party would be retained and would secure public property, a planned economy, a welfare state and a full-employment economy. The economy would be responsive to consumer demand. To secure higher labour productivity, it would move from the extensive to the intensive form of development. It would play an increasing role in the international division of labour. The repressive forms of political and social centralization instituted under Stalin would be replaced by a greater pluralism of opinions, by greater openness and more humane forms of social relationships. Socialism would be democratic and have a human face.

Gorbachev's version of socialism was vague and similar in style and content to that of the reformist social democracy we noted in the first chapter of this book. The party's programme statement, adopted at the Twenty-Eighth Party Congress in 1990, was subtitled: 'Towards a Humane, Democratic Socialism'. The following, taken from this document, epitomizes its outlook:

> The CPSU is a party with a socialist option and a communist outlook. We regard this prospect as the natural, historical thrust of the development of civilization. Its social ideal absorbs the humanist principles of human culture, the age-old striving for a better life and social justice.
>
> In our understanding, humane democratic socialism means a society in which: humankind is the aim of social development; living and working conditions for people are worthy of contemporary civilization; man's alienation from political power and the material and spiritual values created by him are overcome and his active involvement in social processes is

assured; the transformation of working people into the masters of production, the strong motivation of highly productive labour, and the best
conditions for the progress of production forces and the rational use of
nature are ensured on the basis of diverse forms of ownership and economic management; social justice and the social protection of working
people are guaranteed – the sovereign will of the people is the sole source
of power; the state, which is subordinate to society, guarantees the protection of the rights, freedoms, honour and dignity of people regardless of
social position, sex, age, national affiliation or religion; there is free competition and cooperation between all sociopolitical forces operating within
the framework of the law. This is a society which consistently advocates
peaceful and equitable cooperation among the peoples and respect for the
rights of every people to determine their own fate.

There is no mention here of Marxism, class or class struggle, the
hegemony of the party, consciousness, exploitation, money, the state or
the transition to communism, Hence, on a world scale the Soviet state
now presented no external threat to capitalism. The intended outcome
was to be an ideological, moral, political and economic form of communism qualitatively different from Stalinism and one which would become
once more a beacon for socialist, social-democratic and humanitarian
movements in the late twentieth century.

In terms of practical policy, the Soviet Union would 'rejoin civilization' in its spiritual home in Europe, and the West would have no fears
of communist expansion or aggression. For this to be attained, a transformation would have to take place in Soviet foreign policy, which would
withdraw from confrontation with the West; and, perhaps most important
of all, the Soviet Union's socialist allies in Eastern Europe and the Third
World would have to govern by consent or lose power.

Turning from the theoretical underpinnings, perestroika was an attitude or approach to politics and society. It involved five major strategies:

1 A greater role for money and economic calculation and the acceptance
  of limited market relations;
2 Democratization of the political process, an acceptance of a 'plurality of
  opinions', a quasi-electoral system in which the party had to rule with
  consent and through a revitalized system of Soviets;
3 A policy of *glasnost* which involved greater access to information and
  public criticism;
4 Adjudication of rules, hitherto the prerogative of the party, was to be
  the role of a legally constituted state or *Rechtstaat*;
5 A major shift in foreign policy in which the USSR sought an accommodation with, and a place in, the world political community.

As articulated by Gorbachev in the mid-1980s, the reform programme did not involve privatization of public assets nor did it include the rights of people to form independent political parties. It was a reformed type of state socialism.

An underlying assumption was that if self-interest was allowed to take its course, higher levels of economic and political efficiency would be achieved. This might apply to individuals, who should be given room for initiative and rewarded for achievement; to institutions (enterprises being given greater independence in production decisions and rewarded or penalized for their efforts); even to regions of the country, also to be encouraged to manage their own affairs (hence the legitimation of claims for separatism and sovereignty in the republics). An important shift took place in the organizing principles of Soviet society: from an administered model of the public interest determined centrally by 'the authorities' (presumed to be the embodiment of the working class in the party), it became a model of individuals and groups allowed to express their own interests, these being aggregated through a market. Remember the tenets of Adam Smith? 'It is not from the benevolence of the butcher, the brewer, or the baker, that we expect our dinner, but from their regard to their own interest.'[36]

Such developments were given a guarded welcome by the governments of the West; some were sceptical and viewed the tactics as an attempt by the communists to gain respectability and time to revive world communism. Under President Bush in the USA, advisers cautioned that perestroika could make the USSR a 'more competitive superpower', and the less confrontational policy might 'divide the Western alliance'.[37] The USA and Great Britain demanded a clear commitment to markets, privatization of the means of production and an open political system with competition between political parties; substantial changes were also advocated for Eastern Europe. Western policy moved from one of 'containment' to one of 'integration . . . into the international system'.[38] Here the governments of the West were able to bring pressure to bear from the outside on the character of the reform movement, a topic to which we shall return in the next chapter. The reforms were borne on the currents of events and went much further than originally intended by Gorbachev and his associates.

Gorbachev's economic reforms

Initially, the reforms envisaged by Gorbachev were economic in character: 'acceleration' (*uskorenie*) of the economic mechanism was the goal and few political changes were envisaged. There were two major parts to the reforms: first, the development of market forces and encouragement of different types of enterprise, and second, the reform of the economic administration. The objectives of the reforms were to reduce the 'overcentralization' of the economic mechanism; to use prices and money through the market as incentives for producers, workers and consumers; to retain the benefits of planning – rational forms of investment and a full-employment economy.

The economic reforms envisaged by Gorbachev were similar to re-forms carried out in Eastern Europe and may be summarized as follows: the growth and legitimation of market transactions; an increase in private and cooperative trade; greater authority to production units; adoption of the accounting principle of *khozraschet* (units had to balance their income and expenditure). These measures involved a lessening of the powers of the economic ministries and central control, more uncertainty for manag-ers and workers, and greater use of money as a stimulus. The enterprise was given greater autonomy over its own affairs – within the confines of a plan given by the central authorities. Prices, except in the cooperative and private initiative sector, were not to be subject to the forces of supply and demand but fixed administratively.

The reform of the economic administration was the second and much more significant aspect of the reform policy. The aim here was to limit the power of the centralized ministries – and here Gorbachev moved into the political realm. His policy involved two major changes. First, the powers of the ministries were curbed when 'financial autonomy' was given to production enterprises to encourage 'economic' rather than 'administrative' relations. Second, the central bureaucracy was reduced and greater autonomy was devolved to the republics. Between 1985 and 1988 the number of staff in apparatuses of ministries, committees and departments declined by 543,000, a reduction of 33.5 per cent. Nine all-union ministries and departments had been closed down by March 1989, and in June of that year Prime Minister Ryzhkov announced that the economic union-republican ministries, which operated on a USSR scale, were to be abolished and their activities transferred to the governments of the republics.

Gorbachev here seriously weakened the USSR-wide government, shifting economic power to the market and to the republics. The latter began to adopt policies at variance with those of the USSR government. At the end of 1990 and the beginning of 1991, republican and local Soviets decreed that the assets in their territory belonged to them.

Reform in the economy also operated at the level of the enterprise. In order to reduce the detailed administrative control of enterprises, 'economic' criteria were used and the principle of *khozraschet* was adopted. Under this system of autonomous financial accounting, each accounting unit had to balance its own books. The idea was to allocate to enterprises realistic targets for output, increases in labor productivity and product quality; the objective was to increase economic efficiency by encouraging and rewarding increases in productivity at the point of production.

Gorbachev considered that one of the chief causes of the failure to carry out reforms in the past was the lack of involvement of the workers. *Samoupravlenie* (self-management) gave to the employees more influence in controlling the enterprise, sharing in its achievements and suffering its losses. In an attempt to strengthen the links between employees and the enterprise, it was agreed in October 1988 that securities could be sold to members of enterprises (if sanctioned by the government). It was argued that this would overcome working people's alienation from state property and draw personal savings into production in a democratic way. The issue of securities was also legitimated as one element of a socialist market.

The market under socialism was gradually given a new respectability. Politburo member Aleksandr Yakovlev, in a speech in 1988, pointed out:

> The development of the socialist market is one of the roads leading to the combining of interests and to the shaping of the ideology of the good socialist manager. . . . The market is made socialist or capitalist not by the movement of commodities, capital or even the workforce, but by the social context of the processes which accompany it. . . . The dividing line . . . lies in defining the place of people in society and whether they are using the market for the ultimate goals of society or as a source of profit.

Here Yakovlev is distinguishing between a 'capitalist' and a 'socialist' market. The latter is constrained by the ownership of the major productive forces by the state, by the political hegemony of the Communist Party and by the prohibition of the extraction of profit. As we shall see below, the hegemony of the Communist Party was later relaxed.

In the first few years of reform, while the ministries and 'planning' apparatus were weakened, many of the features of the centrally planned system were retained. The market did not determine, except in a marginal way, the direction and rate of investment. Prices were still for the most part set administratively. It was intended that the State Committee on Prices would eventually control only some 10 per cent of production prices – though these would be strategic ones and would exert a major influence over the cost structure of the whole economy. The negative effects of the market would not be allowed to occur, at least not in any extreme form. When Gorbachev was asked about unemployment, he said categorically that it would not be countenanced as a form of discipline for labour. The bankruptcy of enterprises and the laying off of workers was not contemplated without the agreement of the trade union council or committee. In practice this would have made it very difficult for enterprises to make employees redundant.

Economically, the aim was to strengthen the powers of Gosplan, the central planning body, to increase the initiative and independence of enterprises and to weaken the industrial ministries and party apparatus. In agriculture there was no move to abolish collective or state farms, though leasing and family contracts within the collective farms were encouraged. While wholesale and retail trade was encouraged on a cooperative basis, there was no call for large-scale privatization. Cooperatives were encouraged with rights to decide over what produce to sell and buy. By the beginning of 1991, the number of cooperatives producing goods and offering services had risen to 260,000 and they provided empoyment for 6.2 million people out of a total workforce of 118.6 million. The move to private enterprise was modest.

Gorbachev's political reforms

The stated intention of Gorbachev, moreover, was not to undermine the structure of the system of state socialism. At a speech to the Central Committee on 18 February 1988, Gorbachev reiterated: 'We are not departing by one step from socialism, from Marxism-Leninism . . .' The objective was for a more open political system to operate within the hegemony of a more responsive and responsible Communist Party. As one of the clearest advocates of perestroika put it, the revolution under perestroika 'is being accomplished "from above", on the initiative of the ruling party . . . The upper echelon retains its authority and regulating power: it is only the position of the middle and lower links in the apparatus that change.'[39] In addition, 'transformation cannot transcend the limits of reform' without support 'from below',[40] which is spurred by democratization and *glasnost* (greater public access to information and public criticism). It was not intended to legitimate a multiparty system, which, it was recognized, would lead to dissension and to the rise of national parties which would demand greater independence for the regions and republics and would undermine the central powers of the USSR.

The actual development of perestroika, however, belied these lofty claims and the political system became subverted. Political control, hitherto the prerogative of the party, was to be replaced by law, by a legally constituted state or *Rechtstaat*. Prescribed laws were to guarantee civil rights to the population and to define the legal operation of the state. As Gorbachev put it at the Nineteenth Party Conference in June 1988, 'the process of the consistent democratization of Soviet society should complete the creation of a socialist state governed by the rule of law.' This involved a major shift in the relationship between the individual and society. While individuals had rights, as citizens they would be constrained by law.

Gorbachev recognized that economic reform was dependent on political reform; they were causally related because the Soviet Union was an 'administered economy'. Effective control of the economy was located in industrial ministries headed by ministers and operating on a bureaucratic basis, politics controlling economics – unlike under capitalism, where it is the other way round.

> The main point, comrades . . . is that at a certain stage, the political system . . . was subjected to serious deformations. . . . The command-administrative methods of management that developed in those years had a pernicious effect on various aspects of the development of our society. . . . It is in this ossified system of power, in its form of command and structure of control mechanisms, that the fundamental problems of restructuring are grounded today.[41]

Acceleration of the economy could occur only if the political obstacles to economic reform could be removed. Like the Tsars in the nineteenth century, the reform leadership of Gorbachev was confronted with the power of industrial ministries which had developed into self-regulating bodies with a tendency to inertia and resistance to outside control. Gorbachev is reputed to have quoted John Stuart Mill's opinion of the Russian Empire: 'The Tsar himself is powerless against the bureaucratic bodies: he can send any of them to Siberia, but he cannot govern without them, or against their will. On every decree of his they have a tacit veto, by merely refraining from carrying it into effect' (the quotation was attributed to Gorbachev at the time of his meeting with Soviet writers in June 1986).

Gorbachev here recognizes a major political weakness of state socialism. Rather than politics being in command in the USSR and the state being strong, on the contrary, I would contend, the economy was hegemonic and the state's regulatory power was weak. The industrial ministerial elite, by virtue of its operational control of the economy which led to strategic control, became dominant. Unlike under modern capitalism, however, the distinctive features of state socialism made these masters of the economy members of the state bureaucracy.[42] This linkage of politics and economics has created an endemic problem of Soviet politics – how can political leaders control the economy and its rulers, the industrial ministers? Stalin resorted to purges, at considerable costs, which later leaders could not contemplate. In order to strengthen their authority, first Khrushchev then Gorbachev launched their respective policies of reform. Both failed.

It is in this context that democratization of the apparatus was intended to break up the control of these administrative elites and vested interests. Greater decentralization, an enhanced role for the market and a delegation of decision-making downwards as in *khozraschet* were economic devices which could be used to limit the power of the bureaucracy. In addition, Gorbachev envisaged greater democratization in the answerability of officials to public demands, greater participation on the part of the public and the acceptance of a pluralism of opinions – a quasi-electoral system in which the party had to justify its policy, its leaders had to run for public office and, what was to transpire as the most important measure of all, in which there was a shift in authority from the party to the soviets, the elected parliaments in the USSR, the republics and the regions. In a nutshell, perestroika as envisaged by Gorbachev represented a radically reformed type of Soviet communism. *In fact* it meant a significant weakening of that party-state apparatus which he had claimed would maintain the 'socialistic' character of state socialism.

We noted above that Gorbachev enacted measures which effectively weakened the centrally organized command economy. He also effectively destroyed the power of the Communist Party. This was a consequence of shifting power to the Soviets. At the beginning of his rule, Gorbachev envisaged the Soviets as conduits through which party policy would be channelled. He believed that with correct political leadership the party could maintain its hegemony and legitimate its rule. The party would maintain a monopoly of political organization and in this way would ensure a 'socialistic' context for market socialism to thrive. Its power was seriously undermined in September 1988 when the apparatus of the party secretariat was effectively disbanded. In this way, Gorbachev hoped to undermine opposition from the party elite. At the Nineteenth Party Conference (June–July 1988), Gorbachev ruled out the creation of a multiparty system and the existence of 'opposition parties'. However, he was overtaken by events.

A consequence of *glasnost* and the growing assertiveness of the local soviets had led to the formation of political groups which turned into parties. Reformers in the party argued for a redefinition of the party's role and the leadership responded: the 'leading role' of the party was deleted from the Soviet constitution and the formation of other parties and social organizations was recognized. In March 1990, the constitution of the USSR was changed by the Third Congress of People's Deputies of the USSR; effectively, the Communist Party's monopoly of political power was broken. The cement which held together state socialism disintegrated.

By the beginning of the 1990s, perestroika had gone much further than the political leaders around Gorbachev had intended, and than its critics in the West had supposed was possible. The party had relinquished its constitutional monopoly of political power and the constitution had recognized the rights of other parties to compete for political authority. Marxist-Leninist ideology and its guardian, the party of a 'new type', had collapsed. The government now aspired to a welfare state in a mixed economy. The underlying legitimacy of the system had been destroyed. Economically the reforms introduced by perestroika had failed. The economy had been dislocated. The centralized command economy had been effectively dismantled and nothing had been put in its place. Gross national product fell, productivity declined, price inflation rose, the rouble lost its value, unemployment rose, foreign debt soared, and the country was plagued by strikes (details are given in the next chapter). Unlike in China, where economic reform led to economic growth and personal prosperity, in Russia chaos, uncertainty, decline and personal ruin were consequences of the economic reforms. Also in contrast to China, the economic reforms were paralleled by significant reforms of the polity, resulting in internal war, secession and collapse.

The Failure of Market Socialism

What has bedevilled the 'economic reformers' of state socialism is their inability to resolve a contradiction between the values of socialism (a classless society, equity, motivational commitments to work, equalitarian outcomes and full employment) and the operation of the economic market in the context of a capitalist environment. An assumption of many of the reformers studied above was that the socialist context would prevail in a market society. By this they meant not only the continued existence of state property but also the hegemony of the Communist Party, which would ensure that socialist values would not be eroded. The problem here is that the framework of state socialism is maintained by elites of party and state, and these have powers which often conflict with the operation of the market. Once the framework is weakened, other values dominate over those of the state socialist system, bringing other forms of social exchange. The market motivates people for mercenary ends – for wealth creation and accumulation; it is a form of social control, defining the goods and services people have and should have; it is a criterion for individual success and status; it encourages the striving for personal competitive gain. Economic markets have to operate relatively autonomously to coordinate the factors of production, and under capitalism the 'invisible hand' therefore leads to outcomes not compatible with socialism. Most important of all, as was shown by Gorbachev's destruction of the party apparatus, class forces linked to the market appear, with goals which are not compatible with those of state socialism. In his policy, Gorbachev started out with the second variant of market socialism, discussed above, but – as in the experience of Eastern Europe – political forces pushed it into the first variant, which in turn led to collapse of the system.

The other major constraint acting on the socialist polity was the pressure generated by entry into, or exposure to, the world economy. The world division of labour has implications for the type of economy which a 'market socialist' system can take. To ensure the repatriation of debts and the security of capital, the system of international finance demands internal budget constraints to ensure the value of currency, and the convertibility of currency and foreign investment also require rights of control of property. The world economy as it is presently constituted undermines a socialist society, understood in its classical form and as constructed under state socialism.

In the USSR the radical reformers weakened the party-state framework so much that it was unable to withstand the political demands exerted by market forces. In China, on the other hand, the introduction of the market has been successful economically and the formal apparatuses of communist power have continued. But the reforms have undermined the ability of the state as a distributive agency and have generated political groups which will undoubtedly undermine the socialist infrastructure. Economic interests, occluded by the 'invisible hand', potentially have much to gain from a market system. The political leadership under Gorbachev effectively destroyed the system of planning and party control. The Western powers made demands, which were conceded, undermining 'market socialism'. The political, economic, internal and external context was not favourable for market socialism. The Third Way, between capitalism and state socialism, had failed. Just how it failed is the topic of the next two chapters.

Part II
Denouement

Chronology and Precipitants
of Regime Collapse

Despite the continued presence of communist governments in Cuba, Vietnam, North Korea and China, the era born in October 1917 in Russia ended in December 1991. By then communism had collapsed in Eastern Europe and the USSR. Gorbachev's attempt at a reformed socialism, perestroika, had failed. Post-communist governments moved to 'transition'; to parody the Marx of the 'Communist Manifesto', 'A spectre was haunting Eastern Europe' – the spectre of capitalism.

We turn now to examine how and why state socialism collapsed. In the following three chapters the denouement of the socialist project is considered from three perspectives. In this chapter I outline the political precipitants and the sequence of events which led to the fall of communist governments. In the next I turn to consider, in the light of collapse, the extent to which theories of state socialism are able to explain its failure. And in chapter 8 I interpret the disintegration of the system in terms of a 'social structure' approach, discussing my own theory of class division and combining precipitants of change with underlying weaknesses. Finally, I turn to consider the implications for the socialist project.

Eastern Europe

The underlying developments which created popular movements of opposition go back much further than can be covered here, where only some of the major events leading to the fall of communism are briefly described.[1]

In Poland, the communist government had been confronted by organized opposition for many years: strikes had been episodic from 1956, and in the early 1980s Solidarity, the Church and the intelligentsia had been major forms of opposition. The course of events leading to the formation of a non-communist government began with the strikes in the spring and August of 1988, which threatened to paralyse the country. Round-table discussions began between the various political interests, and compromises were worked out between President Jaruzelski and Solidarity. The Polish government agreed to legalize Solidarity and to allow it to participate in elections. In return Solidarity agreed to unpalatable economic measures (price rises). In the electoral system, the Polish political leadership promised a move to free elections. In this context, it was agreed that the President would retain important powers in a future electoral system and that the communists would be guaranteed seats and key positions in the government. In April 1989 a round-table agreement was made between the incumbent political elite and the leaders of Solidarity. It conceded the need for democratic and constitutional reform and, crucially, competitive elections. Here we have the perfect 'negotiated settlement'. A consequence of the agreement was that the communists were assured of a majority of the seats in parliament and Solidarity promised to acquiesce to the election of Jaruzelski as president. In return, the communists would liberalize the constitution.

In the event, the communists fared disastrously in the elections[2] and Solidarity formed a government in September 1989. Though the communists initially did retain a small number of places in the government, their rule in Poland was finished. The communists handed over power to a government which maintained order and public support. The leading role of the party was expunged from the constitution of the country. On 1 January 1990 the country's name became the Polish Republic and in the same year the Communist Party was dissolved and a new party founded: Social Democracy of Republic of Poland. Following the lead of Hungary, a new chapter opened in the history of Polish communism: the communists became part of a multiparty opposition. In July a bill was passed giving workers the right to buy shares in their enterprises, and a window was opened on privatization of the economy. In December, Lech Walesa was elected President. Communism was ended.

External factors were critical in the timing of the collapse. Until the advent of Gorbachev in the USSR, the government was held together by the political alliance with, and dependence on, the USSR. Poland could not independently leave the Warsaw Pact or Comecom. The Soviet Union had traditionally considered Poland to be a major defence bulwark against the West. The 'new thinking' on international affairs by the Soviet leadership under Gorbachev entailed a change in policy towards Poland. In the context of nuclear war, it was no longer believed that a Soviet presence in Poland was essential to the defence of the USSR. Furthermore, the traditional Soviet role in Eastern Europe was a liability for the USSR policy of entente with the Western powers. The Soviet government, Gorbachev made clear, would not assert military force to defend a pro-Soviet leadership in Poland as it had done in Czechoslovakia. This change in policy by the USSR considerably reduced the potential costs of a challenge to the communist government by the opposition movement. The consequence of all this was that the communist government collapsed and was replaced by a radical reform movement intent on a transition to capitalism.

In Hungary, the abortive rising of 1956 influenced developments. Here anti-communism was strong and the country under Imre Nagy in 1956 had declared for a multiparty system and exit from the Warsaw Pact. In the wake of the crushing of the uprising, the process of reform occurred gradually from the 1970s, when the political elite became more technocratic and professionalized. Hungary adopted the New Economic Mechanism, which allowed considerable private initiative and a limited role to the market. While Hungary moved in the direction of market reforms in the 1980s, there was little public unrest or 'dissident' activity. There was effectively no explicit 'political reform', as in Czechoslovakia in the late 1960s. Political developments were internal to the Communist Party, where critiques of the centralized system and the discussion of the significance of the rebellion and subsequent Soviet invasion in 1956 led to internal division. The more traditional leader, Janos Kadar, who had been in office since 1956, was removed from power in May 1988. New leaders elected in 1988 advocated a more pluralist political system, and the Central Committee agreed on the need to move to a multiparty system. National round-table negotiations took place in 1989 between various factions and the communist leadership, and it was agreed that competitive elections would be held. The party's leading role was revoked in that year and the Communist Party changed its name to the Hungarian Socialist Party; in the competitive elections in the spring of 1990 it was decisively beaten. By now communism in Hungary was defeated. The country moved in the direction of privatization of state property. The freedoms demanded by, and conceded to, the East European states had ramifications right across Europe. Henry Kissinger's domino theory prevailed. The successes of anti-communist parties in Poland and Hungary were models for the rest of Eastern Europe.

The German Democratic Republic was one of the least affected by the movements for political and economic reform before 1989. The economy was relatively successful and the political elite appeared to be stable and in control. The communist leaders in East Germany considered their policy to be the 'leading edge' of the development of socialism and they regarded perestroika as irrelevant to their needs. Reform was precipitated from outside. *Glasnost* was a particularly subversive policy. In October 1989, Gorbachev attended the GDR's fortieth anniversary celebrations and met popular aclaim in the streets. During this visit he made it clear to Erich Honecker, the head of state, that rule could only be legitimated through popular support. Concurrently the outflow of a third of a million refugees from the GDR through Hungary to Austria was accompanied by popular anti-communist street demonstrations and strikes. Party membership also declined and the leadership was unable (or unwilling) to adapt to the policies espoused by Gorbachev in the USSR.

But pressure grew. Erich Honecker, following hospitalization, resigned, and his place was taken by Egon Krenz (first as party leader then as head of state). The economy declined and public protest continued alongside a steady stream of emigration. In November and December the government and the politburo of the Communist Party resigned. An emergency meeting of the Central Committee of the party adopted a New Action Programme. It promised economic reforms, which would be guided by market conditions and, crucially, free and democratic elections. In the short term it was proposed that a coalition government should be set up. Competitive elections were promised and were held in March 1990; the communists were again defeated. New political movements mushroomed. The Communist Party (the Socialist Unity Party) changed its name to the Socialist Unity Party of Germany-Party of Democratic Socialism.

In November 1990, Chancellor Kohl of West Germany's Federal Republic outlined a plan for ending the division of Germany. In the same month in East Germany the parliament elected a non-communist as president and a new coalition government was formed; in this the communists' bloc had 11 out of 27 seats. Opposition parties were legalized, press and travel restrictions were removed and on 9 November the Berlin Wall was opened for free movement between the east and the west of the city. In December, leading members of the former communist state (including Erich Honecker) were arrested and charged with corruption. Concurrently, the GDR government indicated its willingness to move towards greater links with the Federal Republic – though many opposition groups as well as communists were opposed to this policy. The move towards reunification was initially opposed by the USSR; however, in February 1990 Gorbachev agreed to the question of unification being decided by the GDR itself. Consequently, at elections held in March, the former Communist Party, now the Party of Democratic Socialism, received only 16 per cent of the votes. The right-wing Christian Democratic Union emerged as the single largest party, with 40.82 per cent of the vote. The GDR was subsequently absorbed into the Federal Republic of Germany.

As we noted earlier, Czechoslovakia in 1968 had led the movement for political and economic reform. Thereafter, however, the country was not at the forefront of reform initiatives. In the 1980s the relatively small group of intellectuals in Charter 77 constituted an oppositional movement. But in 1989 the velvet revolution broke out. The major disturbance took the form of public demonstrations, notably in Prague in November 1989. Opposition groups appeared and demanded reforms from the government: constitutional government, the revocation of the party's leading role and the resignation of the incumbent president, Gustav Husak. There followed the resignation of the party's politburo and the government. Not only did the USSR not intervene militarily (as it had in 1968), but the Soviet secret service actively helped to organize the demonstrations in Wenceslas Square against the incumbent government.[3] Its leader, Ladislav Adamec, spoke positively about Alexander Dubcek's reforms of 1968 and negotiated with the opposition leaders in Civic Forum (the broad alliance of opposition groups formed in 1989). Popular elections were proposed. By the end of December 1989 a non-communist government chaired by Alexander Dubcek and a presidency filled by Vaclav Havel were in place. In 1990 the communists lost the elections to Civic Freedom and Public Against Violence. The country moved to an era of transition.

In Bulgaria, little public disturbance was shown before 1989. A major cue for change came from the USSR, whose television was directly received there. In 1989 dissent centred on flagging economic production, concern at environmental pollution and the expulsion of the Turkish minority by the Todor Zhivkov government. That autumn mass demonstrations took place against the government and criticisms were made of the leader within the politburo. The politburo split, with Zhivkov being opposed by the defence minister, the army chiefs of staff and the foreign minister. In November, after heading the party leadership for 27 years, Zhivkov resigned, and in December he was expelled from the party. A new government was installed and announced comprehensive reforms. From 1990 the constitution defined the country as a parliamentary republic, and the hegemony of the Communist Party was abrogated. As in other countries, the party changed its name, becoming the Bulgarian Socialist Party. Changes here were effectively an internal coup and many of the prior members of the communist elite have remained in power.[4] In electoral terms, though the reformed communists lost their overall majority in the 1991 election, they were still the second most popular party, having 106 seats out of a total of 240 (the United Democratic Front had 110 seats).

Developments were not quite so peaceful and free from political violence in Romania, where Nicolae Ceausescu had ruled since 1965 as a personal dictator, with many positions of state held by members of his family. Whereas he had adopted an independent position vis-à-vis the other countries of the Soviet bloc in foreign affairs, there had been little internal liberalization before 1989. Of the East European communist leaders, he had been the most outspoken against the policies of reform in the USSR and Hungary. In 1989, he reasserted the traditional communist belief in the leading role of the party and the importance of class struggle. The costs of dissent were extremely high and there was no visible opposition movement. Nevertheless, anti-government demonstrations took place in December in Timisoara, and the security forces opened fire on the crowds.

Later in the month, Ceausescu called a mass rally in Bucharest. Here he faced a hostile crowd and demonstrations. A state of emergency was declared. However, opposition leaders resisted the leader and declared the National Salvation Front to be in power. Ceausescu and his entourage fled, were captured and later executed. In the uprising it has been estimated that 10,000 people were killed. Following the upheaval, competitive political parties were allowed and reestablished. In Romania, however, it is believed that counter-elites in the intelligence apparatus engineered Ceausescu's downfall. In competitive elections in May 1990, the National Salvation Front (a coalition in which former communists were a leading force) was elected to power. The developments in Romania were more an internal coup than a popular revolution.

In Yugoslavia in 1989 the League of Communists was under pressure. In Slovenia in January an independent party, the Democratic Alliance, was founded. In December the League conceded the need for a multiparty system, and the 'leading role' of the communists was renounced in January 1990. Elections followed in the various republics: in Serbia the reformed communists maintained power, though in the other republics anti-communists controlled the governments. By 1991 the federation that had combined such diverse elements into one Yugoslavia was dissolved. Once the organizing principles of state socialism and Titoism were subverted, nationalism (and religion) became the only form which could legitimate the elites of the republics. Since the communists were associated with the pan-Yugoslav state, which was increasingly linked to the hegemony of Serbia, anti-communism took a nationalist form. In July 1990, Slovenia declared itself an independent republic. In the same month the Serbs in Croatia declared their own sovereign republic, followed in December by the Croation Assembly's declaration of sovereignty. From 1991, the assertion of independence by states within the Soviet Union – and the recognition of their independence – strengthened the claims of local political and economic elites to form their own states. It was in the economic interests of Croatia and Slovenia to break away from Yugoslavia (the Serbian minorities dissenting), and their independence as states was declared in June 1991; it was later recognized by Germany, then by other Western countries. Except in Serbia, the power of the communist political class was broken and Yugoslavia disintegrated into warring national entities.

The Albanian People's Republic, under the rule of Enver Hoxha, had maintained a strictly isolationalist role – from Western societies in general and from the Eastern European states. The events of 1989 led to mild demonstrations but essentially the regime was unscathed and its government denounced the revisionist regimes around it. In 1990, as in Hungary the year before, some people claimed political asylum in foreign embassies and they were allowed to leave the country. In addition, reformers in the party gained some concessions in the form of marginal political and economic liberalization (the ban on religion, for instance, was lifted).[5] Anti-government demonstrations took place in 1990 and the leadership conceded the right for competitive elections, which took place in 1991. The communists secured a majority, but conceded a large number of seats to the opposition Democratic Party. Further elections followed in March 1992 and the communists lost office. As in other East European countries, a new constitution was declared in 1991: the communist party's hegemony was ended and competitive political parties were legitimated. The Party of Labour of Albania (the communist party) changed its name to Socialist Party in 1991; private property was to be respected and a move to a market economy supported.

By the end of 1990 the communists had effectively lost their power of command in all the major countries of Eastern Europe, though in Romania, Serbia, Bulgaria and Albania members of the old elite still had important positions. In the USSR, the reform leadership of Gorbachev was still in power. The old communist rulers had not been removed by violent revolution but had negotiated their withdrawal. Neither were they replaced by unitary political movements with a clear intention of creating a new society. The opposition movements which came to power were composed, to use Schopflin's term, of 'conglomerate parties'.[6] These included a wide range of political interests which were united in opposition against the dominant communist leadership but had no common policies. They were predisposed to pluralist democracy and to market reform. After gaining power, these groups were to splinter over the direction and rate of change. But they all, more or less, accepted ideas of competitive political parties and a move to a market economy.

Clearly the external environment had had a determinant effect on the internal politics of the Eastern European countries. Were these unanticipated consequences of perestroika or did the Soviet leaders believe that the likely effects of their action would be the fall of communism in Eastern Europe?

The Effects of Perestroika in Eastern Europe

Gorbachev believed that perestroika would lead to reform within the parameters of Soviet socialism. In Eastern Europe, where communist governments were less securely grounded than in the USSR and where there was considerable public opposition, his policies had more profound consequences for the integrity of the regimes. The authority of their communist leaders was undermined by the critique of state socialism endorsed by Gorbachev and by his policy in foreign affairs. Perestroika demanded reform not only in economics but also in politics. The governments of the East European states either adopted *glasnost*, democratization and pluralism as policies, or the people of those countries took them for themselves. If one was 'modelled' on the Soviet Union, how could one not follow its lead? The effects of Gorbachev's policy were twofold: in all societies, the political elites were prone to lose confidence; and public disquiet grew. The collapse of state socialism was a mixture of elite-led withdrawal and popular movements for change.

A reformation in Soviet doctrine influenced policy in foreign affairs. Before Gorbachev, priority was given in Marxist-Leninist theory to class interests, and this was interpreted by Soviet leaders to justify the political identity and unity of the socialist bloc. Attempts by Eastern European governments to weaken economic and political links were threatened by intervention of the USSR, as happened in 1968 in Czechoslovakia. Perestroika replaced this by giving a priority to state sovereignty over class. Gorbachev insisted that the leadership of the people's democracies and socialist states would have to secure its own legitimacy. In 1989 it was made clear that the USSR would not intervene in the affairs of other states, even if they were in the same alliance.[7] This completely reversed the 'Brezhnev doctrine' – that governing communist parties were responsible not only to their own people but to those of 'all the socialist countries'.[8] It was a logical extension of Gorbachev's policy that if the ruling communist parties lost their hegemony in Eastern Europe, the countries would be allowed to adopt their own socioeconomic formation, whether it be reformed socialist or capitalist. This policy significantly lessened the potential costs of independent reform in the Eastern European countries. Ideologically it paved the way for the legitimacy of national and anti-communist groups and parties to subvert allegiance to the USSR, and to its socioeconomic system. When exposed to free elections, the communists lost out to opposition parties, most of which took an anti-communist stance.

Consideration of Western policy explains why state socialism disintegrated when it did. To secure American and European support for his policy of disengagement from the Cold War, Gorbachev had to meet the demands of the Western leaders. As Gorbachev sought to put his policy in place, the Western powers increasingly raised the stakes of compliance. Helmut Kohl, the West German Chancellor, made it clear that Russia would not be allowed into its 'European home' unless the GDR arrived there first as part of a united Germany. The British prime minister, Margaret Thatcher, also raised the level of expectations when she insisted on the introduction of competitive elections in the USSR in the context of a multiparty system.[9] As Dawisha has put it: 'Increasingly, Western responses would shape East European futures . . .'[10] The Soviet leadership had set in motion a process which would guarantee to the West that the people of Eastern Europe would have certain rights and freedoms: the success of this policy led to the downfall of communism in Eastern Europe. It was one of the costs that Gorbachev and his advisers were willing to pay for a real and effective entente with the West.

Did, then, the Gorbachev leadership realize that its policies would lead to the end of communism in Eastern Europe? This does seem to be likely: as Michael MccGwire argues, the 'desanctification of Marxist-Leninist dogma . . . the emphasis on democratising both the state and the party, the plans for unilateral force reductions and the withdrawal of Soviet forces, each on its own was a radical development. In combination their implications were revolutionary.' He concludes that 'the Gorbachev leadership deliberately set in motion the process that would lead to the collapse of communist rule throughout Eastern Europe by the end of 1989.'[11] But Gorbachev did not so readily anticipate the consequences of his policy on the destiny of the USSR.

The Failure of Perestroika within the USSR

Though initially, in 1986, Gorbachev was not confronted by a popular political crisis, with time the effects of his policy gave rise to profound criticism at home.[12] His wager on securing 'acceleration' of the economy through his reform programme had failed dismally. In 1990, gross national product in the USSR declined by 1.5 per cent; in 1991, it fell by 15 per cent. Price inflation in the late 1980s rose significantly: from an average of 5.7 per cent for the period 1981–5 to 7.4 per cent in 1987, 8.4 per cent in 1988 and 10 per cent in 1990. In 1991 it reached three figures, with estimated rates of inflation from 140 per cent to 300 per cent per month. The value of the rouble plummeted: dollars and cigarettes (Western) became a medium of exchange. People's savings became worthless. In 1989, by official figures, 44 million working days were lost through strikes. Exports declined by 12 per cent; the earning of foreign currency fell. In a period of five years the net foreign debt had risen sixfold – from 10 billion dollars to 67 billion. In 1991, Western estimates put the rate of unemployment at 10 per cent.[13]

In the urban areas there was a significant growth of private business and the rise of a new stratum of 'rouble millionaires'.[14] The collapse of the economy strengthened calls for a more rapid move to the 'market'. On the basis of interviews with top officials in the Soviet system, Ellman and Kontorovich write:

> economists were peddling market myths, ignoring any possible ill effects of their proposals (as did the designers of the reforms . . .). Market and democracy emerged in their writings as flawless arrangements unrecognisable to anyone who has seen the real thing. Some of these authors were almost certainly seeking the destruction of the Soviet system first and foremost. We know that the younger generation of economists who came into the government right after the collapse considered the rapid destruction of the old institutions as almost the chief benefit of their policies. The same motivation must have operated for some of them when they were still the opinion makers.[15]

Perestroika was a policy of self-destruction: when the old system of central planning was destroyed, nothing was put in its place except uncertainty and ambiguity.

Perestroika led not to economic renewal but to fundamental questions about Soviet institutions and practices. Moreover, its mobilizing principles were rent with contradictions: between market and plan, between administrative and popular control, between the forces generated by civil society and the dominant party, between demands for private property and state ownership. As demands amplified for a market economy, so did the ramifications with respect to other forms of social organization and the motivational attributes of a market society. The reformers learned again from Adam Smith, who, writing 200 years before perestroika, said: 'A person who can acquire no property can have no other interest but to eat as much, and to labour as little as possible.'[16] The call for private ownership came on to the agenda.

A major political contradiction between the leading role of the Communist Party and the elected soviets became evident. Who was to govern and control the government: the party or the soviets? As the latter were elected on a republican and regional basis, their role was potentially disruptive of central control. The initial changes – in ideology and political practice – were put into effect by the Gorbachev leadership. Unlike in the Eastern European states, they were not a consequence of direct public pressure. The movements for radical reform capitalized on the policy and ideological stance taken by the political leadership in Moscow.

The policy of *glasnost* legitimated a critique of Stalinism which in turn questioned the structure of the Communist Party and its leadership. Soviet writers, in attempting to attribute deficiencies to the 'administrative command system', at first sought to locate the sources of decline in the personal inadequacy of the leaders. This followed a tradition going back to Khrushchev's critique of the 'cult of personality' of Stalin. Gorbachev widened this to include the administrative apparatus, particularly the government ministries. Privilege and corruption and the malfunctioning of the welfare state were disclosed. Critics were able to expose these deficiencies as a consequence of Marxism-Leninism. These criticisms had the effect of destroying the myths created about the legitimacy of leadership under socialism and destabilized the social and political order. Old grievances about the incorporation of the Baltic states into the USSR became a focus of their nationalist movements. In 1988, in Latvia, demonstrators declared: 'No occupation' and 'The independence of Latvia is Lenin's national policy'.

In the same year, the republics and regions demanded greater independence from USSR-level control over the enterprises in their areas, and claims were made for the formation of republican ministries of foreign affairs. Bear in mind: the USSR Constitution stated that the republics had the right to secede; the republics had their own parliaments and governments; the administration was 'national in form' – it was the party and the USSR ministries which provided the unity in the system. In the late 1980s the reform movement, legitimated in terms of a 'plurality' of opinions, succeeded in characterizing the Soviet model of development as 'totalitarian', with all its negative features, and linked Stalinism to fascism.

Democratization gave rise to an authentic pluralism of opinions and interests, which led to demands for different parties to articulate grievances and policies. In March 1990 the USSR parliament voted to amend the article giving the Communist Party of the Soviet Union (CPSU) the 'leading role' in the political system. The party's own apparatus was seriously weakened by the Gorbachev leadership in its quest to give more power to the soviets. The political changes here were led from above by a faction around Gorbachev. In turn, the collapse of the party as a ruling power led to a shift in authority to the soviets. Ellman and Kontorovich, on the basis of interviews with top officials from the previous administration, point out:

> The failure of the centre to protect its own officials in the localities from sharp criticism from the local media and local politicians and sometimes even public humiliation was another important factor weakening the Union. Since the local officials could no longer rely on support from the centre, they naturally had to try and gain local support. This meant in

many cases compromising with that local nationalism that they had previously . . . denounced. This gave a major boost to the disintegration of the USSR.[17]

Power shifted from the centre to the republics. Democratization took an institutional form with the spontaneous formation of political associations and proto-parties: in 1990 in the Russian Republic alone 20 parties were formed; by 1991 the number had grown to 100 and there were some 11,000 'unsponsored' organizations in the USSR. Moreover, in the elections which took place in the republics in 1990 and 1991, many people voted for deputies who sought to disband the communist system.

Once the right had been conceded for contested elections, anti-communist forces gained strength and governments hostile to the Union were elected in the Baltic states, the Caucasus, Moldavia and the Ukraine, while Russia's two leading cities (Leningrad and Moscow) had anti-communist administrations. The Supreme Soviet of the RSFSR (the Russian Republic) became dominated by radical reformers and, in the first ever popular election for a president, the Russian Republic elected an anti-communist and populist, Boris Nikolaevich Yeltsin. These developments reflected major conflicts in ideology and aspirations among the governing elites about how reform should proceed. The political leadership in the republics – now constituted largely from politicians with authority in their Supreme Soviets – sought independence and the dissolution of the USSR. Nationalism became a unifying ideology of dissent. This was a view, however, not universally shared in Russia, where, in the referendum held in March 1991, 76 per cent of those voting on an 80 per cent turnout were for the preservation of the Union. In the Ukraine in October 1989, only 20.6 per cent favoured self-determination for the republic – a figure which had risen to 90.3 per cent by December 1991.[18]

The failure of perestroika to lead to economic improvement, and the rapid destabilization of society, led to open conflict between the supporters of the traditional system and the reformers. Divisions also appeared in the ranks of the reformers themselves – between the insurgent forces of radical reform and the defenders of a reformed state socialism. There were three main groupings. The traditionalists, like Egor Ligachev, have been dubbed 'conservatives' in the West (in the sense that they wished to conserve elements of the past). They sought to move towards limited market relations in the economy in the framework of a strong state sector, but wished to renew and strengthen the party and to revitalize Marxist-Leninist ideology. Others, like Gorbachev, sought to square the circle: to keep the essentials of the traditional system, particularly the hegemony of a reformed Communist Party, in the context of an economic market and a pluralist polity with a civil society. Finally, there arose the radical systemic reformers, like Yeltsin, who were ideologically opposed to the hegemony of the party and to the command economy and advocated a fundamental move to the organizing principles of capitalism: competitive political parties, private property and a market-led economy.

The incumbent political elites were sharply and irreconcilably divided about the course of reform. On the basis of interviews with 116 members of the Gorbachev elite, I distinguished between those seeking fundamental change of the regime and those who wanted reform. Of the political elite 41 per cent regarded the Soviet system as 'fundamentally sound, requiring reforms', 40 per cent believed that it was 'basically flawed, though significant reforms could have been achieved' and, most important of all, 19 per cent thought that the system was 'basically unsound and should have been completely replaced'.[19] Within-system reform, as contemplated by Gorbachev, could never have succeeded concurrently with political stability because the political elites were divided about the fundamental nature of the Soviet system. While members of the political elite universally attributed blame for the failure of reform and for the collapse of the USSR to Gorbachev himself, it was also a consequence of major disagreements between the elite actors themselves about the nature of the Soviet system and the possibility of reform. Though many of the party elite and elected legislators concluded that the system was basically flawed, and favoured radical reform, a large number of leading government executives believed that the Soviet system was 'fundamentally sound'. The political space between the components of the political elite was too wide for a 'negotiated settlement' (associated with transition to democracy) and consequently the transition from state socialism was one of systemic breakdown.

In the late 1980s and early 1990s, major destabilizing elements became apparent. Four major ingredients for radical change surfaced: first, widespread dissatisfaction with economic and social conditions; second, ambiguity among the leaders and the lack of a definite plan to overcome the discontent; third, increased political activity among the masses; fourth, independence movements in the republics and regions. To precipitate a major revolutionary change a fifth factor was needed: a clear political alternative and leaders intent on achieving it, together with a lack of will on the part of the incumbent elite. This final dimension became apparent in August 1991.

The Final Sequence of Collapse

Developments in Eastern Europe, described above, hastened the process of radical reform in the USSR. Given the lack of intervention in Eastern

Europe, the rejection by the people there of communist rule appeared as a precedent for, and a legitimation of, the secession movements in the republics of the USSR. Their demands for independence were amplified. Local political elites, often supported by public demonstrations, asserted their authority against the central powers headed by Gorbachev. The United States, which had never recognized the incorporation of the Baltic states into the USSR, warned the Russians against the use of force. In March 1990, Lithuania declared itself independent. Initially, this was opposed by the Soviet leadership under Gorbachev, and the Soviet Union imposed economic sanctions; this led to the USA withholding the normalization of economic relations promised by President Bush in his meetings with Gorbachev in Malta the previous year.

In the Russian Republic, following the election of Yeltsin as chairman of its presidium, the Supreme Soviet declared the republic's sovereignty in June 1990, and Russia began to enter into political and economic agreements with other republics. By the end of 1990 all the constituent republics (and many other regional areas) of the USSR had declared their own sovereignty. Faced with increasingly hostile governments in most of the republics – not only refusing to yield tax revenues to the USSR, but also claiming the priority of their own laws over those of the centre – Gorbachev formulated a proposed treaty between nine of the republics in which the USSR would become a confederation of states in place of a federation.

In August 1991, Gorbachev took his annual holiday in the Crimea. This proved a fatal miscalculation. The leading members of his own political elite placed him under house arrest, announcing that he was ill. In an attempt to halt the disintegration of the Soviet system, a state of emergency was declared by the State Committee for the State of Emergency; this was a bid to replace Gorbachev as President of the USSR. The members of the State Committee who took command were the most powerful men in the USSR and all had been appointed to leading positions in the state bureaucracy by Gorbachev: the Vice-President of the USSR, the Prime Minister, the chief of the KGB, the Interior Minister, the chief of the military-industrial complex, the head of the Peasant Union, the president of the association of state industries. None had a position in the party apparatus (Gennadi Yanaev had been in the politburo when elected, but later resigned). The Cabinet of Ministers of the USSR supported the coup. The statements of the coup leaders, however, lacked ideological grounding: they were couched in terms of maintaining 'law and order' and saving the USSR as a corporate state. They sought to halt the process of democratization, marketization and indecisive political leadership. In turn, however, they too became irresolute: they hesitated to use armed force and when they did so, it was too late and ineffective.

Yeltsin, now elected President of the Russian Federation and ensconced in the Russian parliament, proclaimed the declaration of the state of emergency to be unconstitutional. He and his supporters resisted arrest and defied the leaders of the Soviet state, now clustered around the State Committee for the State of Emergency (GKChP). In this Yeltsin had crucial support from the United States Embassy in Moscow, which passed information from the US National Security Agency disclosing conversations between Vladimir Kryuchkov (Chair of the KGB) and Dimitri Yazov (Defence Minister). 'An American communications specialist was seconded to help Mr Yeltsin secretly contact wavering military commanders without risk of detection.'[20] The putschists were unable to muster sufficient armed support to take the Russian parliament building where Yeltsin and his supporters were lodged. Crucially, KGB special forces, internal troops and the army refused to use force against the government of the Russian Republic. The leaders of the State Committee for the State of Emergency gave up and were arrested.

Yeltsin assumed command over the USSR and the Russian parliament assumed control over all-union institutions and state property in Russia. Gradually, Russian ministries took over Soviet ones within the territory of the Russian Federation. This constituted an effective countercoup. Yeltsin and his supporters did not adopt a policy of reform, but one of radical political and social transformation. The leaders of radical reform in the other republics also declared control over the assets of the USSR government in their areas. In September the USSR Congress of People's Deputies (its parliament) dissolved itself. In most republics the Communist Party was proscribed, its property confiscated and its newspapers and journals ceased publication. The new liberal leadership promised speedy marketization and privatization of the means of production. The new radical leadership under Yeltsin did not negotiate with the deposed communist elite, they destroyed it. There was no political pact. On his return to Moscow, Gorbachev – though he had resigned from the general secretaryship of the Communist Party – was held by his opponents to have been responsible for aiding the coup. With his political base in the party undermined, his government under arrest and the assets of the USSR requisitioned by the republics, his position was untenable. He was politically isolated and defeated.

In December 1991, the Supreme Soviet of the Russian Federation took control of the property previously subordinate to the USSR and Russia recognized its own president in place of the USSR president. The other member states gained their independence: in September the Baltic republics, in December the Ukraine. The Commonwealth of Independent States was founded in 8 December and enlarged to include the remaining states of the USSR (excepting the Baltic states and Georgia). On 25 December 1991, Gorbachev resigned as president of the USSR, the red flag was hauled down from the Kremlin tower. On 31 December, the Union of Soviet Socialist Republics existed no more. Russia was recognized internationally as the successor state to the USSR. International recognition of the post-communist governments in the new states of the former USSR and in Eastern Europe soon followed. The symbols of the revolution and Bolshevism – statues of Lenin, the red flag, the hammer and sickle, and the places named after communist leaders (Prospekt Marksa) – were gradually removed. The era of state socialism had ended.

Precipitants of Collapse

Who and what then precipitated the fall? The views I collected from the previous political elite are illuminating. The most popular reason for the collapse mentioned was the leadership of Gorbachev.[21] Of the respondents, 70 (60 per cent) regarded his inadequacies as of great importance, and this view was also shared by those interviewed from the 'core' political leadership (his advisers, members of the politburo, party first secretaries and members of the presidium of the Supreme Soviet). Second came the need for the 'renewal of the system', with 41 saying that it was of 'great importance', and third was the role of internal political reformers (27). This was followed by the influence of Western political leaders (25); public dissatisfaction with conditions (19); and at the bottom of the list came the dissident movement (only 9 responses). Of great significance here is the perception of the need for renewal and of the inappropriateness of the structures of the command economy, together with the role of Western leaders. Other research by Ellman and Kontorovich into elite perceptions also identifies the faults in the leadership of Gorbachev as a precipitant of collapse. A point worth making here is that, whereas in revolutionary activity the positive role of political leadership is often emphasized, in this case it was deficient leadership; to paraphrase Bunce,[22] political leaders do make a difference, not only in government but in its collapse.

In chapter 4 we noted the different ways in which the leaders of state socialism came to power. Collapse has been most rapid and complete (in the sense that political and economic institutions have been replaced at the same time) in those states which had little social support and where the communists were installed by foreign states; Poland, Hungary, German Democratic Republic. In those where the communists fought their way to power (Soviet Russia, Yugoslavia, China, Vietnam, Cuba) significant change has either not occurred or has been secured only partially through an economic reform, as in China – or led to disintegration as in Yugoslavia and the Soviet Union. In Romania, public revolt led to bloodshed and an internal coup. Only in China, in Tiananmen Square, did a popular people's demonstration end in bloodshed and defeat. In China the political character of the apparatuses of power has remained and change has been focused on the economy, while in Russia the political apparatus was destroyed first, before major economic reform took place.

In this chapter, we have described the precipitants of regime collapse. We do not here discuss the underlying causes. Undoubtedly the changes set in motion by Gorbachev's policy of perestroika were the major triggers. Perestroika undermined state socialism economically, ideologically and politically: the organizing principles of the centrally managed and controlled economy were cast in doubt; Marxism-Leninism was subverted; the party, as the dominant political institution, was destroyed. These policies weakened internal and international solidarity. In the USSR, such policy was led from the top, by a fraction of the political leadership around Gorbachev. Subsequently, the potential costs for potential insurgents were significantly lowered and the potential benefits were increased.

In Eastern Europe, the thrust was 'from below' or from already established counter-elites vying for power. The communist leadership in Eastern Europe had been mortally weakened by the ideological and strategic stance of the Soviet leaders. They effectively resigned to the opposition, abdicating power. This was the decisive change: previously public unrest would have been met with force, as in Berlin in 1953, Poland and Hungary in 1956, Czechoslovakia in 1968. A negotiated pact characterizes the initial transition from communism. In Poland, the Czech Republic and Hungary there was a 'negotiated settlement' between the various players in the political elite and counter-elite; in Romania there was a 'pre-emptive coup'.[23] In the USSR, the legitimate political elite was divided: Gorbachev had undermined the traditional leadership: at a crucial period in the coup of 19 August 1991, its leaders lacked unity and the resolve to use force against the insurgents intent on the destruction of the USSR. Once elite disintegration was clear, alternative forces perceived that the potential benefits of insurrection outweighed the potential costs: successful insurgency appeared possible. Not only would the incumbent powers yield but a critical mass of anti-communist popular support was mobilized to ensure that the new incumbents would be able to legitimate their power.

Unlike in Eastern Europe, however, in Moscow the incumbent leaders and the insurgents did not negotiate a pact. The breakdown of the USSR was not a revolution driven by forces in society, it was a consequence of failed political reform, propelled from the top, essentially by Gorbachev and other colleagues within the elite of the CPSU. The Soviet leadership was not only severely internally divided but it contained significant individuals, including the head of state, who were intent on total reconstitution of the regime. Hence a negotiated settlement with ascendant elites pushing for reform and making 'pacts' with the incumbent elite – which is the typical scenario of 'democratic transition' – was not achieved. Elite dissension created a political vacuum which was filled by the democratic movement led by a fallen elite member, Yeltsin. This was essentially a negative anti-communist movement rather than an organic outcome of the modernization process – though certainly Yeltsin and his associates had significant levels of popular support. The leaders of the August coup were imprisoned, and the CPSU was banned and its assets sequestrated. The leadership under Yeltsin renounced the Soviet system. They also had foreign assistance and support, and this was a crucial factor both as a determinant of Gorbachev's policy and in support of the movements for radical reform which brought down the communist governments in Eastern Europe, as well as that of the USSR itself.

While the precipitants of change help us understand how state socialism disintegrated, we do not learn from them about the underlying causes and motivations. What were the structural conditions and social prerequisites which led the incumbents to relinquish power and impelled the insurgents to take it?

Explaining State Socialism

In chapter 3, I outlined the Soviet Marxist version of state socialism; since it was a form of legitimation, it provides no theoretical basis for an explanation of state socialism's collapse. With the hindsight of history we may turn to alternative explanations of the system's structure and process. Were the inherent weaknesses of 'socialism' responsible for its fall? What were the underlying dynamics of change? What, if any, class forces were at work? The answers to these question may be considered in terms of two different paradigms: those of Marxism, and those of contemporary social science. These approaches may be grouped into four major theories, all differing in some important respects concerning the development of state socialism. After a discussion and critique of these positions, none of which, it is contended, is adequate to explain the collapse, we turn in the next chapter to consider a multicausal approach and I develop a theory of class structure under state socialism which furthered its fall.

First, the major paradigm in the West has been that of 'totalitarianism'. Though this is a non-Marxist theory, many Marxists subscribe to it. In the states where state socialism collapsed, it has become the major paradigm utilized by the post-communist leadership during and after the process to characterize the previous communist society. I shall argue that this theory has weak explanatory power with respect to the collapse of state socialism.

According to the second theory, Soviet-type societies were not 'socialist' but were in practice state capitalist; the strategy of revolution followed by the Bolsheviks and their supporters was essentially at fault. It is contended that, following the revolution of 1917, the state was dominated by a capitalist class which pursued the development of (state) capitalism. Despite many insights, this theory crucially fails as a Marxist account in important respects.

Third, I examine the notion of a 'transitional society', one between capitalism and socialism. It is a peculiar social formation rather than a mode of production. There are two versions: that of the Fourth International, the best-known advocate of which is Ernest Mandel; and that of the journal *Critique*, and particularly its editor, Hillel Ticktin. While superior, as a Marxist theory, to that of state capitalism, it is also found to be inadequate as an explanation of the system's fall.

Fourth, the notion of convergence is a sociological approach which regards state socialism as a mode of transit to industrial society. While again having many insights, the theory needs considerable amendment to explain collapse.

Totalitarianism

Whereas critical Marxism assumes that a socialist type of society is possible and desirable, the paradigm of totalitarianism evolved in the West has rejected the Marxist-Leninist version of socialist society. Western politics has focused on the absence of a division between state and society, which has led to a particularly autocratic and despotic type of society: a politically organized society, a totalitarian state.

Though the concept of 'totalitarianism' has gained enormous popular acclaim, it has been peripheral to political science and sociology. It does not involve or appeal to any of the traditional concepts – Marxist, functionalist or behaviouralist – of mainstream social science. It has consisted of a listing of a 'syndrome' of characteristics which, it is contended, grasp the reality of the authoritarian relationship between the modern state and society. For writers such as Erich Fromm and Hannah Arendt, the major political movements of the twentieth century – fascism and Leninist Marxism – are not mere aberrations and marginal developments but reflect the subjugation of the individual under conditions of modern tyranny. Totalitarianism was popularized by two American academics, Karl Friedrich and Zbigniew Brzezinski.[1] The essential characteristics of societies of the Soviet type were defined as 'a system of autocratic rule for realizing totalist intentions under modern technical and political conditions'.[2] Hannah Arendt, in generalizing about the human condition under communism and fascism, emphasised 'The permanent domination of each individual in each and every sphere of life.'[3]

By the 1970s, however, after the fall of explicitly fascist regimes and the reform of Stalinist ones, the concept of totalitarianism went out of intellectual favour. 'Totalitarianism' was regarded at best as an outmoded ideological relic. The entry by Herbert J. Spiro in the *International Encyclopedia of the Social Sciences* suggested that the term had become 'an anti-Communist slogan in the cold war'.[4] In the 1980s a revival occurred, with a development of the concept. Not only Western writers, such as

Adam Westoby and Claude Lefort,[5] but also reformers in Eastern Europe and the Soviet Union turned to 'totalitarianism' to define the kernel of the system created by Stalin. At the same time they sought to update the approach by recognizing features which had developed since the 1960s.

Adam Westoby, in assessing communism as a world movement, considers that 'the most *general* characteristic of communism (sometimes, it seems, the only one) [is] "Leninism".'[6] A major characteristic of the movement is 'the tendency to pursue and accumulate power for its own sake, independently of social wishes which it might satisfy'. It sets 'the acquisition and retention of power, and especially state power, above satisfying the desires from which support springs'.[7] The essence of totalitarian regimes is the absence of civil society as a result of domination over society by the state. While not much different from earlier versions, Westoby brings out the absence of 'civil society'.

Jeffrey Goldfarb defines totalitarianism as 'the cultural form necessary for modern tyranny . . . The projects of totalization and absolute command emanate from totalitarian culture.'[8] This approach signals an important difference from the paradigm developed by Arendt and political scientists such as Brzezinski and Friedrich. Physical repression and terror, as instrumentalities of domination, are replaced by Newspeak, which is the 'linguistic equivalent of the master idea of the official ideology'.[9] This is 'a fundamental cultural instrument of totalitarianism'.[10] Cultural control is ubiquitous.

In their analyses of movement from pre-industrial to industrial society, social scientists have assumed the simultaneous growth of social complexity and the differentiation of society epitomized in Durkheim's distinction between organic and mechanical solidarity. This development is put in question by Goldfarb. Leaders in totalitarian states attempt to create a 'dedifferentiated society on the grounds of a supersimplistic view of the world'.[11] The party-state is the crucial political apparatus and 'ideology is the core of totalitarian culture.' Ideology in turn is based on force. While the earlier generation of theorists of totalitarianism emphasized the direct application of violence to the individual, Goldfarb points to its indirect use. Since Khrushchev, it is conceded, there has been totalitarianism without terror. Goldfarb, moreover, argues that the change encompasses more than that. A new form of legitimacy has arisen: 'legitimation through cynicism'. Newspeak promotes tyrannical social relations, but also suggests its opposite, 'living in truth'.[12]

A major part of Goldfarb's work is to emphasize cultural resistance to totalitarianism, and ways of transcending it. As cultural control is regarded as the major component of totalitarianism, true resistance to it has the character of an alternative critical culture. 'Post-totalitarianism', which evolved in Eastern Europe and the Soviet Union (and eventually led to the collapse), includes the 'whole complex of totalitarian culture and the distinctive post-totalitarian voices and actions of resistance'.[13] Here totalitarianism could be broken down by marginal and marginalized intellectuals through the formation of subcultures – the assertion of human rights, youth subculture, the peace movement, jazz, and the formation of secondary associations on the basis of common interests. The growth of such a 'second society' would hasten the fall of totalitarianism.

Whatever its merits in bringing attention to the pervasive use of force in modern society, the totalitarian approach is faulted. It tends to conflate the striving of Marxist-Leninist states to exert total control with the actual division between state and society. Martin Mali (writing as Z), for instance, shifts the goalposts when he defines totalitarianism as the 'aspiration' for total control over the population.[14] For Arendt, a defining feature of totalitarianism was the kind of technological and psychological control made possible by modern society; this is what made it different from other forms of autocracy. The leaders not just aspired to, but were successful in imposing total control. As Kornhauser put it: 'Totalitarian dictatorships involve total domination, limited neither by received laws or codes (as in traditional authoritarianism) nor even by the boundaries of governmental functions (as in classical tyranny), since they *obliterate the distinction between state and society.*'[15]

'Intentions' of political elites are not only ambiguous but strip the idea of totalitarianism of any analytical rigour: by analogy, would the democratic 'intentions' of dictators make their rule democratic? Whereas in the notion of totalitarianism the dynamics of modern society lead to the growth and strengthening of the tentacles of universal control, the view taken by the author is quite the opposite: as societies modernize, their structure becomes more differentiated, precluding omnipotent political control.[16] It is also questionable whether Marxism-Leninism has ever been the comprehensively (as contrasted to nominally) dominant ideology in Eastern Europe and whether the party-state has ever in practice penetrated society very deeply. (We noted, for example, resistance in the case of Poland in chapter 4.) Societal demands and opposition to state control also increased considerably as these societies modernized. Totalitarianism as an interpretation makes no distinctions between the different stages of development of Marxist-Leninist states: hence revolutionary, developmental and industrialized phases are all conflated. Many of these points are conceded by the emphasis on the formation of subcultures leading to countercultures, stressed by Goldfarb. Moreover, such developments are evidence of differentiation. The developmental phases which bring about new occupational groups and higher educational levels – which in turn create demands and an impetus to political change – are ignored.

Hence the theory is static and cannot explain political change. If the 'totalitarian state' is all-powerful, how can it be changed from within? As

Richard Pipes has pointed out, people did not expect it to collapse. 'Professor Merle Fainsod concluded his influential *How Russia is Ruled* . . . with the unqualified assertion that totalitarian regimes died only when power was wrenched from them – in other words, that they were immune to self-destruction.'[17] As the society is held together by force, it is not susceptible to a legitimacy crisis, for it has no autonomous sets of values on which it can be judged. By definition, totalitarianism implies that not only open dissent but even group stratification is prevented from developing; thus the triggers for change cannot be found in society. As Friedrich and Brzezinski conclude: 'Our entire analysis of totalitarianism suggests that it is improbable that . . . a "revolution" will be undertaken, let alone succeed . . . When the characteristic techniques of a terroristic police and of mass propaganda are added to the monopoly of weapons that all modern governments enjoy, the prospects of a revolutionary overthrow becomes practically nill.'[18] The rise of national secessionist movements under totalitarianism would not be seen to be linked to the structural and cultural forms of state socialism and would not pose a threat to the stability of the regime; indeed, in discussing national movements, they are dismissed as 'hopeless resistance to totalitarianism'.[19]

Consequently, the outlook adopted by theorists of totalitarianism is not useful in understanding either the various reform movements which characterized the politics of the more developed Marxist-Leninist states, or the ways in which its leaders abdicated their political and economic power. Even in the Goldfarb version, something more than opposition to pollution and the formation of jazz bands is required to account for the fall of a 'totalitarian state'. Paradoxically, it was forced industrialization and development which brought in its train more sophisticated, differentiated and demanding strata (the intelligentsia), which questioned the centralized system of management and control and in doing so, perhaps ironically in this context, utilized 'totalitarianism' as a counter-ideology to undermine the political order. The changing social structure created an intelligentsia which not only had a demographic density (see chapter 8 below) but also had a moral one in the sense of being able to form alternative subcultures and countercultures. This was the basis of an ascendant class which brought down state socialism – discussed in the next chapter.

Bureaucratic State Capitalism

Bureaucratic state capitalism is a political position shared by many diverse political groups ranging from the Mensheviks through Herbert Marcuse and Tony Cliff to Mao Zedong. The crucial element held in common by this range of theorists is that the state continues to exercise independent political and economic functions. Rather than being an expression of the interest of the working class, as in the views of the apologist of state socialism, these writers claim that the state embodies the domination of a capitalist class. The state therefore performs the historical act of the bourgeoisie, and state officialdom becomes a ruling 'class'. Hence surplus is extracted from the producers to further accumulation and to support the ruling class. Class conflict, usually latent but sometimes manifest, continues under state capitalism and takes the form of an opposition between the working class and the state bureaucracy. Various thinkers have put forward different reasons for this development and there is an important political difference between those who believe that a socialist revolution could not have been carried out in Russia in 1917 and those who believe that the revolution was justified but then took the wrong direction.

The first position is the orthodox Marxist approach adopted by Lenin's opponents, the Mensheviks, even before the October Revolution. This position is based on the prognosis of Marx and Engels that before a new mode of production could arise all the possibilities of development of the previous one must have been exhausted. The often quoted remarks of Marx in the *Critique of Political Economy* are used to legitimate the Menshevik position: 'No social order ever disappears before all the productive forces, for which there is room in it, have been developed; and new, higher relations of production never appear before the material conditions of their existence have matured in the womb of the old society.' Marxists following this line of approach, such as Karl Kautsky and Georgy Plekhanov, argued that the revolution had to come first in the advanced capitalist countries.

Russia in October 1917, it is contended, was not at the stage or formation appropriate for socialism. October finally ended feudalism but it did not introduce socialism. The communist mode of production, it is pointed out, can only arise after capitalism is fully developed. This approach (as we noted in chapter 2 above) emphasizes the primacy of the development of the productive forces and the labour process going with it. Changes in the relations of production (such as the elimination of a class of capitalists and the institution of state ownership) will not lead to a communist mode of production. The logic of this position is that the Bolsheviks became not just classless 'modernizers', as depicted by modernization theorists (see chapter 4), but built capitalism through the state apparatus. State capitalism resulted from October.

The second position recognizes the October Revolution as a working-class event, and many who are critical of Stalinism have supported the

Bolsheviks' revolutionary initiative. Hence they incline to the second position advanced in chapter 2, that the class relations to the means of production are hegemonic in political change. Their argument hinges not on the possibilities of instigating a socialist revolution in Russia, but on the events which followed. They see the 'revolution' as the successful seizure of power, but consider that it failed to put into effect the insurgents' policies. After October, policy led to the degeneration of the regime – which allowed it to sink back to capitalism.

The best-known advocate of this position is Tony Cliff in his book *Russia: A Marxist Analysis* (1964). Here he argues that October ended feudalism but did not introduce socialism. The success of the October Revolution indicated that the world was ripe for socialism; it was a legitimate seizure of power on behalf of the working class and should be supported; but Soviet Russia alone could not build a socialist society. A proletarian revolution on a world scale (or at least in the major industrial countries) was a necessary condition for the rise of a socialist state.

As the proletarian revolution did not occur subsequently in the West, for Cliff 'the central problem in post-October Russia with its low level of national income [was] the fulfilment of the bourgeois tasks of the development of the productive forces.'[20] This was not the conscious intention of the Soviet leadership: 'They thought [that] the five-year plans would take Russia far in the direction of socialism' but 'the historical mission of the bourgeoisie [in] outright contradiction to the wishes and hopes of the actors themselves' had to be carried out by the Soviet bureaucracy.[21]

The process of capital accumulation entailed the forcible extraction of surplus from the working class. This was the *raison d'être* of the repressive state apparatus, and its controllers, the bureaucracy, took on the character of a ruling class. This development was aided by the destruction of the already small working class during the civil war, which weakened the proletarian character of the regime, by the isolation of Soviet Russia and by the need to compete militarily with the advanced capitalist states, which were threatening the new regime. With time, the bureaucracy's supremacy in the relations of production led to privilege in the relations of distribution and consumption: a new ruling (state capitalist) class was born.

An important distinction is made here between the intentions of Marx and Lenin and the growth of Stalinism, which is associated with the rise of capitalism. To quote Callinicos writing in 1991, 'a qualitative break separates Stalinism from Marx and Lenin. This profound discontinuity can be traced in the historical record, in the process which transformed the Bolshevik Party . . . into the apparatus of power, terrorized and terrorizing, that it became by the end of the 1930s.'[22] The mistaken task of trying to build 'socialism in one country' 'became the foundation of the building of state capitalism'. State capitalism, for Cliff, 'is the extreme theoretical limit which capitalism can reach'; it is 'the extreme opposite of socialism'.[23]

State capitalism, it is conceded, differs considerably from Western bourgeois capitalism. There is no competition between enterprises or competition of capitals. Production is mainly for use rather than for exchange: that is, production is not geared to the production of goods for sale through a market. The making of profit at the level of the enterprise is not required to keep the productive unit in operation. The dynamic force for expansion and capital investment was not intrinsic to the Soviet Union (and by extension to the other state socialist societies) but to the forces generated by the world economy, to 'world competition'. 'The Russian state is in a similar position to the owner of a single capitalist enterprise competing with other enterprises.'[24] Competition takes an international form, and the need for military preparedness also legitimates the state and its economic activities. Under these conditions, the political leadership cannot break out of the capitalist world shell. The capitalist state (like the individual capitalist) has to accumulate in order to survive. Unlike Western bourgeois capitalism, the 'state capitalist' versions (which included the other state socialist societies) did not have persons who are 'capitalists' with a legal right to the ownership of enterprises. Bureaucrats extracted surplus value and their class rights were given by their 'control' of the means of production.

It cannot, of course, be denied that preparations for defence and the priority given to the arms industry under Stalin played an important part in determining the level of accumulation, and it must be conceded that it distorted the economy. However, it does not follow from this that the 'goal of capitalism – production for production's sake' prevailed or that the states of the Soviet bloc became a 'variant of *capitalism*, in which global military competition compelled the subordination of production within the USSR to the goal of capital accumulation'.[25]

Leaving aside the fact that the overwhelming level of output did not enter into the sphere of international competition (in Chris Harman's estimate only between 12 and 16 per cent of national income in the USSR was devoted to arms expenditure in the post-war period),[26] global competition of this kind cannot be said to be equivalent to that of the competition of capitals. Without such competition, capitalist societies would collapse and so would the infrastructure of capitalist markets and the dominant class. This was not the case in the state socialist societies. Take away global military competition and the bureaucratic and class structure does not change.

The state capitalist theorists such as Cliff and Callinicos, it is contended here, are unable to point to any distinct revolutionary break in the development of the relations of production in Soviet Russia – or in the other state socialist societies prior to the events of 1989. The major institutional forms and processes were initiated by Lenin. The party and its control and direction over society were held supreme by Lenin: even in *State and Revolution* he spoke of the party as 'the vanguard of the proletariat [which is] capable of assuming power and of *leading the whole people* to socialism, of directing and organizing the new order, of being the teacher, the guide, the leader of all the working and exploited people in organizing their social life without the bourgeoisie and against the bourgeoisie'.[27]

The implication of this position is that the collapse of the Eastern European and Soviet regimes between 1989 and 1991 is irrelevant to the socialist project. State capitalism was a phase in the development of capitalism. Chris Harman asserts: 'The transition from state capitalism to multinational capitalism is neither a step forward nor a step backwards, but a step sideways.'[28] The theory does not point out why the shift should have occurred after over 50 years of 'class power'. There is an implication that 'control' did not give rise to a ruling class in a Marxist sense – if it had, there would have been no need to change it. Also, if state socialism was the 'extreme theoretical limit capitalism could reach', then a shift to multinational capitalism is surely a step back. There is, too, a presumption that the ascendant class should be the working class, whereas in fact the working class was marginal to the political events occurring in the collapse of state socialism. But this school does have the valuable insight of locating state socialism in the context of global capitalism, a point we shall take up below.

The Transitional Society

These arguments are taken up and rejected by the second school of Marxists mentioned above, that of the transitional society. The classic statement of this interpretation was put by Trotsky in his work *The Revolution Betrayed* (1937). Here the Soviet Union was defined as a 'contradictory society, halfway between capitalism and socialism'. Where Trotsky and his followers differ from Cliff is over the class nature of the USSR. Classes are 'characterized by their position in the social system of economy and primarily by their relation to the means of production'.[29] Since Cliff denies any competition of capitals and does not identify a class of persons who enjoy a source of income derived from legal ownership of property, the class boundary of the 'state bourgeoisie' is undefined. For Trotsky, the ruling group has its basis of privilege in control of the administration; it is bureaucratic in character, rather than economic. Indeed, while it may be true that bureaucratic position gives rise to economic privilege, it does not give the right to ownership of the means of production and their transfer through the family – which ensures the reproduction of bourgeois capitalism.[30]

Ernest Mandel has elaborated this paradigm.[31] He has argued that Soviet-type societies are not modes of production but 'transitional societies' combining elements of capitalism and communism. The form of ownership and direction of the economy was socialist because there was no alienation of labour power, no production of exchange value (that is no profit realized by a social group through the purchase and sale of commodities). But the system is 'bourgeois' in so far as distribution is carried out through the market. There is then an 'antagonistic logic' between markets of commodities and labour and the plan for the macro ordering of the economy. The end stage of 'transition' for Trotsky and Mandel was indeterminate; it could lead to socialism, or degeneration could result in a capitalist restoration. From this point of view, and contrary to Harman and Callinicos, the privatization of property under state socialism would appear to be a step backwards rather than one sideways; it entails the creation of a bourgeois class with legal rights to property.

Trotsky and his followers, however, are at odds with the political formation of Soviet-type societies, which, they contend, are not characterized by workers' power but by bureaucratic rule. The political leadership is not the true representative of the working class, but a degenerate political grouping. Their power is not altruistic: the party has been displaced through forms of 'bureaucratic deformation' caused by the cultural backwardness of Soviet Russia and by capitalist encirclement.

This social formation was considered to be unstable: optimists prior to the 1990s considered that it might grow into a socialist society. Mandel defined six simultaneous factors which would have to occur for this to happen: the growth of productive forces; the institution of workers' self-management; political democracy; the withering away of the commodity–money relationship; a continuous revolution in daily habits, morals, ideology and culture; and finally, 'international development of the revolution, which alone . . . is capable of creating the necessary preconditions for a conclusion to the process of constructing a socialist society . . .'[32]

A more pessimistic scenario was drawn by Hillel Ticktin and his collaborators in the journal *Critique*. Hillel Ticktin has persevered over the years with an original development of what might be termed a post-Marxist critical interpretation of the evolution of Soviet society. Derived from Marx, it utilizes the concepts of surplus product, contradiction and class, to which Ticktin adds notions of atomization, disintegration and elite. The result is a novel paradigm of Soviet-type societies. Analogously to Mandel, Ticktin sees the Soviet Union and similar societies as 'a new form of hybrid . . . the product of a transitional epoch between modes of production . . . but [one in] an historical blind alley . . . without itself having any tendency of motion towards the new mode of production'.[33] Marxist-Leninist society is not a mode of production and has the character of 'a historical accident'[34] subject to systemic instability.

In Ticktin's view the dynamic of Soviet-type formations has been 'the enormous levels of useless productive consumption or waste that result from the instability of the system'.[35] 'The central economic feature of the USSR . . . [was] its economic wastefulness.'[36] Waste, moveover, is but a 'symptom and a result of more profound forces at work'.[37] A major contradiction in 'the system' is in the labour process: control is only partially achieved by 'the elite' through the atomization of the workforce (an idea derived from totalitarianism and, for Ticktin, originating under Stalin), which leaves 'the worker' with control over the work process. This is the cause both of underproduction and the production of 'defective use value', that is, shoddy or unwanted goods. Ticktin parts company with the traditional Marxist interpretations of Soviet society: there is no class system but 'the elite' and the atomized workforce. The former attempts to derive surplus product from the latter to fund its privileges, and the relationship therefore is exploitative. In contrast to class power, which is based on socially legitimate ownership of property and the extraction, under capitalism, of surplus value, the transfer of surplus value through bureaucratic means, as in the USSR (and by implication other state socialist societies), is illegitimate. Hence a major cause of the disintegration of the system was the incapacity of 'the elite' to extract surplus, to promote growth and to meet needs. Also the 'elite' had no legitimate rights of ownership and inheritance of property.

The working class, while not in power, nevertheless had an important role under state socialism. Its effective control over the production process made it difficult for the elite to extract surplus and this was exacerbated by its lack of legitimacy. In a book published in 1992, Ticktin wrote: 'The whole dynamic of the system is toward its own demise and overthrow by the workers.'[38]

With the hindsight of history, Ticktin must go down as one of the few specialists on state socialist society who correctly analysed the weaknesses and potential for disintegration of Soviet-type society. This context provides the major explanatory variables for reform and social change under Gorbachev. In a nutshell, politically astute sections of the Soviet elite sought to introduce the market to preserve their own position. If established, the market and its associated institutions of private property and exchange of labour value – and (one might add) civil society and a bourgeois ideology – will legitimate a new ruling class. The strength of his analysis, however, is not to be found in a strictly Marxist understanding. Nowhere do we find in his work any discussion of the class character of the society. 'The elite' is a dominant stratum, but it is not a Marxist concept; its class character is undefined and not linked to the social formation. Also, class consciousness and class action are underdeveloped and not theorized. No evidence is given (and none exists) to show the rise of working-class political consciousness as an instrument to overthrow the system. We may say that the 'dynamic of the system [was] toward its own demise', but we shall see that the leadership forces of 'reform' were from the intelligentsia, or groups within the bureaucracy, and that their world-view was to create capitalism, not to move to socialism.

Convergence and Industrial Society

It is pertinent to recall that following the Second World War some of the most influential sociologists believed that what I have called the 'organizing principles' of state socialism could not be sustained – even in a totalitarian jacket. It was denied that public property, collective welfare and equality, a dominant public sphere, planning and central control could for long underpin the development of the productive forces of an industrial society. It was held further that the socialist 'alternative' would either lead to collapse or to the recognition of, and transition to, the superior mode of operation of the Western capitalist countries. More charitably, some writers wrote in more ideologically neutral terms referring to the exigencies of 'advanced industrial society' and the notion of 'convergence', though in practice the theories entailed a one-way convergence from state socialism to capitalism, to polyarchy or democratic pluralism.[39]

Unlike advocates of the totalitarianism interpretation, who placed Western democratic pluralist societies and state socialist ones at opposite ends of a continuum, Pitirim Sorokin in 1944 stressed the similarity of psychological, cultural and social values between the USA and the USSR.[40] In 1949, Talcott Parsons described 'capitalist and socialist industrialisms . . . as variants of a single fundamental type'.[41] He described the Soviet Union as a 'counterpoint' of the capitalist West, as a 'specification'[42] of the more general pattern of 'instrumental activism'. Parsons was joined by Clark Kerr, who postulated the theory of an 'industrial society'.[43] These conclusions were grounded in the Durkheimian theory of structural differentiation. 'Evolving adaptive capacity' led to the formation of complex forms of organization requiring market exchange and the division of labour; structural differentiation involved the development of organic solidarity, stratification and social pluralism. The 'inclusion' of units in the party/state would have to give rise to democratic forms of government which ensure solidarity. The development of the productive forces (the process of 'adaptation') is dependent on adjustments in the value (belief), political and social systems. A consequence of the increasing division of labour is the necessary development of pluralism. Economic inequality is a necessary incentive to promote growth and economic efficiency.

Such writers, who were largely but not exclusively American, believed that the evolution of world history led to societies of an 'industrial type'. Evolution would lead to developing countries copying the structural and functional features of American society. As Parsons put it: 'The United States's new type of societal community, more than any other single factor, justifies our assigning it the lead in the latest phase of modernization . . . American society has gone farther than any comparable large-scale society in its dissociation from the older ascriptive inequalities and the institutionalization of a basically egalitarian pattern.'[44]

Moreover, this school anticipated fundamental changes in the communist states. The United Sates, as the most advanced society, would become a model for the rest of the world. The implication of Parsons's theory was that the possibilities for the creation of an essentially different kind of advanced society – such as communism or totalitarianism – were limited. The 'totalitarian' character of the USSR was not, he claimed, compatible with an effective industrial-type system. One of the most important consequences of increasing social and political differentiation, derived from the advanced division of labour, involves the weakening of undifferentiated societies. 'It can . . . be definitely said that the further this differentiation of the social structure proceeds, the more difficult it becomes to press it into the mould of a rigid line of authority from the top down.'[45] The political hegemony of the state (its domination, and its control of property and resources) was essentially a systemic variable of the communist societies which would have to be modified for a modern society to work efficiently and effectively.

Based on this approach, the present author pointed out that the development of state socialist societies led to increases in levels of structural differentiation and to 'exchange between the various sub-systems [becoming] more reciprocated'.[46] Without such changes, evolution would not occur and society would not develop: it might stagnate or decline. Parsons in a prescient passage anticipated that the communist societies would 'either make adjustments in the direction of electoral democracy and a plural party system or "regress" into generally less advanced and politically less effective forms of organization'.[47]

Such views were echoed by many other writers, particularly Daniel Bell and J. K. Galbraith. Bell in an influential work cogently argued that the 'end of ideology' had arrived,[48] and here he anticipated much recent writing about the 'end of history'. The radical's conception of a utopian order (communism), of a classless society, would be replaced by the striving for individual advancement and status differentiation. Politics would become a matter of administering industrial society, reconciling group interests and managing tensions, rather than being the expression of class struggle or ideological preferences. (The 'end of ideology' Bell had in mind was that of the counter-ideology of socialism, rather than the dominant ideology of capitalism.) Bell was unique in applying this concept to the states of the Soviet camp.[49]

Galbraith, who was less ethnocentric than Parsons, took a dual convergence approach, anticipating the growth of enterprise autonomy in both systems. He saw the independence of business undertakings from the bureaucracy under state socialism as being analogous to the 'exclusion of the capitalist from effective power' in Western firms.[50] Ownership of the means of production vested in the state had to be split from control of the means of production. Galbraith doubted whether the market exchange characteristic of capitalism could continue to be effective and he believed that the state as a coordinator would become a more important feature of both capitalism and socialism. Galbraith correctly foresaw that under state socialism the party activist would follow the shareholder in relinquishing direct control of the industrial enterprise.

Unlike the American writing of the 1960s, which had been deeply influenced by the writing of Talcott Parsons, the dominant trend in British sociological thought has been to insist on the diversity of types of industrial societies. Alex Inkeles represented the inspiration for this school of British sociologists. While he analysed Soviet society in 'industrial society' terms, he concluded that the industrial order was compatible with either 'democratic or totalitarian political forms'.[51] John Goldthorpe, in an influential article, 'Social Stratification in Industrial Society',[52] insisted that social stratification and economic order may be subject to '*political* regulation', ensuring that industrialism may take a totalitarian form.

> The experience of Soviet society can be taken as indicating that the structural and functional imperatives of an industrial order are not so stringent as to prevent quite wide variations in patterns of social stratification, or to prohibit the systematic manipulation of social inequalities by a regime commanding modern administrative resources and under no constraints from an organized opposition or rule of law.[53]

Goldthorpe, basing his views on empirical data derived from specialists working in the field of Soviet studies, generalized his position by arguing against common features of differentiation, consistency and mobility in industrial societies. He was contending against the Parsons/Kerr idea that Soviet-type societies should be placed on a 'lower' level than the United States.[54]

European sociologists have generally been more sensitive to cultural division, and have emphasized the difference rather than the superiority of the American model. Anthony Giddens saw capitalism and state socialism as encapsulating 'alternative frameworks' for the development of the 'industrializing process'. 'The state socialist societies . . . have genuinely succeeded in moving towards a classless order, but only at the cost of creating a system of political domination rather than in any sense diminishing it.'[55] In Giddens's view, divergence lay in the institutional structure. Capitalism ensured a division between economy and polity. This separated out conflicts between labour and capital, which are restricted to struggles of an economistic type. Under state socialism, however, the fusion of economy and polity made the system more unstable. Economistic demands had no boundaries and in seeking economic improvements, labour challenged the whole system. Rather than stability, as in the totalitarian paradigm, Giddens detected an institutional precariousness.

British sociologists then sought social bases for conflict under state socialism. Giddens emphasized the role of political domination and exploitation[56] and Frank Parkin attempted to revive the notion of a Marxist ascendant class (the intelligentsia) struggling against a ruling bureaucratic class.[57]

Industrial society theory in essence entails the view that the industrializing process has many different forms and that state socialism, therefore, was not a qualitatively different type of society, as Marxist-Leninists would imply. Capitalism and state socialism shared many features in common: inequality and stratification, domination and exploitation. The fusion of polity and economy and the lack of pluralistic forms under the hegemony of party control lead to instability – this is an important insight. Many convergence theorists pointed to the incipient pluralism and the need for reform of the institutions and processes of state socialism. None, however, was able to understand how or when collapse would occur. The main agents anticipated by the Marxist view of revolutionary change – the entrepreneurs heading new economic institutions, and the working class – were minor actors. Such interests, of course, may have had effects in creating more amorphous demands shaping expectations, but they did not impinge as direct political forces.

None of the theories we have discussed pointed to irreconcilable contradictions or tensions which would have led one to anticipate collapse and revolution. State socialism in the mid-1980s appeared to be firmly set as an alternative form of social organization to capitalism and there was no reason to suppose that collapse, rather than reform, would happen. We turn then in the next chapter to consider the underlying structural features and the precipitants of change. There we combine different elements from each of the paradigms considered above and locate a major tension in its class structure. It is argued that state socialism was distinguished by two conflicting classes: a political class – dominant in the developmental stage – deriving power from administrative control; and an ascendant class (with potential power in mature state socialism) based on the possession of social capital or intellectual assets, particularly skill and education.

8

The Fall

While the theories outlined in the previous chapter and perceptions of the precipitants of collapse described in chapter 6 can illuminate the process of change and give insights into the structural factors responsible for the dramatic outcome, none can provide a comprehensive and realistic account. In this chapter, a systemic and structural approach is adopted and linked to the precipitants of change. It is contended that there was no one single cause or set of causes to explain the collapse.[1] The fall of communism has to be considered as multicausal phenomena involving internal and external factors. We consider the underlying factors which pervaded and weakened the system and the catalysts which induced change.

A Systemic Approach

To survive and to reproduce themselves effectively and efficiently, modern societies have to solve a large number of problems. These may be analysed in terms of four major sets of institutions and related processes within them: the economy, the system of government, values and beliefs, and the system of social integration. An important assumption of a systemic approach is that these systems are interrelated: a change in one has ramifications for all three other systems. We may add yet another important factor. Modern societies are not autonomous units; they operate in a global environment and enter into relationships with the external economic and political actors.[2]

It is when there is a concurrent failure in several of these sectors and interchange systems that severe instability may occur. In certain circumstances a political order may collapse, leading to revolutionary change – as defined in the introduction to this book. But even serious systemic imbalances may not give rise to insurrection. Revolutions occur not only when there are severe disequilibrating forces, but also when potential insurgents have a collective vision of an alternative regime (economic, political and social), when they have a will and capacity to bring down the incumbents of power and when the defenders of the old order give up or are eliminated. These conditions were fulfilled in Eastern Europe and the USSR in the period 1989–90. They were not fulfilled in China.

Many of the tensions unfolding under state socialism were noted when we considered movements for economic and political reform. Here we analyse the cumulative effect of five major systemic problems.

1 The mobilization of resources. This involved a long-term decline in the rate of economic growth and the development of a popular 'expectations' gap.
2 The maintenance of loyalty, solidarity and commitment. Here we consider the modernization of the social structure – the growth of a skilled non-manual class and the cultural and social maturation of the population – which gave rise to a new pattern of demands which were not congruent with what the state could supply.
3 The nature of the political support system. We note a change in the political elite structure, the rise of potential counter-elites and a fundamental change in occupational and educational levels, weakening the supports of the established elites and strengthening counter-elites.
4 The crisis of legitimacy. The political leadership under Gorbachev in the USSR denigrated the centralized command system in politics and economics, which consequently led to the disintegration of Marxism-Leninism. The renunciation of the dominant ideology by the leaders of the reform movement in the political elite created an ideological vacuum.
5 Relationships with the outside world. Internal problems led to changes in foreign affairs. In essence, policy was transformed to one of joining the world capitalist system rather than one of competing with it. The terms of joining were set by the West and these impacted on internal political and economic policies.

Finally, we consider the interaction of structural and contingent factors leading to the breakdown of the socioeconomic order.

Economic Decline

Probably the most important long-term underlying insufficiency of the state socialist societies was the fall in the rates of economic growth. In chapter 5 I referred to the decline and its effects in individual countries. Figure 8.1 indicates that this was a systemic characteristic of state socialism in Eastern Europe and the USSR. (We shall consider other comparative figures later in this chapter.) In the earlier periods, particularly before 1960, rates of growth were spectacularly high; since 1975, however, they have fallen considerably and the average rate of growth in the later 1980s was under 4 per cent. Even the most favourable statistics produced in these societies, for all the East European states and the USSR, show a persistent long-term fall.[3] In China economic decline was halted by reform. After the Cultural Revolution, between 1979 and 1990, China's gross domestic product grew at an annual rate of 8.8 per cent. As Minxin Pei points out, this rise had a 'cushion effect' on the erosion of political authority.[4]

However, these figures, even for the Eastern European states, are positive overall and they involved the growth of the retail sector and a rise in the circulation of money. The market became relatively more

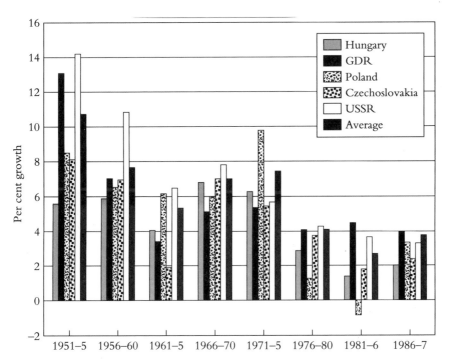

Figure 8.1 Growth of national product in Eastern European countries and the USSR, 1951–1987 (average percentage growth per year)

important in terms of the distribution, exchange and consumption of commodities and labour. Private trade in services and commodities developed in all the state socialist societies, albeit associated with 'corruption' and the growth of 'grey markets' (that is, semi-legal commercial activity). The 'market sector' of the society increased in importance and there was a rise in the number of people involved in market-type transactions. Although it was only a quasi-market limited to the political class and the administrative system,[5] it created latent and unmet demands in an aspiring 'acquisition' class for whom potentially a fuller market would give greater opportunity.

The power of the socialist bloc in the world economy was weakened. From the late 1980s, the Soviet Union yielded to Japan its position as producer of the world's second largest gross national product after the USA. A wide technological gap became evident between the Western advanced powers (and even the new economies in the Pacific rim) and the socialist societies. Consequently, the latter countries overstretched their resources to compete militarily with NATO. They 'drained the pond to catch the fish', as the Chinese proverb puts it. Such outgoings reduced the availability of goods and services for public consumption and thereby weakened the legitimacy of the polity as provider.[6] The 'Star Wars' (SDI) initiative launched by President Reagan was an even stronger military, technological and economic threat. Suppressed inflation led to shortages on the retail market, and to increased levels of savings. (Suppressed inflation occurs when demand for goods and services exceeds supply at current (fixed) prices.)

Such figures in themselves are interesting and indicate serious problems in countries such as Czechoslovakia (1961–5), where they precipitated the reform movement of the late 1960s, and in Poland and Hungary from 1976. But the figures are not sufficient in themselves to account for a major crisis: they indicate performances which are not so different from those of advanced Western European countries during the 1980s. For the period 1980–5, for example, Britain had a growth rate of only 1.2 per cent and the German Federal Republic 1.3 per cent – though overall OECD countries did better on average than the Comecon countries (see also table 8.6 on p. 177).

Underlying this decline were a number of economic factors, which the reforms (discussed in chapter 5) attempted to correct. Productivity of labour and capital declined. Whereas in the early period of economic development, *extensive* economic growth (involving increased inputs of labor, land and raw materials) had been effective, in a more complex economy, with a reduction in the supply of labour and the growing cost of natural resources, the economy had to move over to *intensive* growth (to utilize the factors of production more efficiently). In grappling with this problem, economic reformers attempted to improve labour discipline and introduced various incentives to increase labour efficiency. Changes were made to improve economic planning and the use of the market.

Many of the reformers in the USSR under Gorbachev, however, regarded the whole system of central planning to be obsolete. Command economies, it was believed, could not provide effective labour incentives, the efficient allocation of resources or a proper stimulus to innovation. This was a major thrust behind the move to a market economy.[7] A conclusion was reached that the exchanges necessary for economic efficiency (as anticipated by the industrial society model above) could not be achieved under central planning.[8] Hence the Soviet leadership cautiously followed the lead of the reformers in Czechoslovakia, Hungary and China with the introduction of the market. Whereas in the latter two countries the reforms worked well, in the USSR the economic effects of perestroika were disastrous. The reforms demolished the old system but failed to introduce a new one. The resource management system collapsed, production declined, inflation and unemployment rose. Once started, radical reform led Gorbachev's policy intellectuals, such as Tatiana Zaslavskaya, to define the process as a revolution. Economic reform was augmented by political reform. Gorbachev's radical critics were to extend his reasoning to call for systemic change – to move from state socialism to capitalism and multiparty democracy.

But something more than economic decline has to be invoked to explain the widespread repudiation of the state socialist political and economic system. Expectations had been generated by the political leadership of the state socialist societies. Remember: Khrushchev had boasted of the decline of capitalism and the inevitability that the socialist states would surpass the standard of living of the West (chapter 5 above). While these public pronouncements were toned down by successive leaders, the legitimacy of the government rested on fulfilling a high level of public expectations. General public dissatisfaction with the standard of living was a major impetus for reform; in all the state socialist societies it led to an emphasis on economic reform to increase productivity and output, proposals within the parameters of state socialism. This discontent was itself a reflection, not just of a fall in the rate of growth, but of changes in levels of expectations of a more demanding population. Insufficient growth in living standards was a cause of public frustration and a stimulus for economic reform. The failure of that reform in Russia exacerbated economic conditions and led to further political and ideological reform.

The Problem of Loyalty, Solidarity and Commitment

The inadequacy of resource management led to a crisis in the loyalty-solidarity system. Put simply, significant groups of people felt that the rewards (material and psychological) did not match the required expenditure of energy and commitment. This incompatibility from the perspective of certain social strata was a consequence of the modernization of the social structure.[9]

Sociologists would point to the deep-seated and long-term changes which have taken place in the social structure of state socialism. By the term 'social structure' we mean an array of positions or statuses, the conditions that shape them and a network of relationships between people and groups. Statuses give rise to patterns of behaviour, to norms and expectations; they are focuses for people's sense of social and individual identity. Statuses include occupations and social groups, which may be divided into many categories, such as by sex and age, urban and rural, ethnic and religious, white collar and blue collar, professionals and collective farmers.

The state socialist societies of the late 1980s were significantly different from those in which the communists took power. Major features have been the growth of population and the rise in levels of urbanization and the quality of education. There has matured a substantial urban population with higher education. As a consequence of industrialization, the occupational structure has shifted away from jobs in the primary to those in the secondary and tertiary sectors. Important generational differences are linked to these changes, younger people being more influenced by the modernization of society than older ones. Psychologically, this has disposed the younger generation to be more receptive to ideas of the market.

Table 8.1 shows the long-term pattern of growth of the urban population in state socialist societies. In 1950 only the GDR and Czechoslovakia had more than half of the population living in towns. By 1987 the average (excluding Vietnam) was well over 60 per cent. By the 1980s the USSR was an urban industrial society comparable in many respects to advanced Western societies (in 1989, 66 per cent of the population was urban). China was well behind the European societies, having 13.6 per cent living in towns in 1964 and only 26 per cent in 1990. By way of comparison, in the mid-1970s North America was 72 per cent urbanized and the north of Europe had an urban population of 83 per cent. Only in the early 1960s did the USSR become mainly urban, a condition reached in Britain before the mid-nineteenth century. The growth of an

Table 8.1 Rise in urban population of state socialist societies, 1950–1989 (per cent of total population)

	1950	1960	1970	1980	1987	1989
Bulgaria	27.5	38.0	53.0	62.5	66.2	67.6
Hungary	37.8	41.7	49.9	56.8	59.2	62.0
Vietnam	0	0	20.7	19.1	19.8	21.4
GDR	70.9	72.0	73.8	76.6	76.8	76.6
Cuba	0	0	60.5	68.4	72.3	73.5
Poland	36.9	48.3	52.3	58.7	60.9	61.6
Romania	25.2	32.4	36.9	45.8	50.6[a]	53.2
USSR	40.2	49.9	56.9	63.4	66.4	66.0
Czechoslovakia	51.5	57.4	62.3	72.6	75.7	–
Yugoslavia	–	–	–	–	50.2[b]	–
China	–	13.6[c]	–	18.9[d]	–	26.0[e]

[a] Data for 1986.
[b] Data for 1987 cited in Minxin Pei, *From Reform to Revolution* (Harvard University Press, 1994), p. 59.
[c] Data for 1963.
[d] Data for 1979, from Pei, *From Reform to Revolution*, p. 59).
[e] Data for 1990, calculated by the author from *Chinese Statistical Yearbook 1994* (Beijing: 1994), p. 47.

Source: *Statisticheski ezhegodnik stran – chlenov soveta ekonomicheskoi vzaimopomoshchi* (Moscow: 1988), p. 18, and the same yearbook (Moscow: 1990), p. 59.

urban population in the USSR in the past 65 years is remarkable; the total number of urban dwellers rose from some 22 million in 1922 to 100 million in 1959, and to 186.8 million in 1989.

There was a shift of employment from the agricultural sector to the industrial and service sectors. At the same time, there was a massive decline in the traditional peasantry. Table 8.2 shows that by 1981 manual and non-manual workers accounted for over 80 per cent of the population in most of the East European states (only Romania had 68.9 per cent). These figures refer to people in paid employment including workers and employees of agricultural state farms; the residual figure is of collective farmers, individual craftspersons and peasants working solely on individual plots.

The number of employees categorized in the data as in 'non-productive'[10] work activity is an index of non-manuals employed in the economy. Table 8.3 shows the doubling of numbers in the developing East European countries. To give one example: in Poland in 1950 only 385,000 people were employed in the sectors of science, education, culture, health, insurance and tourism; by 1987 the number had risen to 2.001 million. In the USSR the comparable figures were 6.265 million

Table 8.2 Growth of population by social groups of manual workers and non-manual employees in state socialist societies (per cent of total population)

	1950–65	1977–85
Bulgaria	43.9 (Dec. 56)	94.2 (Dec. 85)
Hungary	72.8 (Jan. 65)	80.5 (Jan. 80)
GDR	80.5 (Dec. 64)	87.8 (Dec. 81)
Cuba	75.5 (Jan. 55)	81.7 (Sept. 81)
Poland	52.5 (Dec. 50)	77.6 (Dec. 84)
Romania	37.0 (Feb. 56)	68.9 (Jan. 77)
USSR	68.3 (Jan. 59)	85.1 (Jan. 79)
Czechoslovakia	72.8 (Mar. 50)	88.6 (Nov. 80)

Source: *Statisticheski ezhegodnik stran – chlenov soveta ekonomicheskoi vzaimopomoshchi* (Moscow: 1988), pp. 21–2.

Table 8.3 'Non-productive' employment in state socialist societies, 1950–1987, as percentage of workforce

	1950	1960	1970	1980	1987
Bulgaria	5	9.2	13.1	16.9	18.2
Hungary	16.4	14.3	15.2	19	21.1
Vietnam	0	0	7.1	7.1	6.8
GDR	14.4	15.3	18.8	19.4	20.7
Poland	8.6	11.6	14.4	16.4	19
Romania	6.4	7.6	10.2	12.4	12.7
USSR	12.4	15.2	20.3	22.9	24.3
Czechoslovakia	10.6	13.6	17.8	20.1	21.4

Source: *Statisticheski ezhegodnik stran – chlenov soveta ekonomicheskoi vzaimopomoshchi 1988* (Moscow: 1988), pp. 409–13.

and 23.812 million.[11] All these data indicate the presence of a large professional middle class, known in these countries as the intelligentsia. By the late 1980s this group had a demographic and a growing moral density. This development had a profound impact on the political support system, which we discuss below.

In China, a somewhat different picture prevails. In table 8.4 we note that nearly 3 million people are engaged in the countryside as rural labourers. Rural municipal enterprises also account for more employees

Table 8.4 Labour force in China by type of activity, 1993

	Number (millions)	Percentage
Urban employees		
State-owned enterprises	109	68
Collective owned	33.9	21.25
Joint owned	0.66	0.4
Joint stock	1.64	1.0
Foreign	1.33	0.83
Other ownership	0.18	0.11
Private enterprise	1.86	1.16
Individual	9.30	5.81
Total★	160	100
Rural workforce		
Township enterprises	123	27.8
Private enterprise	1.87	0.42
Individual	20.1	4.5
Other rural labourers	297	67
Total★	442	100
Total urban and rural	602	

★ Totals do not sum due to rounding and other categories.

Source: *China: Statistical Yearbook 1994* (Beijing: China Statistical Information, 1994), p. 65.

than those in the urban state-owned factories, which, in the urban areas, accounted for more than two-thirds of the employed workforce in 1993. The figures bring out the relatively small number of people employed in privately owned concerns. The economic and social structure in China, being mainly agricultural and rural, was significantly different from that in the Eastern European states.

The rise in educational levels

Linked to these occupational changes were improvements in the cultural levels of the population. One measure of such advancement is the standard of education. In 1926 the Soviet authorities claimed that 51.1 per cent of the population aged over nine years was literate, and by 1939 the figure had reached 81.2 per cent.[12] By 1959, the census showed that by far the largest group of the population had received only an incomplete secondary education. Hence, under Khrushchev, the educational and cultural level of the population was much below that of the advanced European states. But there was a spectacular rise in educational standards during the 30 years prior to perestroika. Whereas in the USSR in 1939 there were only 1.2 million people with a complete higher education, in 1959 there were 8.3 million, and in 1987 nearly 21 million. The number of qualified specialists employed in industry increased from 8.8 million in 1960 to 35.6 million in 1987.[13] Some 20 million graduates of trade schools were added to the workforce between 1960 and 1986 (an annual output of 2.5 million in the late 1980s).

These figures are aggregated for the USSR. It is also important to note that the various nationalities in the republics of the USSR shared this significant development in terms of levels of education, non-manual statuses and urbanism.[14] The USSR government encouraged the diversity of cultures of the nations constituting the USSR. Language competence in the vernacular languages rose during the years of Soviet power.[15] As we shall note below, nationality became a basis of social identification when Marxism-Leninism lost its binding power.

Similarly, in the Eastern European countries there was a significant rise in the numbers of people with tertiary education. Table 8.5 illustrates the growth of qualified non-manuals employed in the economy. Between the early 1970s and mid-1980s, the numbers had doubled: in Poland, from 1.781 million in 1970 to 3.772 million in 1987; in Czechoslovakia, from 1.356 million to 2.177 million. Whereas the intelligentsia had been very small in the early days of communist power, it now had a demographic – and moral – mass. In China, by way of comparison, in 1982 only 1 per cent of the population had higher education and 21.8 per cent had secondary education.[16]

Table 8.5 Numbers of qualified non-manuals (*spetsialisty*) employed in the economies of state socialist societies (higher education and specialist secondary) (000s)

	1968–70	1980–3	1986–8
Bulgaria	521	858	1,013
Hungary	430	868	n.a.
GDR	717	1,412	n.a.
Cuba	n.a.	309	640
Poland	1,781	3,365	3,772
USSR	16,841	28,612	35,693
Czechoslovakia	1,356	2,177	n.a.

Source: Statisticheski ezhegodnik stran – chlenov soveta ekonomicheskoi vzaimopomoshchi 1988 (Moscow: 1988), p. 422.

There was a qualitative rise in the levels of mass communications which directly and indirectly changed people's perceptions of life in the West, which became for them an ideal. Television developed and Western programmes became directly accessible in the German Democratic Republic, Czechoslovakia, Hungary and the Baltic areas; video recorders gave access to Western films on a wide scale. The population's expectations rose: a consumer mentality matured, as did a bourgeoisification of aspirations.[17] We note here the relationship to the external environment, the importance of which we dwell on later.

These developments all led to a population more receptive to the move to a market economy. In the 1980s the intelligentsia was a stratum receptive to an alternative conception of socialism (which in practice embraced many of the practices of contemporary capitalism), to a vision of a future different from that of their parents. As Millar concludes from a study of Soviet immigrants to the United States, 'A long term trend toward privatization is evident, which shows up not only in the evasion of mobilization effort . . . but also in the economic realm. The study reaffirms the pervasiveness of illegal as well as private economic activity.'[18] An underlying cause of this consciousness was the market relationships on which these strata could capitalize (or believed they could capitalize) because of their skills. It was a mechanism to realize intellectual capital in monetary terms. The consumption of commodities in exchange for effort was not in equilibrium: this was expressed in the growth of corruption (behaviour which deviates from accepted public norms to serve private ends). The failure of the loyalty-solidarity-commitment nexus led to moral decay.

Field studies conducted in 1991 confirm that, on the part of the intelligentsia in the post-communist countries, there was a significant negative attitude to socialist principles and a positive attitude to capitalist ones. (Thus there was opposition to income being determined by need rather than merit, government provision of employment, egalitarianism of income distribution and limits on earned income.) One study shows a 'steady decline in support for socialist principles from those with low education to those with higher education. Across all the East European countries, the correlation coefficient between the socialism index and education level is −0.33 . . . non-egalitarian reforms are supported by the more highly educated minority in those societies, who, as it happens, also have the most to gain from such reforms.'[19]

These changes in the loyalty and solidarity of the population are evidence of increasing levels of dissatisfaction, especially among the growing professional classes. It is not being argued here that these demographic changes directly led to challenges of the system of state socialism, rather they created predispositions towards change.

Political Support and Domination

The rise of a large stratum of non-manual urban people had implications for the political support structure. They made demands to which the reform political leadership responded. The recognition of 'deficiencies' and 'shortcomings' in policy was triggered particularly by the lack of fulfilment of the aspirations of groups of intellectuals – professional employees with higher education or specialist qualifications. The policy of *glasnost* was a recognition of a surge of individual and group demands. The support for reform came from the professional classes who became disenchanted with their status under command socialism; they in turn were cultivated by the reform leadership.

There can be no doubt that the 'outputs' of state socialism had favoured the manual working class. After the assumption of power by the communists, wage differentials between social groups fell considerably; the working class was a major beneficiary and qualified non-manuals (the 'intelligentsia') lost their privileged position. Figure 3.1 (p. 45 above) showed the dramatic relative decline in the money earnings of managerial and technical employees and non-manuals in the USSR. This tendency applied to all state socialist societies. On the basis of an exhaustive study, Jean-Charles Asselain concludes that in Poland, Czechoslovakia and Hungary, there took place a 'real deterioration in the standard of living of "intellectual" categories compared to the prewar period'.[20] The members of the political administrative class (including some in the intelligentsia), however, received a disproportionate part of their income in kind (housing, travel, health). Still, there is no doubt that the professional classes were relatively worse off and perceived this deterioration.

By the 1980s, the large educated non-manual urban population changed the social base of politics. In the USSR under Stalin, a peasant mentality was a prop to the regime; under Brezhnev and Khrushchev this mantle fell to the unskilled manual worker. Under Gorbachev, the skilled and qualified non-manual workforce was an ascendant group and the social base on which radical reform policies rested. A 'demographic identity' developed among the intelligentsia. In the East European countries the intelligentsia inherited bourgeois traditions from the pre-communist regimes. In the Soviet Union the maturation of the Soviet political culture led to a significant number of individuals and groups having a positive conception of their own interests. A critical moral mass developed which adopted either an independent appraisal of, or became detached and alienated from, the legitimating ideology of power, and the political class. In all these societies, the real political ballast of the regime moved from the peasantry and working class to the intelligentsia.

The political support system of the traditional political leadership was not appropriate to the changing demographic structure of the country. In the period 1956 to 1961 (under Khrushchev), workers constituted 41.1 per cent of new Communist Party members, their share rising to 59.4 per cent in the late Brezhnev period (1981–5).[21] This gave a solid working-class membership to the party: manual workers constituted 43.4 per cent of the whole membership in 1981 and 45.4 per cent in 1989.[22] However, manual workers and collective farmers were increasingly excluded from positions of authority in the party and the political leadership was filled with those from non-manual and professional social groups. For example, in the USSR, of the total party membership in 1971, 2.81 million (19.6 per cent) had higher education, and this figure rose to 6.8 million (31.8 per cent) in 1986. Concurrently, of the party's leading cadres (members and candidates of central committees and auditing commissions of the party at republican level and of party committees at province (*obkom*) and territory (*krai*) level), 69.4 per cent had higher education. Even at the level of cities, districts and areas, 56.7 per cent of cadres had higher education.[23] These data indicate the inflow of the intelligentsia to positions of influence in the leading institutions of the party.

Another measure which indicates the changing political base for the new leadership is the changing social background of the membership of the Supreme Soviet of the USSR. In 1979, workers constituted 34.8 per cent of the members of the Supreme Soviet of the USSR.[24] This figure rose slightly to 35.2 per cent in the Supreme Soviet elected before the reform leadership was in command. After Gorbachev came to power, there was a massive decline of working-class representation. The share of workers among the deputies to the Congress of People's Deputies in the 1989 election came to 18.6 per cent, collective farmers received only 11.2 per cent of the seats (compared to their earlier 16.1 per cent) and the proportion of women fell considerably from 32.8 per cent to 17.1 per cent.[25] The number of deputies in the professional classes with higher education rose from 7.8 per cent to 15.7 per cent.[26] These data are illustrative of a shift in the basis of power of the leadership towards the non-manual professional strata. The implication here is that a dual class structure was developing in which 'intellectuals' and professionals had much potentially to gain from a market-type system. They had marketable skills and were not dependent on a 'nomenklatura' system. We return and develop this point below.

In Eastern Europe, an important indicator of support for the traditional communist elites from the manual working class is the influx of manual workers into the party and representative institutions after political crises. In Hungary after 1956, 'recruitment of active workers into the . . . Party increased substantially . . . together with massive promotion of former workers to administrative party posts. In Czechoslovakia . . . after the events of 1968–69 . . . workers made up 63 per cent of the new members admitted to the Communist Party between 1971 and 1976.'[27] In 1971 in Poland, Eduard Gierek promised to speed up 'the process of integration of the working class in the management of the state'.[28] Another obverse example is the case of Hungary, where in October 1989 the Congress of the Hungarian Socialist Workers' Party renamed itself the Socialist Party of Hungary; its membership, which in 1985 had included 40 per cent workers and 20 per cent peasants, was transformed and by 1989 90 per cent of its members were 'intellectuals'.[29] A new class, an 'acquisition class', I shall argue, had established its hegemony over the political class.

It is undoubtedly the case that the reform leadership of Gorbachev shifted its political fulcrum of support away from the manual working class and the traditional party and state bureaucracy to an alliance with the more technologically inclined and modernizing forces and the intelligentsia. This threatened the traditional alliance between the party executive, government administrators and their supporters among the manual working class. The maintenance and replication of the traditional political elites were further weakened by the rise of market forces encouraged by the reforms. As movements to marketization and democratization progressed from the top, the costs to the intelligentsia of non-support of the existing system fell and the attractiveness of an alternative system rose.[30] Also, the position of people in ambiguous class positions changed: if their authority was being eroded by the political leadership of the political class, then they could look to see if their interests might be better served by support for the market. Marketization would provide great opportunities: previous members of the political class would be in a position not only to benefit from their intellectual capital, but also potentially to gain from the acquisition of physical assets as a consequence of the privatization of state assets.

Here then we identify class interests which were dividing state socialist society and which were crucial in putting weight behind political change. These groups formed part of the 'counterculture' referred to above by writers such as Goldfarb, and they also would be characterized by Mandel as constituting 'bourgeois' strata in terms of their consumption patterns. They were a latent class interest under state socialism, kept 'in place' by the political class which controlled the state and party apparat.

Class dynamics under state socialism

Class analysis in socialist revolutions is usually conducted within a Marxist framework. Unquestionably, Marx defined class in terms of the ownership of property and the extraction of surplus through exchange value.

'The historical task of the socialist revolution is to eliminate that form of exploitation due to differential ownership of alienable assets.'[31] Neither private property nor the production of exchange value existed under state socialism. As John Roemer has pointed out, it is the possession of 'physical assets' that constitutes capitalist exploitation, and he suggests that because of the abolition of private ownership of assets, exploitation of such assets did not characterize state socialism.[32] The 'state capitalist' theorists have to conflate class, in the sense of ownership, with control of productive assets. Hence it is seen as a characteristic of state socialism that a capitalist class not only did not exist but was prevented from forming.

The exploitation which occurred under state socialism had a much wider significance than that defined by Marx, and it may be subsumed under the Weberian concept of domination. Rather than extracting surplus value to further capital accumulation, the bureaucratic 'controllers' dominated society. Such people may seek to turn their political power into monetary rewards, but this is not surplus in a Marxist sense. I would agree with writers such as Giddens[33] and Feher, Heller and Markus[34] that relations of domination are more than class relations. Rather than attempting to distort the Marxist concept of 'exploitation' to interpret the class structure of state socialism, I would suggest that there were two major and competing forms of class stratification which permeated the whole of the social structure. Political class determined by political position and an acquisition class (*Erwerbsklasse*) given by market position. And here I use the term 'class' in a Weberian sense of a market relationship determining a person's life chances.

Under state socialism there were two concurrent and contrasting organizing principles: the administrative and the market. The major criteria for class stratification are control (political class) and marketability (acquisition class). In state socialist bureaucratic systems, political position and economic position were administratively defined. This is described cogently by E. O. Wright: 'Exploitation is based on bureaucratic power: the control over organizational assets defines the material basis for class relations and exploitation.'[35] I would suggest that this new social formation has the character of a modern form of political domination.[36]

This relationship has been grasped by writers such as Rudolf Bahro, who refers to the 'politbureaucratic dictatorship'.[37] The mechanism of exploitation is the 'planned appropriation and distribution of surplus based on hierarchy'. There was a hierarchy of posts which gave control over the means of production, distribution and exchange: it gave the rights of control of property. The *nomenklatura* included not only elite positions, but positions of authority at lower levels. Positions in the party and trade union hierarchies and executive positions in government institutions were also dependent on the *nomenklatura*. Hence there may be a vertical binding of members of the *nomenklatura*, with movement between *nomenklatura* posts. This was a vertically structured class system – rather like capitalism, where capitalists range from relatively small-scale entrepreneurs to wealthy shareholders and top directors. These positions were not only forms of employment: they included political positions associated with the work process (trade union secretary) or with political organization in any association, such as a secretary in the Young Communist League (Komsomol). Movement through such positions determined the careers of persons in the political class. However, many persons occupied positions in the party structure which were symbolic and nominal and they were also members of the professional classes (examples being representatives of academia, the media and the military in the Central Committee of the party).

The ascendant class

A systemic form of class stratification was also linked to the market. This is similar to the process of Western capitalism though there are important differences. Employees had to sell their labour to a state enterprise or institution: the state had a monopoly of hiring, and it strongly influenced wage rates and conditions. Labour productivity was encouraged through the incentive for monetary reward. This gave rise to a market for labour and for goods. People competed for jobs which were distinguished by a hierarchy of conditions and an uneven distribution of income. The exchange of labour power for money remained a feature of state socialism, and income derived from employment was important in the determination of life chances. Roemer theorizes this form of inequality in Weberian terms. It gives rise, he says, to a class being in possession of 'skill assets', which leads to structural inequality.[38] The intelligentsia, defined by levels of education, gave rise to what I contend should be described as an acquisition class.

The structure of state socialism (the control exercised by the political class), however, prevented the intelligentsia from exploiting this position. The functioning of the labour market and the exchange of commodities were severely limited by the political class, and there was no market for property. To allow a market to operate would have seriously weakened the political class and strengthened the economic one. This was the traditional view of the nexus between property, market and class noted in chapter 5 above. Moreover, administrative privilege (also shared by some strata of the acquisition class) also had its attendant forms of access to goods and services. Hence the class system had, as argued by Mandel, ramifications in the system of distribution. The existence of this quasi-market goes some way to explain the ways that detailed empirical comparisons between socialist and capitalist countries have indicated partial forms of convergence.[39]

The political (or bureaucratic) class is defined by its position in control of administrative statuses, whereas the acquisition class is demarcated by possession of skill (intellectual) assets. Hence, in a Weberian sense, class is defined for these groups by the possession of power or marketability of skills. Bureaucratic position and skill/knowledge were two competing principles of class allegiance under state socialism. The intelligentsia (all employees with higher educational qualifications, or 'professionals') have better 'market' chances than 'bureaucrats' (those dependent on the *nomenklatura* for position), who endorse administrative redistribution. The latter class was not simply composed of people 'extracting surplus', but rather of persons with a commitment to a system of state ownership and control under a state socialist regime. Politically, they would seek 'to better' the administrative command system, rather than to replace it.[40] Many from this administrative stratum, however, would potentially be able to benefit from a market system, if it were available. This defines their ambiguous class location.[41] During the terminal period of the USSR, as noted in earlier chapters, the political class was undermined by the reforming leadership of Gorbachev.

At its core, however, were the key sectors of the government bureaucracy of the USSR – the military-industrial complex, the ministries with control over the means of production. Their relative autonomy defied penetration by the Gorbachev party leadership and they opposed market reforms.[42] It is important to emphasize too that the 'intelligentsia' or the professional administrative strata was not a unitary class, but contained layers with varying degrees of identity and commitment to the political class. Depending on the likelihood of political success, they would endorse one or the other system of power. Under Gorbachev's leadership, the party's own professional cadres were among the first to shift their allegiance away from the political class to the acquisition class.

There were then two systems with contrary classes in operation under state socialism: a planning and administrative system controlled by a political class and a quasi-market system with an incipient class linked to the possession of intellectual assets. We may define class boundaries operating on the basis of these two criteria of stratification (control and marketability of skills). Behind the reform process were the interests of these two competing classes: state bureaucracy and mainly middle-class occupational groups whose life chances were linked to the marketability of their intellectual capital.

Class identification

To illustrate this form of class identification, I give four examples. First, support for market reforms and its associated values, and opposition to socialist norms, was associated with the intelligentsia. A survey of Russian immigrants who arrived in the USA in the 1970s indicates

> an unambiguous and negative relationship between the level of educational attainment and the level of support for various political and economic institutions of the Soviet system. The level of support for state control and management of major sectors of the system declines with each increase in the level of education attained, and this is true even for attainments in primary and secondary school. The same pattern is evident in responses to questions that juxtapose individual rights and the power of the states, such as the provision of civil liberties. As education increases, support for state power relative to individual rights decreases. . . . [T]his same group of 'the best and the brightest' also was the most likely to be involved in 'unconventional' behavior – refusing to vote, listening to BBC and foreign broadcasts, reading and distributing *samizdat*, reading foreign fiction and nonfiction, and participating in other unsanctioned activities.[43]

Support by this stratum for market reforms and the values of the market has also been confirmed by interviews on an Eastern European basis reported by David S. Mason.[44]

Second, Lane and Ross have examined the voting on five crucial issues of the political elite of the parliament of the USSR between 1989 and 1991. Of those who voted with the radical reformers, 'almost half were professionals, but only 4 out of 34 voting with the leadership were from this group'. Those loyal to Gorbachev, then opposing radical reform, included 'the large number of directors of production associations and enterprises and members of the CPSU and Komsomol apparat'. On the other side, 'Only one [enterprise] director [was found] in the opposition and there [were] no members of the party apparat and only one member of the Komsomol apparat [voting for the radical opposition].' Yeltsin's support among the Supreme Soviet (USSR) elite came overwhelmingly from 'members of the liberal intelligentsia'.[45] In the country as a whole, the conscious political support of Yeltsin's market reform came from this class.

Third, Thomas F. Remington has traced 'a deeply and universally cited distinction' in Soviet society between 'party people and nonparty people', between those in the *nomenklatura* (the political class) and others.[46] In 1990, during the terminal period of the USSR, he points out, 'the single strongest determinant of voter intentions . . . was a populist desire to vote against candidates considered to be part of the "bureaucracy" and to vote for those opposing it.'[47] The *nomenklatura* group 'occupies a distinct and thoroughly resented place in popular consciousness'. A study by Marc Garcelon of the Democratic Movement[48] in Moscow between 1989 and 1991 shows that its membership was dominated by the intelligentsia: only 7 per cent of a sample of members were industrial workers; entrepreneurs came to 4 per cent, service workers 8 per cent and 'specialists' (professionals with higher educational qualifications) 80 per cent.[49] Garcelon points to the two streams of the movement for the market and democracy: from academia and from reformers in the Communist Party. The second group were obviously in the position of class ambiguity, and these included lecturers and editors in the party's own institutions. Perestroika pushed them into the acquisition class.

Finally, interviews with members of the political and economic elite under Gorbachev report that he relied on the intelligentsia to undermine state socialism: 'the intelligentsia was used by Gorbachev intensively in the ideological taboo-smashing stage of his rule (1986–89). This was one group on which he could rely . . . Professional opinion of social scientists was strongly weighted toward market-like forms of organisation, and against the classical Soviet model.'[50] Renunciation of the norms and values of the USSR not only undermined supporters of the traditional order, but also pushed them in the direction of the acquisition class. In my own study of influential people's opinions on the reform process, I found that the intelligentsia was ranked the highest of social groups and forces as an influence on reform.[51]

The ambiguous class position of the managerial and executive strata had been a major factor inhibiting a move to the market: as long as the mainstays of the political class were united and determined to keep the administrative system, they had potentially more to lose than to gain by pledging support to its demise. The leadership of Gorbachev was decisive in changing this relationship: he indicated that the acquisition class had more potentially to gain than it had potentially to lose.

A great weakness of the ascendant acquisition class was its lack of political power and its weak organizational resources. The political class had secured economic and political power, a point emphasized in the 'totalitarian' concept of state socialism. As we have noted above, the confidence of the political class varied between different state socialist societies, depending on the way in which power had originally been achieved. Whereas in Eastern Europe latent opposition included people who had experienced capitalism, and the image of capitalism was much clearer, this was not the case in the USSR or China, where generations had not known the phenomenon or where a significant indigenous capitalism had not developed. Whence then the origin of a thrust for a capitalist market system and a pluralist parliamentary type of democracy?

There were two main sources: first, the leadership of Gorbachev (division within the political class); second, exogenous forces. Members of the acquisition class, particularly in Eastern Europe, provided a third.

The Legitimacy System

Ideology defines what is ethical and desirable; it provides a basis for social solidarity on which political legitimacy may rest. As Rousseau aptly put it: 'The strongest is never strong enough to be always the master, unless he transforms strength into right, and obedience into duty.'[52] Legitimacy occurs if the political elites and a significant part of the people subscribe to the values and institutions of the system, even though many may not (all modern political systems have dissenting groups, often large ones).[53] Crucial to the legitimacy of a social system is the extent to which the elites remain confident in their exercise of power and maintain the myths enshrined in its ideological charter. When such beliefs break down, a critical mass of dissent is necessary for a legitimacy crisis to occur, articulating an alternative ideology on which a new social solidarity may arise.

In the countries of Eastern Europe the failure of the economic resource management system coupled to the weakness of political supports led to public dissatisfaction. When the system of central command was denigrated by the leadership under Gorbachev, discontent led to a crisis in legitimacy. This was not the case initially in the Soviet Union, where Marxism-Leninism was the official ideology which sustained the political order from Lenin to Chernenko. While the saliency of ideology weakened under Khrushchev, it was not discredited until the advent of perestroika, which not only amplified public dissatisfaction through the policy of *glasnost*, but also gave sustenance to a counter-ideology. The superiority of state ownership of property and central planning and the notion of the inevitable world victory of communism were either rejected by the leadership of the reformist Marxist-Leninist states, or these sentiments were quietly dropped from doctrinal statements. The erosion of the legitimating ideology was now under way.

In the USSR, moreover, the failure of economic policy and the political direction taken under Gorbachev had ramifications affecting the political structures of the command system and then impacted on political legitimacy and aggregate political support. Economic reform, entailing the growth of markets, undermined the leading role of the party and the system of command planning. The Soviet Union and the other Eastern European states moved from the fusion of politics and economics to a more pluralistic structure. This process began before perestroika and was defined in Western political science as a kind of 'socialist pluralism'; these developments, however, were contained by the political class. Marxism-Leninism was a handicap to the reform leadership in its search not only for a new internal order but also for a different place in the world community. This weakening of ideology was a long-term development which was amplified during perestroika.

In a way which would have been unthinkable earlier, Marxist-Leninist ideology was broken by the political leadership under Gorbachev. Ideological dissent within the political leadership radicalized: some members, initially grouped around Gorbachev himself, lost confidence in the party and communist institutions of power and they publicly discredited the legitimating ideology of Marxism-Leninism. As we noted in chapter 6, a significant section of the political elite believed that the institutions of Soviet power had to be completely replaced. As Aleksandr Yakovlev – member of the party politburo and special adviser to Gorbachev – put it in October 1991:

> At the end of the day Marxism has brought us to the abyss, to backwardness and to the destruction of one's conscience . . . Any person on earth knows that Marxism in the first place is a teaching of the annihilation of both private ownership of the means of production and the material, legal and spiritual foundations for Western civilization . . . Marx as long as he lived remained loyal to the *Communist Manifesto*, this guide for the proletarians to destroy everything that had until now safeguarded private ownership . . .[54]

The USSR Minister of Health, at the Nineteenth Party Conference in 1988, berated the national health system by pointing out that the level of infant mortality in the USSR was next to that of Barbados and that average life expectancy in the USSR was thirty-second in the world; in Uzbekistan, he pointed out 'milliards of roubles' were squandered and 46 per cent of the hospitals were in buildings which were below the minimum standards of sanitary hygiene. The point here is not whether these statements were true or false, but that such statements are never made by ruling elites, even or especially if they are true, because they undermine the moral capacity of the leaders to rule. (Previously sponsored 'self-criticism' was directed at negative phenomena at variance with the communist system, not, as here, with gross faults generated by it.)

The break with Marxist-Leninist ideology was a consequence of a conscious decision to delegitimate the past and to move to a new market type society. It was a clear signal to those in ambiguous class positions to 'jump ship' to join the forces of the economic class.

The media, legitimated by the policy of *glasnost*, further undermined the myths about the regime. This is illustrated by Ligachev (member of the party politburo and critic of Gorbachev) when he recalled:

> [*Glasnost*] created a gloomy atmosphere in the country. It affects the emotions of the people, their mood, their work-efficiency, when from morning to night everything negative from the past is being dumped on them . . . [O]ur own cultural figures have published more lies and anti-Soviet things than our Western enemies ever did in the last seventy years combined . . . An avalanche is falling on our party. So many worthy communists, leaders, prominent representatives of science, culture, and literature have been slandered in recent times . . . Under the flag of democracy and *glasnost*, the ideological and moral pillars of society are being washed away. The destructive work of the opposition forces coincides with hostile forces from outside. They have set as their goal the breakup of the USSR, after Eastern Europe, to ruin the social transformation along the lines of scientific socialism, and switch our country to the tracks of capitalist development. As to the mass media, along with the great creative work they are doing, some publications, television studios, and radio programs openly trample our past and present, inciting tension in society . . .[55]

The collapse of Marxism-Leninism entailed the weakening of the regime to an extent not anticipated by the Gorbachev reformers. Somewhat incomprehensively for persons with even a cursory knowledge of Marxism, Gorbachev and his advisers – still seeking to maintain party hegemony – appeared insensitive to the class interests, defined above, which would be strengthened by the market. The ways of maintaining social solidarity were misjudged and the destabilizing effects of *glasnost* and pluralism, when linked to a qualitative change in participation, were not foreseen. The old slogan of 'unity of party and the people' was replaced by a plurality of interests, which in the transition period of 1989–90 lacked consensus and forms of solidarity. The changes envisioned by the political leadership of Gorbachev required a new ideological shell to legitimate reform socialism – and this was lacking.

As the radical reform movement (critical of Gorbachev's commitment to the renewal of state socialism, particularly the hegemony of the Communist Party) grew in pace, it looked to Eastern Europe and generated its own counterculture. There, the crisis of legitimacy led to revolutionary claims – the Eastern European countries had an alternative: in Heller's words, 'the overwhelming majority of the population [*did*] have an image of an alternative order, namely that of the West European or North American liberal-legal state . . .'[56] The traditional political 'conservatism' of these countries was implanted in an authoritarian peasant-type political culture which had been destroyed by communism, and thus conservative ideology could not legitimate a transition to democracy and the market.[57]

Nationalism, religion and the values of capitalism gradually filled the void in thinking in the territories of the USSR and some of the Eastern European states. Nationalism and religion provided their own form of legitimation to the counter-elites. As ideologies they provided a legitimation for opposition to Soviet power and to communism. It was an ideological vehicle ridden by the acquisition class. As Beissinger has put it: 'in the Soviet case groups which were the most economically developed were actually those that pressed the hardest for the breakup of the Soviet Union, while least developed groups were practically the last to support their own independence.' He further points to a correlation between non-violent protest and levels of urbanization and education of a nationality.[58] The politicization of the peoples on the basis of nationality developed rapidly in the period 1988–9. The idea became a cause, the cause became a movement. As Walzer has put it: 'nationality [is] an idea, nationalism a program. The program is conceived in difficulty; it aims to mobilize the nation so as to overcome some deficiency in its common life.'[59] Where people had no nationality, they soon invented one.

Compare again the position in China. The political leadership did not renounce the legitimating ideology of Marxism-Leninism-Mao Zedong Thought. Market economic reforms occurred without political reforms. Does this mean that the Communist Party will continue its hegemony in a privatized market economy? It might be argued that many countries in South East Asia (Singapore, South Korea, Taiwan, for example) have moved to a market economy concurrent with an authoritarian government not unlike that in China. The answer depends on what one means by hegemony. If one means control over the economy and the absence of a capitalist class, the answer must be negative. The difference between the developing countries in South East Asia and state socialist ones is that the former countries already have a capitalist class and the institution of private property. As we noted in chapter 5, an incipient bourgeois class is already in place in China and the political leadership responds to its interests. This class is likely to generate further demands on the political system. The constellation of political factors (the relatively small intelligentsia, the large peasantry, the powerful interests of the armed forces and a secure leadership) has maintained the formal rule of the party while its power has been undermined. The political class has maintained its power because of its relative strength, confidence and the will to rule. It has not provided conditions in which the potential advantages of revolt by those in ambiguous class positions outweigh the potential losses.

The divisions I have pointed to between the political and acquisition classes in the USSR are paralleled in China. Walder points out, for example, the distinction between 'elite professionals and elite administrators'. Professionals, he suggests, 'do not receive the returns to education that they would in a market economy . . . Therefore [they] might reasonably expect that a transition away from central planning and party dictatorship would bring them authority and material compensation more consistent with their education and occupational prestige.'[60] The development of market forces, which it has encouraged, will strengthen the economic class; and the erosion of the power of the political class will eventually lead to its downfall. It seems likely that a process will occur in China similar to that in the East European societies: professionals in an ambiguous class position will, when conditions are ripe, join forces with the rising business class.

' "Bourgeois" in outlook, national in form'

The changing social structure is one of those crucial variables in the provision of support or opposition to a given political leadership and system of rule. Social structure has multifactorial effects, a change in social structure influencing norms, values, institutions and processes. The major 'push' for a movement to the market came from those who had most to gain from the institution of a market system and the weakening of the administrative planning system: the intelligentsia and those who had marketable skills, what I have defined as the acquisition class. The development of national interests and the creation of national consciousness were essentially a consequence of local elites reviving nationality as a basis for their own legitimacy. The management of the all-union Soviet political and economic institutions formed the core of the political class – those in charge of the control of the economy; those in the republics were in an ambiguous position. The weakening of ideological controls and the discrediting of Soviet institutions and their legitimating ideology created conditions in which the republican elites had potentially more to gain than to lose by advocating a move to the market and to their own sovereignty. As a consequence of the weakening of the Soviet political class, control (and, in future, ownership) of assets would come under their control.

The movement for radical reform had a nationalist/regional form. From the time of Stalin, '*korenizatsiia*' had been the basis of nationality policy; this entailed that local cadres would be recruited from the indigenous nationalities. A consequence here was that the commanding posts of the political institutions were manned by members of the local peoples. Soviet policy on the nationalities had the effect of heightening the awareness of the dominant republican nationalities. Underlying the rise of consciousness was the increase in educational levels, and the stratum of professionals provided the leadership of the nationalist movements. The greater urbanization and higher levels of communication brought nationalities closer together. In conditions of slow economic growth and rapid population increase, competition between strata – for education, occupational status and political power – escalated, and this competition took a national form. While in the theory of Soviet socialism, ethnicity was a legitimate form of cultural identification, it became a form of 'social closure' in which language, religion and skin pigmentation became a code to identify social groups and to allocate privilege, power and prestige. People had in fact two forms of national identity: Soviet and nation, linked to geographical area or linked to language. Hence when the Soviet identity (area) was disowned (by the leadership of perestroika), nationality (language) became the basis of legitimation of the political reform movement. The republics had a constitutional right to secede.

However, it is important not to conflate the reform movement into a nationalist movement; the latter legitimated the former. In the East European countries, ethnically homogeneous societies – GDR, Poland and Hungary, for example – developed their reform movements independently of the national movement. The assertion of the rights of the Russian Republic (led by Yeltsin) did not, in the first instance, have a *nationalist/ethnic* base; the move was political, based on the interests of the ascendant acquisitive class. Nation was revived and/or created and turned into a movement (nationalism) for reform. Nationalism then was a conveni-ent form of legitimation for the reform movement: it has crucial social and political cementing effects. As Gellner has pointed out: 'A nation is a large collection of men [and women] such that its members identify with the collectivity without being acquainted with its other members, and without identifying in any important way with sub-groups of that collectivity.'[61]

But a social structural analysis in terms of a society's internal dynamic alone cannot explain the variation of support for an alternative to the state socialist regimes. In the case of the Eastern European and Baltic societies, proximity to the West and traditional forms of national identity are important variables which give rise to alternative political ideals and to support for a new regime. In these societies, the West, in the form of the advanced industrial states of Europe and the USA, constituted the environment in which state socialism had to develop and reform. In the absence of a home-based bourgeoisie, it had a major impact on the reforms and provided support and impetus for the internal transition to capitalism. The external environment, to which we now turn, had a determinant effect not only in shaping politics but in influencing values, norms and the ways the transformation was to proceed.

The External Environment

Capitalism on a world scale has proved to be more successful as a system of production and consumption than anticipated by a succession of communist leaders from Lenin to Brezhnev. As we have noted in an earlier chapter, the 'developmental model' of state socialism had positive effects in Eastern Europe and the Third World immediately after the Second World War. But from the 1980s the rise of the capitalist South-East Asian economies such as Taiwan, Malaysia and South Korea provided an alternative for the developing societies of the Third World.

The economic model of state socialism did not fail absolutely; it fell relative to the world economy. In 1986 the USSR accounted for 12 per cent of world manufacturing production, coming third (after the USA and Japan) in the world ranking; China was fourth, and East Germany eighth.[62] Table 8.6 illustrates the relative decline in the 1980s. Until the 1980s, the ratio of growth rates was balanced between East and West Europe; in the period 1971–80, the ratio even favoured state socialism, East to West Europe being 1.13 and state socialist to capitalist core countries being 1.08 (see bottom of table). The 1980s, however, saw a considerable fall in growth rates and a decline in the ratio of state socialist to the capitalist core (0.86) and East to West Europe (0.70). The table also emphasizes the enormous success of the Chinese reforms: the middle part of the table shows consistent growth in the three successive periods (4.05, 5.7, 8.68). Even the Eastern European states still had respectable industrial growth rates: in the period 1980 to 1987, the USSR had an annual growth rate of industrial production of 3.7 per cent, East Germany 4.0 per cent, Romania 4.8 per cent, Poland 1.4 per cent and Czechoslovakia 2.8 per cent (China's was 12.6 per cent), comparing favourably with Germany (1 per cent), France (−0.5 per cent), the United Kingdom (1.3 per cent) and Italy (0.9 per cent) (the figure for the USA was 3.9 per cent).[63]

The state socialist societies had borrowed advanced technological processes and techniques from the core capitalist countries. They could not surpass them, but they had become industrial countries producing aircraft, computers, space satellites, advanced military equipment and electronic systems. In Wallerstein's terms, state socialism was not just a group of states on the 'periphery' of the world system. State socialism had the effect of moving Russia from the periphery 'into a much more core-like place'.[64] Undoubtedly, the level of technology stayed below that of the West and the 'technology gap' was not closing;[65] consequently one of the reform leadership's objectives was to join the world market in order to improve technological capacity. Whether the Soviet Union and the East

Table 8.6 Economic growth in the capitalist core and state socialist societies, 1961–1988

	Annual average real GNP growth rates (%)			Percentage change in growth rates		
	1961–70	1971–80	1981–8	1960s–1970s	1970s–1980s	1960s–1980s
Capitalist core[a]	4.95	3.20	2.62	−35	−18	−47
Western Europe[b]	4.75	3.0	1.79	−36	−40	−62
USA	3.8	2.95	3.02	−22	+2	−21
State socialist[c]	4.7	3.45	2.27	−26	−34	−51
Soviet Union	4.9	2.85	2.08	−41	−27	−58
Eastern Europe	3.85	3.4	1.26	−12	−63	−67
China[d]	4.05	5.7	8.68	+40	+52	+114
Comparative ratios state socialist to capitalist core	0.99	1.08	0.86	+9	−20	−13
East to West Europe	0.81	1.13	0.70	+40	−38	−14

[a] OECD countries (1976–80 also includes Israel, South Africa and non-OECD Europe).
[b] European Community.
[c] China, Eastern Europe, North Korea, Soviet Union, Yugoslavia.
[d] Gross domestic product continued to rise in China during the early 1990s – an average of approximately 8 per cent in 1990–3; *Financial Times*, 6 January 1996.

Source: *Economic Report of the President 1985–89* (Washington, D.C.: US Government Printing Office, 1989), cited in T. Boswell and R. Peters, 'State Socialism and the Industrial Divide in the World Economy', *Critical Sociology* 17:1 (Spring 1990), p. 7.

European states would join 'the core' of the capitalist world economy or fall into the periphery is an open question.

There is little evidence to suggest, moreover, that Asia's newly industrializing countries were *perceived* to be a threat or an alternative model to the political leadership. In my study of the opinions of 116 members of the Gorbachev elite, they were asked whether there was any foreign country which could be a model for the development of Russia. It is clear from the responses that the members of the political elite had no agreement about the country which could be used as a model. The most frequently cited country was China (15), followed by Scandinavia (13), Germany (12) and the USA (11).[66] By far the majority of the elite respondents (66) believed that Russia had to find its own way, and spontaneously declared that no other country could be used as a model. There was clearly no generally held vision of a movement to capitalism on the model of the Western countries. It is clear that the political elite had no clear, positive idea of the kind of society which it sought as a replacement for state socialism. Finding a 'Russian' path is a sure formula for muddling through. It is somewhat surprising that corporatist societies like South Korea and Taiwan received little recognition as possible ways forward. While the improvements in the newly industrializing countries of South-East Asia were certainly one of the arguments used to criticize the traditional communist leaders and were of concern to the political leadership, they were not really decisive.

In Eastern Europe, the image of the consumption effects of capitalism was a constant reminder of the comparative weakness of state socialism. The level of living standards in the West could not be bettered by the socialist states – they could only be copied by inferior models. It was the subjective evaluation of the West which was an important 'push' factor for reform. The artifacts of capitalism captured the minds of the people: the fulfilment of social and emotional needs was sought through the continual and renewed consumption of an infinite variety of goods and services. This expression of consumer society – symbolized by a supermarket mentality, television as mass media, the motor car as status symbol, rock music and sex as immediate gratification – were forms of cultural contamination that state socialism could neither match nor control. As a member of Democratic Russia put it in an interview with Marc Garcelon, 'In general, the program of the democrats in Russia for a very long time . . . was simply: "We'll make life here like it is in America." '[67] The 'cultural counterculture', with affinities to Western liberalism, also undermined ideology. The external environment of the society had a determinant influence over its values, forms of integration, means of political commitment and methods of adaptation. In a Marxist sense, the isolation of the Soviet bloc from the world economy had the appearance of a 'fetter' on the development of the productive forces. Military competition was also an intolerable drain on the resources of the USSR and the Eastern European countries. The time had come to join the capitalist core.

Capitalism's changing image

The capitalist world had also changed significantly. Between 1914 and 1945, world capitalism experienced two savage major world wars, structural unemployment, and autocratic and dictatorial rule culminating in fascism. The defeat of fascism in the Second World War discredited the political right, and socialist ideas – planning, the welfare state – were put into practice by many post-war European governments. From the late 1970s, however, the *democratic* aspects of capitalist society expressed in human rights, free elections and competitive political parties enhanced the image of capitalism.[68] A moral rearmament of capitalism took place: the USA cloaked its foreign policy in terms of human rights and the United Nations pursued 'peace keeping'. 'Capitalism' became a politically incorrect term and was supplanted by reference to pluralist and free democracies. These symbolic aspects of capitalism became more important in the foreign policy stances of Western leaders, particularly Jimmy Carter; investment, loans, trade and military help were increasingly tied to civil rights issues.[69] The transition from autocracy to democracy in South Africa, Spain, Portugal and eventually Argentina and Chile provided an alternative political scenario, not only to authoritarian capitalism but also to the bureaucratic formations of state socialism often negatively labelled as 'Stalinist'.[70] The latter was a generally less attractive proposition than the image portrayed of successful Western democracy. The spectre of capitalism – dynamic, rich, democratic and charitable – overburdened communism.

The advent of the political leadership of Ronald Reagan in the USA and Margaret Thatcher in the UK had brought with it a combative anti-communist rhetoric: the USSR was an 'evil empire' driven by Marxism-Leninism and intent on external expansion. Containment could only be achieved through confrontation and military superiority. In 1982, Reagan began his 'crusade for freedom' to liberate all people living under Marxist-Leninist regimes.[71] In his address to the British parliament in June 1982, he called for a 'global campaign for freedom . . . a plan and a hope for the long term – the march of freedom and democracy which will leave Marxism-Leninism on the ash heap of history'.[72] This was part of American policy to promote democratic change in both communist states and other authoritarian non-communist societies (such as South Africa). These aims were promoted by many agencies and means. Samuel Huntington lists the following: the National Endowment for Democracy, statements by the President, the broadcasts of Voice of America and Radio Free Europe/Radio Liberty, economic pressure and sanctions in many countries, negative votes and abstentions with respect to loans by multilateral financial institutions, diplomatic action, and material support for democratic forces funded through the CIA. This included support for Solidarity in Poland and insurgents in Chile in 1988, in Nicaragua in 1990, military action, including activity in Grenada, Panama, the Philippines and El Salvador (to deal with Marxist-Leninist insurgents), support of anti-communist forces in Afghanistan, Angola, Cambodia and Nicaragua. 'In effect, under Carter, Reagan, and Bush the United States adopted a democratic [sic] version of the Brezhnev doctrine: within its area of influence it would not permit democratic governments to be overthrown.'[73]

With respect to Eastern Europe and the Soviet Union, there were three aspects to this policy: 'a sustained attempt to achieve military superiority . . . a general militarization of the international arena . . . a massive "psychological" attack against the socialist community . . .'[74] This involved the development of space-based weapons, special forces to be used in East Europe and the exercise of economic sanctions through trade policy and advanced technology embargoes. In 1983 the Strategic Defence Initiative (SDI) was adopted to further American military superiority. Aid was promised to Eastern European states (such as Hungary and Romania)[75] as reward for movement away from Soviet influence.[76] A psychological war against the Soviet bloc was intended to prepare the people in capitalist countries for military action against the socialist states and to subvert the trust of the people there in their governments.[77]

Richard Pipes points out that the 'systematic policy of subverting the Soviet Union, largely through the use of the CIA' made a decisive contribution to the collapse of communism.[78] He argues further that SDI 'accelerated the decline' of the USSR and that CIA policy succeeded in persuading Saudi Arabia to lower oil prices, which severely affected Soviet foreign currency earnings, and that support to the Afghan partisans helped to defeat the USSR in Afghanistan,[79] which in turn exacerbated internal decay. In 1989, during the critical turn of events which led to calls for independence in the Baltic states, the US National Endowment for Democracy gave financial assistance to pro-Western groups in the Baltic republics, the Ukraine and the Caucasus.[80] To this one could add, as noted earlier, the subversion which took place in Cuba and Poland, and the success for the US of the policy of 'covert operations in Chile and Nicaragua'.[81]

It was under these ideological and political conditions that the reformers in the USSR sought to join the world community. Translated into different political terms, the international context of collapse is defined by Halliday as 'class struggle on an international scale'.[82]

The outward civil rights stance of American policy not only gave capitalism a democratic image but also had internal ramifications in the socialist countries. In signing the Helsinki Human Rights Agreement, Brezhnev legitimated Western individual rights as criteria for the conduct of practices in the states of Eastern Europe and the USSR.[83] As Schopflin has noted: 'The insistence on the introduction of human rights into the Helsinki process resulted in the slow but inexorable diffusion of the principle into Soviet-type politics and contributed qualitatively to weakening the legitimating force of Marxism-Leninism.'[84] The Conference on Security and Cooperation in Europe (CSCE) had moved 'from commitments to a limited number of human rights [in 1975] to endorsement of the full range of democratic liberties and institutions'[85] – democracy, political pluralism, the right to form political parties, and free and fair elections. Such rights were to become the first conditions for the acceptance of the socialist states in the world community and these policy positions defined the conditions on which the states of the socialist countries could join the global community. One direct consequence of this policy was the commitment of the reform government in Hungary to the right of people to emigrate. Thus they allowed the East Germans to move to West Germany through Hungary, so weakening the authority of the GDR.

The West as an ascendant capitalist class

Transitions from autocratic rule in countries with established markets and private property are usually seen to stem from endogenous forces in which the ascendant bourgeoisie plays an important contributory role. As Barrington Moore in his work on the origins of dictatorship and democracy has tersely put it: 'No bourgeois, no democracy.'[86] Moore, of course, was concerned with modern parliamentary-type 'bourgeois democracies' – not all forms of democracy are dependent on the formation of a propertied market class. The bourgeoisie has a stake in the institutionalization of private property, on which legal rational norms are based. Furthermore, a parliamentary type of democracy is dependent on a private entrepreneurial class whose interests are furthered by a limited state and, initially at least, representative parliamentary-type institutions. As Charles Lindblom has pointed out: 'The history of democracy is largely an account of the pursuit of liberty.'[87] The constitutional movement was the means by which the rising middle class of entrepreneurs and merchants sought to protect wealth, property and economic freedom from arbitrary state action. 'State capitalism' – as Cliff and others have pointed out – had no interest in furthering representative institutions, since coordination may be secured by the state apparatuses. Moreover, the leaders of the political class in the communist states would not support competitive elections and representative institutions, which might challenge the hegemony of the state through demands for individual rights and civil society. In the USSR, the 'new industrial and commercial bourgeoisie' under Gorbachev was exceedingly weak and played an insignificant role in influencing the reform process[88] and is generally discounted as a significant factor in the impetus for reform.[89]

Exogenous factors in transitions to democracy and markets are deemed by most writers to have played a minor role. Though acknowledging that international factors may 'condition and affect the course of transition', O'Donnell and Schmitter regard as 'fruitless' the search for 'some international factor or context' which 'cause[s] regimes to collapse'.[90] This position in general underplays external factors, not only in terms of the role of international corporations, but also the part played by the foreign policy of the metropolitan powers and international agencies, such as the IMF and the World Bank, whose purpose it is to influence economically the internal developments in countries to which they give loans. Focusing on the 'fluctuating cleavage between hard-liners and soft-liners'[91] evades the analysis of interests to which these actors are responding. The difference between the move to capitalism in the countries of southern Europe and Latin America and the post-communist societies is that in the latter there was no indigenous bourgeois class. Like the move to capitalism in Germany and Japan, in the USSR under Gorbachev a revolution was pursued from above. Gorbachev precipitated change not only in alliance with the intelligentsia, but with the support of the dominant exogenous forces of capitalism.

The leadership of both Gorbachev and Yeltsin (in the early period of his rule) was pushed into dependence on outsiders to support the move to a capitalist economy; this in turn intensified elite instability and further weakened solidarity. As a former adviser to Gorbachev has cogently put it:

> The task of [Gorbachev's foreign policy] was not to protect the USSR from the outside threat and to assure the internal stability but almost the opposite: to use relations with the outside world as an additional instrument of internal change. He wished to transform the West into his ally in the political struggle against the conservative opposition he was facing at home because his real political front was there.[92]

Ironically, perhaps, dependence was on Western powers who had sought to undermine the previous communist government and its political and economic order. The politically conservative leaders of the leading Western nations advocated a policy of competitive markets in the polity (parties and elections) as well as in the economy (privatized production for the market and profit, and money which would be negotiable in international markets). Both these policies clearly had implications for 'transition' in the USSR and Russia: the rise of parties and elections led to the break-up of the USSR; and a marketized form of exchange paved the way for the induction of Western products and capital and the exploitation of the indigenous labour force. The linkage with foreign interests provided the ballast in the process of capitalist transition – in the place of an indigenous bourgeois class or, as in early capitalism, a landed aristocracy with a commercial and bourgeois outlook. It is important here to note that there is no evidence to suggest that the previous dominant institutions (KGB, military, *nomenklatura*) performed a surrogate role for

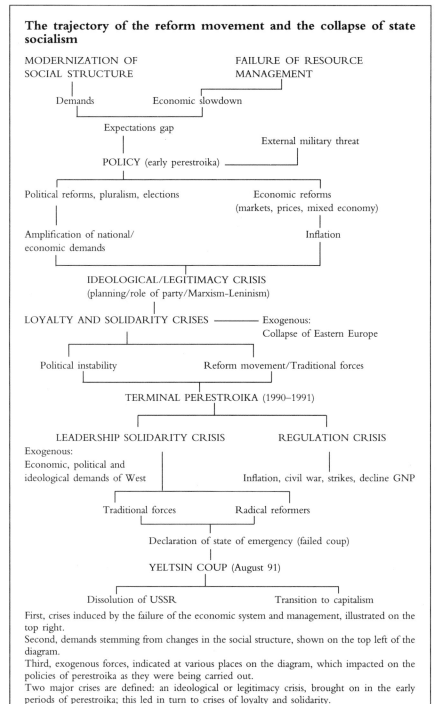

The trajectory of the reform movement and the collapse of state socialism

MODERNIZATION OF SOCIAL STRUCTURE

FAILURE OF RESOURCE MANAGEMENT

Demands   Economic slowdown

Expectations gap

External military threat

POLICY (early perestroika)

Political reforms, pluralism, elections

Economic reforms (markets, prices, mixed economy)

Amplification of national/ economic demands

Inflation

IDEOLOGICAL/LEGITIMACY CRISIS (planning/role of party/Marxism-Leninism)

LOYALTY AND SOLIDARITY CRISES ———— Exogenous: Collapse of Eastern Europe

Political instability   Reform movement/Traditional forces

TERMINAL PERESTROIKA (1990–1991)

LEADERSHIP SOLIDARITY CRISIS   REGULATION CRISIS

Exogenous: Economic, political and ideological demands of West

Inflation, civil war, strikes, decline GNP

Traditional forces   Radical reformers

Declaration of state of emergency (failed coup)

YELTSIN COUP (August 91)

Dissolution of USSR   Transition to capitalism

First, crises induced by the failure of the economic system and management, illustrated on the top right.

Second, demands stemming from changes in the social structure, shown on the top left of the diagram.

Third, exogenous forces, indicated at various places on the diagram, which impacted on the policies of perestroika as they were being carried out.

Two major crises are defined: an ideological or legitimacy crisis, brought on in the early periods of perestroika; this led in turn to crises of loyalty and solidarity.

the bourgeoisie. Therefore, if a necessary condition of bourgeois democracy is a bourgeoisie, it is clear why such a democracy has not developed in Russia and why Western interests are given such a prominent place in the views of the political elites.

The process of internal reform provides a classic case in which the radical reform leadership, first under Gorbachev and then under Yeltsin, sought a pact with foreign world actors to further its policy.[93] A consequence – in a state which had a relatively autarkic form of policy-making – was to amplify elite dissension. Under Yeltsin, transition involved the suppression of the former communist elite and later a physical assault on the legislative elite (in the Russian parliament), which is invariably the base of a 'democratic' transition. The dominant elite which emerged under Yeltsin in August 1991 was dependent in its strategy on creating an image of legitimacy to the leading countries of the West.

This was a consequence of his dependence on foreigners, on the importance of a 'demonstration effect' to the West to secure his legitimacy as a true reformer building a post-communist system with a bourgeois character. The implication for systemic collapse is that the political preferences and alliances of incumbent political elites are salient issues in understanding regime change. Moreover, demands on such leaders have to take into account the policy of dominant actors in the international arena who have their own political interests.[94]

The combination of systemic imbalances and the interplay of political leadership caused the fall. From a sociological point of view, Western policy impacted on values – freedom became a symbol of liberation; and on integration – community was replaced by competition. In the polity, competitive parties and civil society succeeded democratic centralism; in the economy, private ownership and the market were to supersede state ownership and a planned economy. The chart on p. 183 summarizes the impact of these various factors together with the sequence of events discussed in chapter 6.

Precipitants of Collapse: The Cumulative Effects

These confrontational policies of the Western powers *in themselves* did not cause collapse, as writers such as Pipes have argued. But they did have an important contributory effect in undermining the Soviet system and in motivating and supporting the kind of reform movement acceptable to the West.[95] The timing of the collapse was linked to the policy initiatives of the West. Rather than 'the match that set the fire alight', in Pipes's terms, it was the last straw that broke the camel's back. It is in the wider global context that these policies have to be evaluated. While the USSR remained a major world power claiming a quantitative gross national product and military capacity second only to the USA, the country in both internal and international affairs had experienced a steady decline. Since the end of the Second World War, the Soviet Union had lost its hegemony over the world communist movement, which itself was in disarray.[96] The non-ruling European communist parties were distancing themselves from identification with Soviet-type regimes, which had become an electoral handicap, and had adopted 'eurocommunist' social-democratic strategies.

Gorbachev, in formulating policy, was not only influenced by Margaret Thatcher and other Western leaders, but also by the heads of socialist and communist parties. In seeking a model for a revision of communism, he was no doubt influenced by eurocommunism and particularly by Felipe Gonzales (socialist premier of Spain), who was the 'foreign leader whom Gorbachev felt closest to' and with whom he had spent many hours discussing politics.[97] Gonzales, it will be recalled, had converted his party from Marxism to support for privatization, the free market and NATO and had also secured success at the polls. His policies have been described by the British conservative weekly *The Economist* as 'somewhat to the right of Mrs Thatcher's'.[98]

Within the communist bloc the Soviet mould of socialism had been openly challenged by diverse forces such as the Czechoslovak reform movement, Solidarity in Poland, and market reformers in Hungary and China. Even in the Soviet Union, the political leadership was aware of the decline in economic productivity and the weakness of the Soviet bloc in its competition with the advanced capitalist West – both in a military and an economic sense. In short, it was widely recognized that Marxism-Leninism was losing its credibility as capable of creating a sociopolitical system more advanced than capitalism. However, the position was not desperate. The Warsaw Pact had a well-equipped land army and was in possession of nuclear weapons. Economic growth was positive. The alternative capitalist system also had its own problems.

The political leadership under Gorbachev did have an alternative. It could have formed a bloc between reformist groups in the political class and the traditional supporters of state socialism: the working class. It could also have appealed to those likely to lose from a movement to the market, the armed forces, and to public employees, to retirees (a large and influential group, in support of state socialism) and to women. Marxism-Leninism still had some internal binding force; it could have been revised, as under Khrushchev. Another alternative would have been to have conducted a reform along the lines of that in China. This was widely expected in the West,[99] and – as we noted above – this policy had considerable support within the Soviet political elite. That Gorbachev did not do so must be explained in terms of the greater salience of the other forces we have discussed in this book.

It was under these circumstances that the confrontational policy of Ronald Reagan and Margaret Thatcher succeeded and led to President Bush's policy of 'beyond containment'. This was a final straw which led the Soviet leadership to abandon its traditional political policies in order at least to save what it could of state socialism and at best to create a new paradigm of communism. While the underlying forces of change created the conditions to which state socialism would have to adapt whatever leader was in power, Western policy precipitated the changes under Gorbachev: nothing less than a transition to a Western-type democracy with competing political parties and a market economy was demanded.

Perestroika was supported by the US government because it provided 'leverage to help move the Soviet Union in directions the United States wanted it to go'.[100] Gorbachev's objectives in the terminal period of the USSR were to secure support for his policy from the West, to end discriminatory trade restrictions and to facilitate integration into the world economic system. He responded to the West by abandoning the Brezhnev line of external socialist intervention in Eastern Europe, confirming this in his discussions with Bush in Malta in December 1989, by reducing Soviet military help to Third World countries, especially Nicaragua, and by unilateral disarmament. In February 1990, Gorbachev reversed policy on Germany and accepted reunification. The policy was hailed by George Bush as a 'triumph for "Western" democratic values'.[101] The Soviet Union and Eastern Europe gained some relaxation of controls on the import of technologies, but the West held out for internal changes before a 'normalization' of trade could take place. In June 1990, for instance, President Bush vetoed lending by the European Bank for Reconstruction and Development and other economic assistance until economic reforms were 'in place'.[102] In July 1991, the Group of Seven (the large industrially advanced states: USA, UK, Japan, Germany, France, Italy, Canada) at its special meeting with Gorbachev did not give the aid requested and full membership of the International Monetary Fund was not given. At the same time, President Bush made it clear that support for perestroika, for the 'new Soviet revolution', was dependent on 'real reform'.[103]

It was well understood in the West that the consequences of Gorbachev's position would lead to systemic collapse. Economic efficiency, Brzezinski pointed out,[104] needs competition, competition requires markets, and valorization requires private ownership. From this standpoint, perestroika would defeat communism.[105] To modernize the economy, the market called for political pluralism and this in turn entailed democracy. *Real* pluralism meant the autonomy of political activity in general, and competition between political parties in particular. A failure of the Communist Party was that it could not successfully enter into this competition. Thus the political market would lead to a representative-type democracy with interest groups and competing parties; the distinctive features of state socialism (the centralized Marxist-Leninist party and state planning) would be destroyed. To ensure a material basis to civil society, private property would have to be legitimated. When these were conceded, the Cold War was won by the West. It was not won by armed combat: the maturation of the ascendant intellectual acquisition class ensured a positive reception for these policies. The people voted down state socialism. Whether those who made revolution in this sense were to gain from it is another question.

The World of the Comrades: An Appraisal

What then is the significance of these momentous changes for the socialist project? It is unwarranted to evade the question by adopting the standpoint that the state socialist societies were not 'truly socialist'. As noted in the first chapter, socialism stands for many ideologies and movements and Bolshevism must be considered to be one of them, and in political terms the most influential. Socialism is a political movement and must be considered in its various political expressions.

A tradition in socialism has ended. While the prognosis of the Webbs that Soviet Russia was a 'new civilization' comparable to the shift in history from feudalism to the 'modern world'[1] seems a little hollow, state socialism survived the claims of capitalist critics that an industrial society could not operate without private property, competition and the market. As Richard Pipes has noted: 'Communism was, without a doubt, the most audacious and most determined effort in the entire history of mankind to reshape human nature and redesign human society.'[2] Whatever the social and political costs of the October Revolution, Western socialists took heart from the fact that economic growth and mass public welfare could be achieved through a system of planning. As C. B. Macpherson put it in 1965: 'it is now possible, as it was not possible in the heyday of capitalism, to conceive of a system in which high productivity does not require the transfer of powers from non-owners. Not only is it *possible* to conceive of such a system; it *has* been conceived, and is being attempted, in the socialist third of the world.'[3] In 1982, John Roemer echoed the sentiments of many commentators when he pointed out that *capitalist* exploitation had been eliminated under state socialism.[4]

Such an optimistic perspective has not been shared by many critics of state socialism. Already just after the 1917 revolution, Max Weber expressed his scepticism: he warned that 'the audacious Russian experiment would bereave socialism of its reputation and authority for a hundred years.'[5] Moreover, it was not only liberals and capitalists who were critical of the new society. By the fiftieth anniversary of the revolution, even Western Marxist writers who had supported pro-Soviet communist parties had seriously begun to doubt the achievements of Soviet power and its capacity to achieve socialist emancipatory goals. Harry Braverman in 1967 sums up the tenor of Western Marxists when he writes: 'the ebbing of the Soviet purpose to create a society of a distinctly new type is clear.'[6] Anthony Giddens, in the 1970s, pointed to the pernicious effects of exploitation under state socialism, where 'a system of political domination . . . has altered the character of social exploitation rather than in any sense diminishing it.'[7] By the 1980s, the economic, political and moral leadership of the Soviet Union and its model of socialism had been almost completely eclipsed. In 1983, Feher, Heller and Markus in their book, *Dictatorship Over Needs*, remark that the 'word socialism has . . . deservedly lost its reputation'.[8] By the middle of the 1990s, 'socialism', in its traditional and widely accepted sense of a movement which aims to 'create a "classless society" or, in one form or another, a "society of associated producers"',[9] had become a politically incorrect 'S' word. In this process the degeneration (and final collapse) of state socialism played an important part.

But however critical one may be of state socialism, its breakdown cannot be ignored or considered as irrelevant to the socialist project: its fall is not simply 'a step sideways'[10] rather than a step backwards. This line of reasoning considers the collapse of the state socialist regimes to herald a transition from state capitalism to multinational capitalism. Similarly, contemporary social-democratic commentators conflate socialism, social democracy and democracy: 'It is important to understand that Soviet-type systems [had] next to nothing in common with socialism as this was defined in the West . . . Socialism has traditionally involved commitment to equality, social justice, respect for the individual, widening choice and access to the decision-making processes that govern the life of a community.'[11] While it cannot be denied that the Soviet form of state ownership and control from a socialist standpoint had many deficiencies, these conclusions are not justified. Socialism, I noted in chapter 2 above, may be defined in terms of a set of ideological suppositions, as a political movement and as a post-revolutionary phenomenon. The denouement of state socialism has seriously weakened the first: beliefs are dismissed as irrelevant superstitions. As for the second, it has effectively destroyed the communist tradition. And as for the third, the pillars of political action, the Marxist-Leninist communist parties, have been demolished.

It is not only those on the triumphant right who recognize the true significance of the collapse of state socialism. For Fred Halliday, the collapse of such societies has been 'nothing less than a defeat for the Communist project as it has been known in the twentieth century and a

triumph of the capitalist'.[12] On a world basis, the collapse of the communist system and the recognition of its inadequacies have had a profoundly
negative effect on the quest for a socialist society. They have contributed
to the moral, intellectual and political disintegration of the left. As John
Saville puts it: 'Without question, there has taken place a major defeat of
the socialist idea and ideal . . . in many important matters we have indeed
to begin again, and the process in historical terms will be long and
bitter.'[13] The experience of state socialism, its failure – economically,
politically and morally – has lessons on which positive future policies may
be constructed.

I am not arguing here that these societies encapsulated an acceptable
form of socialism – the 'end product', as it were, of the socialist project
– and many of the criticisms ranging from Braverman to Callinicos are
well taken. But we must evaluate the objectives of these states and
consider the effects of their collapse in the terms of the movements for
radical reform which are replacing them. In doing so, we need not
idealize their past, but neither should we dismiss the advances which were
made or the objectives of the founders of the system. From their errors
may come new strategies and policies. What are the implications for the
'socialist idea and ideal'? What has been lost for the socialist cause by the
collapse of state socialism?

The World We Have Lost

State socialism put politics in command over the economy; it broke the
autonomous power of private capital. Its collapse has weakened the claim
that to meet human needs, collective political control can be superior to
the market. What has been put in question here is the idea that all persons
have a right to employment and an occupation, to contribute their labour
positively to society, and to receive as of right a comprehensive range of
social services, having their needs met collectively, in an economy organized without the necessity of a pool of permanently unemployed people
to provide 'motivation' to work. Furthermore, the fall of state socialism
has led to policies modelled on the views of Western conservatives
adopting a 'new right' philosophy: the privatization and denationalization
of publicly owned assets, the monetarization of health services, the introduction of a labour market with its consequent high levels of unemployment, the growth of excessive income differentials and of poverty,[14] the
weakening of the rights of women and, most important of all, the rise of
a capitalist class.[15] From a socialist perspective, this is undoubtedly a step
backwards not a step sideways.

Public ownership through the collective agency of the state has been a major component in the socialist project. It has been widely contended that only public ownership can provide the basis for the abolition of alienation of people from the means of production and thereby provide the basis for individual freedom and equality. It is also argued that a necessary condition for a democratic society is the control of economic power through public ownership in which the state – organized collectively – has a large role. In repudiating the role of the state to achieve social emancipation, the radical reformers of state socialism have undermined collective agency and replaced it with individualistic competitive activity. It should be made clear, however, that the denouement of state socialism does not rebuff the socialist arguments against rights for private property. Richard Pipes, for instance, has asserted that 'because the nationalization of all wealth was at the center of the communist program, it doomed communism to failure as well.'[16] In my discussion of the fall of the communist systems, there was no evidence that the *nationalization* of property was a cause of collapse. Had this been the case, state socialist societies would never have been able to survive in the first place, let alone for nearly three-quarters of a century. The ways public property has been organized and the effects of planning may be put under question, but the assertion of Macpherson, cited above, is not put in jeopardy.

State socialism and the ideology of Marxism-Leninism, however attenuated in practice, was predicated on the Marxist idea of class. The motivation for bringing about the Russian Revolution was inspired by class analysis and state socialism was instrumental in significantly changing the class structure. Class was a major component in the analysis of the trajectory of contemporary industrial society. The collapse of what were 'workers' states' and the theories which underpinned them has undermined such class analysis. In place of class is being put either an atheoretical empiricism or concepts of status, elite, national, environmental, gender and ethnic interests as a basis of political analysis. Fukuyama, for instance, has suggested that the context of class struggle, a central tenet of Marxist analysis, has been resolved in the liberal state.[17] The discussion in this book does not justify such a conclusion. Firstly, I have argued that an incipient bourgeoisie in the form of an 'acquisition class' played an important role in the collapse, and secondly, that capitalism has to be considered as a global system.

State socialism attempted, again in an uneven and inconsistent way, to encourage participation in society as a citizen, as a 'comrade'. It was assumed that conviviality and cooperative relationships would pertain between people. Ultimately, this should have entailed public control over the economy. The political value system endorsed public activity 'for the good of the cause'; it promoted altruism. Whatever the shortcomings of the system, these values have been repudiated. The world of the comrades is ended. The values of the societies now 'in transition' to capitalism minimize a collective contribution to society. The marketization of relationships weakens any altruistic commitment to and by society, except through private (and public) charity.

The system of state socialism should have operated on a commonality of interest between leaders and people: 'the unity of party and people', as the communist slogan put it. It must be conceded that personal and bureaucratic interests have driven these societies, not completely perhaps but enough to cast in doubt collectivism and cooperation as organizing principles. The fall of state socialism has reinforced the belief that a society cannot be organized on rational forms of collectivism and cooperation and that leaders cannot act altruistically on behalf of society. Forms of bureaucratic control have to be considered a major obstacle to public participation under socialism. Weber's distinction between purposive-rational (*wertrational*) action and instrumental-rational (*zweckrational*) action is appropriate here. The state socialist form of organization may be faulted in pursuing the latter and having insufficient mechanisms to ensure the former. This caused inadequacies in the mobilization and solidarity networks of society.

The communist states were atheistic in values. The idea of a secular society has been significant in many important components of the socialist tradition. One of the consequences of state socialism was the secularization of life and the support of the idea that people can have a human conscience independent of gods and religions. This view has been denied by the leaders of the reform movements and religion has been revived and legitimated as a system of values. As a result, the socialist ideal that human beings may not only understand but determine their life chances has been thwarted and an arena of mysticism and irrationality has once again been revived. To argue, however, that the absence of religion created a 'spiritual vacuum' which further weakened 'an already weak sense of communal allegiance'[18] does not entail that religion is indispensable. As Pipes rightly points out, religion avoids the comparison between 'promise and reality', 'comparisons which true religion avoids by relegating rewards to the next world'.[19] Why should not citizens be aware of the reality between what is promised and its fulfilment? The collapse of state socialism points to a failure in socialization. The leadership promised too much, too soon. Socialist education and the form of socialization in the family were inadequate and inappropriate. The family as an institution continued to reproduce access to intellectual (and social) assets. The social and political altruism of the early period of state socialism was replaced by a materialism which the system could not fuel. Socialism, which was traditionally steeped in a moral critique of capitalism, with time lost its bearings.

What has been lost in the fall of state socialism is the vision of an alternative social and political system to capitalism – that is the message of the 'end of history'. What gave state socialism its character and appeal was the fact that it was not just a variation of capitalism, but a different social system claiming to combine industrialism with rationality and equality. Socialists believe that there is no necessary contradiction between efficiency and social justice; society should (and can) be arranged to ensure both. No other political strategy of the twentieth century can compete with the Marxist-Leninist movement in this respect. In the place of a socialist critique of capitalism, the liberal reformers in the East European states seek a political and economic system modelled on market structures championed by the right. The possibility of within-system change, a Third Way, has been significantly diminished. What has been advocated and is being adopted in the process of transition in the post-Soviet societies is a dual system of power: a political assembly with a popular franchise and an economy with ownership[20] of assets responsive to a market. Such a system weakens the extent of political control and will in time result in a society driven by a capitalist class in control of the economy.

Most important of all perhaps, what has been weakened is public confidence in the possibility of the socialist project. A major cause of collapse was public disapproval. When given an electoral choice, people voted out state socialism and in so doing denied many of the values defined above. This had the effect of weakening faith in socialism, not only in the post-communist societies but also in the West. A word of caution is appropriate here: not all voted against the system and many who did so approved of the political stability it had brought and its welfare policies. The end of the Cold War has indeed liberated the peoples of Eastern Europe and the USSR in many ways, particularly with respect to individual rights and freedoms. In this respect those state socialist societies may be genuinely faulted. The leadership failed to keep pace with the demands of an urban, educated population. The system did not provide forms of intellectual expression and spiritual consumption required by the younger generation. The leadership was strapped in a straitjacket of traditional authoritarianism; as socialist critics argued, here we had a negation of principles. Whether such authoritarianism was an outgrowth of communism or had more traditional causes in the political cultures of these societies remains to be seen.

The fall of state socialism has buttressed the claims of writers such as Brzezinski[21] and Fukuyama[22] that communism, as a form of political and economic order, and Marxism, as theory, are finished. It has stimulated rightist critics, such as Pipes, in their view that societies cannot survive without private property and religion.[23] It has led to Dahrendorf's pronouncement: 'Socialism is dead.'[24] The collapse of state socialism, in my own view, does not justify these conclusions. It may also be premature to pronounce on history. It remains to be seen whether the revolutions in the post-communist regimes lead to a successful transition to stable liberal democracies and whether the state socialist societies will indeed move to capitalism, or whether history will propel them into a new form of socialism, or to a permanent state of retarded development. The question may also be posed of the infinite progress and prosperity of world capitalism. Not only the post-communist societies, but also India, Africa, South and Central America have still to make a successful transition to the stable, democratic, capitalist type of societies.

The failure of Leninism

While the collapse of state socialism may have cast doubts on the efficacy of the socialist movement, does it also mean that Marxism has failed? What is at issue, in the fall, is the Leninist interpretation of revolution and political strategy. Lenin, and even more so Mao and Castro, took a voluntarist approach: a socialist revolution could be started in a backward country, it could be led by a party of a new type and it would spread to the capitalist countries. In the absence of revolution in the advanced Western societies, the state socialist regimes attempted to outstrip the capitalist countries, to build socialism. This process was called by Western socialists such as the Webbs an 'experiment'. In this venture, socialism failed: but this is a crash of Bolshevism rather than Marxism. Contemporary writers often conflate Marxism as a theoretical doctrine with Bolshevism, which was a political movement and an institution of political power.

Where Bolshevism succeeded was in providing a model for breaking out of the stagnation of feudal or early capitalist regimes; it broke dependence on the metropolitan capitalist states. State socialism as a strategy of development has been relatively successful in initial periods of mobilization and industrialization. Leninism was a theory of revolution, and Marxism-Leninism became an ideology of development. This explains its appeal to countries of the developing world. To countries on the periphery, it provided an alternative: they would not be dependent on the metropolitan countries and could devote their resources to internal industrial development. In this respect, Marxism-Leninism has had some successes: rapid economic growth, a full-employment economy, a comprehensive welfare state, and enhanced military capacity expressed in the Second World War against fascism. In international affairs, the socialist bloc also provided a countervailing power to the hegemonic political and military ascendancy of the USA.

It is clear that state socialism was not able to compete economically with capitalism. On this critics such as Brzezinski are correct.[25] On Lenin's authority we may say that: 'In the final analysis the competition and struggle between capitalism and socialism will be resolved in favor of the system that attains a higher level of economic productivity.'[26] The material forces of state socialism remained at a lower level than in the West. Planning did not triumph over the market. The increasing globalization of capital and the expanding wealth of the capitalist states have proved too strong for the state socialist societies. State socialism did succeed in one way: it provided full employment and a universal system of welfare which have been positively evaluated by the population. Too much so, for public expenditure on welfare services and the production of consumer products could no longer match expectations. There were also important ramifications on the economy from the sphere of international relations: the US escalation of military confrontation under Reagan gave rise to burdens which could only be borne at an intolerable internal cost.

All the state socialist societies have been plagued by backwardness. Despite the mobilization effects of education and mass media, the general level of human and physical capital has not kept pace with their growth in the advanced Western states. Backwardness also infused the political culture of Bolshevism: Soviet collectivism and authoritarian control had their roots not just in Stalinism, but in the socioeconomic formation of pre-revolutionary Russia. The balance sheet of the socialist project contained serious and unjustified debits. Revolution led to arbitrary rule, tyranny and the horrors of Stalinism in Russia, to the famine of the Great Leap Forward and to the chaos of the Cultural Revolution in China. The 'export of revolution' to Eastern Europe was inappropriate as a socialist strategy (though it had advantages for the USSR): it led to dictatorship – quite the opposite of socialist democracy.

Modernization led to the collapse of social solidarity under the traditional type of communist party leadership. Lenin's 'party of a new type' suffered a crisis of legitimacy: it failed to meet the ideal aspirations of a more participant political culture. The political class, generated by administrative control, met its antithesis in an ascendant acquisition class, not a socialist one. In this context, class identification – a core tenet of Marxism – has been displaced by national identity; and religion has reasserted itself as a social focus.

The intellectual leadership of the world communist and socialist movement must also be faulted. It failed to generate an intellectual critique of the revitalization of the world capitalist system in its ideological, economic and military domains. Intellectual leadership in the East may also be faulted in respect of its capacity to define how socialism should develop after Stalinism. Perestroika was the last attempt to compete with capitalism on revised communist terms. It was a policy poorly thought out and hastily implemented. The inadequacy and the incompetence of the political leadership to cope with systemic imbalances was an important contributory factor in the collapse. Gorbachev's political alliance was made with the intelligentsia, which was seeking to undermine the political order. As Huntington pointed out in 1968, 'reforms directed at the urban middle class are a catalyst of revolution.'[27] Had the political leadership of Gorbachev supported reformist elements within the political class (including the military), and relied on support from the working class and those with positions in the public sector (such as teachers and health workers) and pensioners, there would have been an alliance which would have backed within-system reform and would have opposed a radical (and uncontrollable) move to the market and the privatization of assets. The reformers could have rallied support around the socialist principles of a welfare state, emphasizing the limitations of possessive individualism in securing comprehensive assurance.

China has adopted a course of economic change without political change. This has been successful in terms of economic growth and prosperity. In the short run, a similar policy would have secured time for the Soviet political leadership and it could have gradually moved to political reform. It has taken centuries to build the conditions for stable democracies in the West. The policy in China, however, cannot be considered a long-term strategy to maintain state socialism. The market reforms in China have made considerable inroads into the redistributive nature of the Chinese state and the current political leadership has little in common with what is traditionally regarded as a Marxist-Leninist state. The Communist Party adapted to the market and privatization and China is increasingly becoming like the autocratic regimes of the other Confucian 'little dragon' economies of South-East Asia. China too has a much less developed social infrastructure than the East European societies: it has a small intelligentsia and an impotent civil society. The Communist Party leadership may be transformed into one adopting a liberal ideology, legitimating a mixed type of multinational and state capitalism.

The failure of perestroika in the USSR was caused not only by internal forces but by exogenous ones. The terms of reform, of joining the world market, were determined by the West. The Soviet bloc has been confronted since its inception by hostile external states. Gorbachev encountered embargoes on the import of new technology; the socialist states faced not only an increasing military threat from the USA but also a Western mass culture which de-ideologized the younger generation. The Group of Seven states (particularly the USA) made it clear that a reformed communist society would not be admitted to the world market unless 'real reforms' took place: that is, political and economic competition in conditions of private property and the market. The Helsinki process endorsed Western principles of the rule of law, democracy, political pluralism, the right to form political parties and the necessity of free and fair elections. These external constraints put the leaders of state socialist societies under great pressure to put an end to the hegemony of the Communist Party and to the structure of an administrative-command economy. Thus the conditions of within-system reform coupled to participation in a global society were prescribed by the leaders of the West. The 'Third Way' attempted by Gorbachev led to collapse.

It must also be acknowledged that many people in the socialist states rejected the equalitarianism, collectivism, statism and central control which were associated with state socialism and which were a part of the socialist project. The social constituencies of support have waned. The generations socialized under the campaigns for socialist industrialization and in the Spanish Civil War and the Great Patriotic War have either passed away or have reached pensionable age. For the younger generation, people born after 1950, there was an aspiration, generated by their own government's promise of surpassing the affluence of the West, for prosperity and consumer choice. Unreconstructed party and state control led to the decline of the vitality of the political system. Individualism replaced collectivism, diversity was sought in place of uniformity, freedom for equality, private choice rather than public welfare.[28] The elective affinity between personal interest and communist ideology evaporated for the ascendant groups of intellectuals and professionals – the acquisition class – who fashioned the revolutions. There are clear parallels here with the changing political culture of Western states. Individualism, freedom, pluralism and civil society were widely held aspirations of opinion leaders among the ascendant 'intelligentsia' in state socialist societies and such opinions were shared by many (not all) of the population. Indeed, it is important to note that significant parts of the population supported distribution based on need, a strong role for government over the economy and a full-employment economy.[29] Ironically, while 'statism' was widely unpopular, state provision had come to be accepted. The strength of post-communist parties in Russia, Poland, Hungary, Bulgaria, Macedonia, Lithuania, Romania and Serbia[30] is witness to the fact that many people have suffered under the transition and were 'better off' under state socialism.[31]

The possession of individual intellectual assets (intellectual capital), for

those who had them, led to an identification with the market rather than
with collective property. It is again important to distinguish between
different groups in the population: the 'intelligentsia', in general, were
more in favour of a market-type society than the rest of the population;
studies have shown that those with higher education are more likely to be
opposed to state provision than those with lower levels.[32] Whereas state
socialism deprived the population of the ownership of physical capital
assets (property), these findings point to the ubiquitous influence of the
family as an institution which transmits differentially cultural capital. The
leaders of the reform movement sought to transform such personal intellectual assets into physical ones. But, in the final analysis, the communist
parties did not command support in elections. However unpalatable for
socialists, it must be accepted that people – particularly young people –
voted down state socialism. Whether the acquisition class, which made
the revolution, and the people who supported it will gain from it remains
to be seen.

Marx predicted these developments in the *Communist Manifesto* when
he wrote: '[The bourgeoisie] compels all nations, on pain of extinction, to
adopt the bourgeois mode of production; it compels them to introduce
what it calls civilisation into their midst, i.e. to become bourgeois themselves. In one word, it creates a world after its own image.'[33] It is worth
noting that Talcott Parsons and Karl Marx came to a common conclusion: one cannot have a 'socialist system' conjointly with another (capitalist) social system at a higher level of 'adaptive capacity' (Parsons) or with
a higher level of 'productive forces' (Marx). The historical mission of the
Bolsheviks has not led to the victory of socialism. Building 'socialism in
one country (or group of countries)' led to their exclusion from the global
order of capitalism. Initially, they were saved from the fate of peripheral
Third World countries and became a form of industrializing society. I am
not saying that state socialism did not work as a political and economic
system – it did; but it did not work well enough, it did not surpass
capitalism. The countries constituting state socialism have now 'joined
civilization': on this Karl Marx and Richard Pipes also have an area of
agreement.

The Challenge to Socialism

What then are the implications for socialist revolution as a means of
change? It is not the intention here to write a book on the future of
socialism. We may however note some of the major implications, even if
only in a negative way, of what the experience of state socialism may

contribute to the future. What the developments in Eastern Europe and the Soviet Union show for Marxism is that political voluntarism was not appropriate as a praxis of socialist revolution. The idea, reaching its climax in Maoism, that the vanguard Communist Party could seize power in a pre-capitalist country, introduce 'socialist' relations to the means of production and then develop the forces of production to a level higher than that of capitalism is now discredited. Underdeveloped countries independently cannot skip the capitalist mode of production. They might do so with the help and cooperation of the capitalist countries: but this is not a Marxist scenario. The concept of socialist revolution must be embedded in the context of the level of productive forces and the class formation in the advanced capitalist states of the West.

One positive result of the collapse of state socialism in the East for the socialist project is that 'existing' socialism will no longer be linked to countries emerging from pre-capitalist formations. The autocratic political culture and statism of Tsarist Russia made a weighty imprint on the Soviet model of state socialism. The power of the industrial ministries were a systemic feature which made within-system reform difficult for the communist parties to achieve.[34] The legacy of Stalinism – itself a product of underdevelopment – has been a millstone around the neck of socialism. When he linked the administrative-command system to the crimes of Stalin, Gorbachev learned to his cost that the latter were associated with the Leninist notion of a society led by state and party. In trying to cut free from Stalinism, Gorbachev went down with it. This heritage of Stalinism was perpetuated by Soviet interests in their domination over Eastern Europe, and the societies there became enveloped under Soviet hegemony as a consequence of war rather than a choice of socialist path. The imprint of the autocratic past which predated Stalinism may be deeper than current reformers and their advisers realize. The assumption, like that of the believers in Cargo Cults,[35] that the boat of capitalism will return all that was taken away and lacking under socialism may on examination turn out to be an empty one. Destroying the communist infrastructure will not necessarily liberate the people; it may lead to stagnation under conditions of dictatorship legitimated by fervent nationalism.[36]

Fukuyama is correct to see the collapse of communism as the failure of a major critique of capitalism. But this does not entail the end of history in the sense of major forms of human conflict. (After the 1905 revolution, Russia appeared to be stable – yet collapse followed in 1917. In 1985, state socialism was universally regarded as a permanent part of the political architecture, yet it disintegrated in 1989.) I have contended that Leninism, in its traditional form, is finished, the conditions which gave rise to it (at least in Europe) having gone away. In place of the Cold War there are now conflicts between the core and periphery, between the rich North and the impoverished South. Religion and nationalism, when driven by ambitious elites, are equally destructive. Inequality has not declined either in a distributional or relational sense, but rather it has changed in scope and in kind. Manifest struggle between classes may reappear not only in the post-communist societies but also in advanced Western ones. It is clear, however, that the possibilities for social change to a socialist form of society are no longer linked to the Leninist type of revolutionary strategy. Bolshevism is ended, not history.

The collapse of communism shifts the focus of socialism as an aspiration once again to the advanced capitalist West in the context of the globalization and internationalization of capital. Traditionally Marx developed the concept of capitalism in terms of the formation of a society and its state apparatus; this has now shifted to a global scale. Socialism, if it has a future, has to be global in character.

It must be acknowledged (as Fukuyama and Brzezinski suggest) that there is currently no effective alternative challenge to capitalism in terms of a counterculture or counterpolitical movement. Evaluation by the left of the 'prospects' for socialism is pessimistic. As Ralph Miliband put it: 'The liberation from capital is nowhere on the agenda of politics.'[37] As we noted in the second chapter of this book, as industrialization has progressed, as capitalism has developed, and as a consumer society has become widespread, the appeal of the socialist project has languished – this is a world-wide phenomenon.[38] While some of the 'outputs' of socialism are still positively evaluated – the provision of public services and employment – the economic system, linked to central planning, and the hegemonic state are not. The fall of Bolshevism may be simply another aspect of this general development. Classical socialism in Europe developed as a reaction of the emerging working class and intelligentsia to their feudal past as well as to capitalism. The class antagonisms of feudalism structured the relations to capitalism. As Walter Dean Burnham has tersely put it: 'No feudalism, no socialism.'[39] The non-socialist United States of America – once regarded as an 'exception' by the socialist left – may become the paradigm of politics in which a socialist strategy has to be rethought.

Unless a new paradigm of socialism is invented, the likelihood is that 'socialism' will be reduced to the issue-group politics of the (American) Democratic Party: that indeed would spell the end of history. Lenin provided the tactics and theory for seizing power in societies which lacked an internal dynamic to move to capitalism. We need a new *What Is To Be Done?* in conditions of post-industrial society, when the hegemony of capital becomes global and when the traditional instruments of change, the political party based on working-class consciousness, is no longer credible. Lenin also distinguished between reforming capitalism (a social-democratic objective) and reform as a strategy to transcend capitalism. In the latter sense, 'reforms are not to be contrasted to revolution.'[40] This approach is undoubtedly the only policy strategy open to the left at the end of the twentieth century.

There is an intellectual challenge: the socialist left needs to redefine its role. The revolutions in Eastern Europe have brought in their train a critique of reason, of human control over history. '[The end of communism] has brought an end not just to the nineteenth and twentieth centuries, but to the modern age as a whole . . . [Its] fall can be regarded as a sign that modern thought – based on the premise that the world is objectively knowable, and that the knowledge so obtained can be generalized – has come to a final crisis.'[41] This is a challenge. In Jürgen Habermas's view, '[The socialist left] can generate the ferment that produces the continuous process of political communication that prevents the institutional framework of a constitutional democracy from becoming dessicated.'[42] This position, which is shared by many writers today, involves 'socialism' becoming part of the radical democratic tradition: 'the task of the Left . . . [is] to deepen and expand [liberal-democratic ideology] in the direction of a radical and plural democracy.'[43] However, reviving and renewing 'constitutional democracy' applies to all parties – liberal, social-democratic and conservative – and groups, and the position occludes what a specific 'socialist' platform' might be. 'Pluralist' democracy has an appealing ring, but pluralism is democratic only if all participant groups in the plurality are equal in resources; if not, 'pluralism' legitimates the powerful interests and the disadvantage of the weak ones. Is it enough for a socialist to be a democrat? Liberals, conservatives, Christians and humanists also claim a democratic allegiance.

One answer is that a socialist type of democracy is not confined to the political domain, to 'parliamentary social-democracy'; it ought to include democracy in and over the economy. Such an extension of democracy would break the dual system of power which is characteristic of capitalism and can provide a form of control over the market. In addition to an extension of democratic policies, three other approaches inform a socialist critique. First is a critical appraisal of *capitalism*, which is marginalized at best and evaded at worst by current political movements stressing such issues as gender, race, nationality, and the environment. I am not saying that such issues are unimportant, but they have to be theorized within the context of the power relations of capitalism.[44] Second, a socialist praxis should indicate how a publicly owned and democratically controlled society would not 'dictate over needs' in the way that a capitalist market society does. It is commonplace to dismiss the 'Soviet experiment' because it took place in a backward country, but if 'socialism' had come to power in Western Europe, would it have survived better than in Eastern Europe? One might be sceptical. Michels's retort, 'Who says organization, says oligarchy,' has yet to be answered in the context of a socialist form of organization. Clearly, bureaucratic forms of domination, which are not dependent on ownership relations, need to be addressed by socialists. How does one ensure that bureaucracies pursue substantive rather than instrumental rationality? Thirdly, socialism has not only been a theory of society but also a political movement seeking political power. Lenin's innovation was to invent a 'party of a new type'. A challenge here is to devise a political movement which is international in scope, radical in objective and able to be an effective instrument of political power. This objective has eluded the revisions of socialism since the end of the Second World War, including both East and West Europe.

It is to the advanced capitalist societies of the West that Marxists must look for the dynamic of socialist social change. It is here that the productive forces are the most developed, the political culture the most mature. In doing so, post-Marxist analysis must take account, in more than a mechanistic way, of the changes which have taken place in world capitalism, in contemporary class formation (the lack of an ascendant class consciousness), in an ideological superstructure infused with bourgeois norms, and in the difficulty of controlling large-scale international bureaucratic organization. Capitalism is now truly an international world system and it cannot be analysed in units of single countries (or even groups of countries). As we have noted in this book, exogenous causes were important in the collapse of state socialism. The political hegemony of capitalism on an international basis makes it impossible for single countries to move to socialism or to combine markets with significant public ownership, as advocated by market socialists. Any movement to socialism requires a significant shift in global as well as in domestic politics. To concur that state socialism did not succeed neither refutes its aims nor denies the chance of future accomplishments. Socialist goals – of a classless society, of equality, of the absence of exploitation (of which economic exploitation is the essence), of the end of war, of democratic control, of a society governed by rationality, of social cooperation and solidarity – have not been compromised by the collapse of state socialism. Indeed, its fall brings these values into sharper focus.

Notes and References

Notes to the individual chapters also contain general references for their subject areas.

Chapter 1   Introduction

1 Richard Pipes at this time was Director of East European and Soviet Affairs in the US National Security Council.

2 See Raymond Tanter and Manus Midlarsky, 'A Theory of Revolution', *Journal of Conflict Resolution* 11:3 (1967), pp. 264–80, discussion of mass revolution, p. 265.

3 Theda Skocpol, *States and Social Revolutions* (Cambridge University Press, 1979), pp. 14–15.

4 Louis Gottschalk in a much earlier definition suggests that revolution is a 'popular movement whereby a significant change in the structure of a nation or society is effected. Usually an overthrow of the existing government and the substitution by another comes early in such a movement and significant social and economic changes follow.' Louis Gottschalk, 'Causes of Revolution', *American Journal of Sociology* 50:5 (1944), p. 4.

5 I use the term 'communist' states in a descriptive sense for states ruled by a self-defined communist party. In terms of their own theory, these societies were at the first (socialist) stage of communism. Communism is a mature classless society in which finally economic abundance would prevail and the state, as an instrument of oppression, would 'wither away'.

6 Gabriel A. Almond and G. Bingham Powell Jr, *Comparative Politics* (Little, Brown, 1966).

7 The Communist Information Bureau was set up in 1947. Its original members were representatives from the communist parties of Bulgaria, Czechoslovakia, France, Hungary, Italy, Poland, Romania, the USSR and Yugoslavia. Its main task was to coordinate and strengthen opposition to the capitalist states. In June 1948 the Yugoslavs were expelled as traitors. It was dissolved in 1956, by Khrushchev.

Chapter 2   The Socialist Project

1 For overviews of socialism see G.D.H. Cole, *A History of Socialist Thought* (5 vols, Macmillan and St Martins, 1956–60); Alexander Gray, *The Socialist Tradition: Moses to Lenin* (Longmans, 1946); Bhikhu Parekh (ed.), *The Concept of Socialism* (Croom Helm, 1975); Z. Bauman, *Socialism: The Active Utopia* (Allen and Unwin, 1976); R.N. Berki, *Socialism* (Dent, 1978); P. Beilharz, *Labour's Utopias: Bolshevism, Fabianism, Social Democracy* (Routledge, 1992); Norberto Bobbio, *Which Socialism? Marxism, Socialism and Democracy* (Polity Press, 1986). For a review of recent developments see Christopher Pierson, *Socialism and After: The New Market Socialism* (Polity Press, 1995); Anthony Butler, *Transformative Politics* (St Martin's, 1995).

2 F. Engels, 'Socialism; Utopian and Scientific', in K. Marx and F. Engels, *Selected Works in Two Volumes*, vol. 2 (Lawrence and Wishart, 1951), p. 107.

3 Political movements are not unambiguously labelled, as many self-styled social-democratic parties are of the 'hard' type (e.g. the Russian Social-Democratic Labour Party, which contained Lenin's Bolshevik faction) and many socialist parties are of the 'soft' type.

4 See F. Venturi, *The Roots of Revolution* (Weidenfeld and Nicolson, 1961); A. Walicki, *The Controversy over Capitalism* (Clarendon, 1969). African socialism of the 1960s was similarly backward looking, the assumption being that before the arrival of the European powers, the society was classless and communal. Socialism was rooted in traditional Africa. See David and Marina Ottaway, *Afrocommunism* (Holmes and Meyer, 1981), esp. ch. 2. On socialist movements in the Third World see Gordon White, Robin Murray and Christine White, *Revolutionary Socialist Development in the Third World* (Wheatsheaf, 1983).

5 V.I. Lenin, 'The Economic Content of Narodism', in Lenin, *Collected Works*, vol. 1 (Foreign Languages Publishing House, 1960).

6 Sidney Webb, in G. Bernard Shaw, *Fabian Essays* (Fabian Society and Allen and Unwin, 1931), p. 29; cited in Tom Bottomore, *The Socialist Economy* (Harvester, 1990), p. 14.

7 For a classic statement see C.A.R. Crosland, *The Future of Socialism* (1956; revised edn, Cape, 1963).

8 A survey of newly elected Labour Party Members of Parliament conducted in 1906 found that, when asked about the books or authors which had most influenced them, none mentioned Marx; the most frequent mention was John Ruskin, followed by the Bible and Charles Dickens. (Hence the party was often labelled as being more influenced by Methodism than Marxism.) In another survey in 1994, Marx came in fourth place, after Robert Tressell (author of the *Ragged Trousered Philanthropist*), R.H. Tawney and the Bible; see 'From Bevan to the Bible', *New Statesman and Society*, 30 Sept. 1994.

9 E. Bernstein, *Evolutionary Socialism* (1909; Schocken, 1961).

10 K. Marx and F. Engels, 'Communist Manifesto', in Marx and Engels, *Selected Works*, vol. 1 (Lawrence and Wishart, 1958), p. 60.

11 According to Leszek Kolakowski, the 'breakdown of Marxism' as a revolutionary strategy dates from the 1920s; cited by Pierson, *Socialism and After*, p. 55, who also has a good discussion of socialism's decline.

12 'Policy instruments' include modified forms of public ownership where efficiency, equality and the public interest require it. However, such policies are endorsed by non-socialist parties, such as the 'wet' wing of the Conservative Party, when industries are threatened with collapse.

13 The classical description is to be found in Werner Sombart, *Why Is There No Socialism in the United States?* (1906), reprinted with an introduction by Michael Harrington (Macmillan, 1976). See also S.M. Lipset, 'No Third Way', in Daniel Chirot (ed.), *The Crisis of Leninism and the Decline of the Left: The Revolutions of 1989* (University of Washington Press, 1991), pp. 209–12.

14 See for example, M. Jacques and S. Hall, *New Times* (Lawrence and Wishart, 1989).

15 On postmodernism see J.-F. Lyotard, *The Postmodern Condition* (Manchester University Press, 1984). For a critique of these trends see Alex Callinicos, *Against Modernism* (Polity Press, 1989).

16 The following are useful introductions to Marxism: E. Mandel, *Late Capitalism* (New Left Books, 1976); G.A. Cohen, *Karl Marx's Theory of History: A Defence* (Oxford University Press, 1979). For modern sympathetic though critical restatements of Marxism see Jon Elster, *Making Sense of Marx* (Cambridge University Press, 1985); John Roemer, *Analytical Marxism* (Cambridge University Press, 1986); A. Callinicos (ed.), *Marxist Theory* (Oxford University Press, 1989). For a critique see L. Kolakowski, *Main Currents of Marxism* (3 vols, Oxford University Press, 1978); K. Popper, *The Open Society and its Enemies* (Routledge, 1962). For a 'capitalist' critique of socialism see F.A. Hayek, *The Fatal Conceit* (Routledge, 1990).

17 On Marxism and socialism see particularly T. Bottomore, *Sociology and Socialism* (Wheatsheaf, 1984), and *The Socialist Economy: Theory and Practice* (Harvester, 1990); Bobbio, *Which Socialism?*

18 An alternative sequence is Asiatic–ancient–feudal–bourgeois–communist. Other modes have also been mentioned by Marxists: Oriental, ancient, Germanic, Slavonic – they need not detain us here. See U. Melotti, *Marx and the Third World* (Macmillan, 1977).

19 Adam Smith, *The Wealth of Nations*, introduced by Andrew Skinner (Penguin, 1986), p. 33.

20 In the *German Ideology* (vol. 1, section I C) Marx pointed out that a precondition for the development of communism was the abolition of the division of labour.

21 *Economic and Philosophical Manuscripts*, see David McLellan, *Karl Marx: Selected Writings* (Third Manuscript) (Oxford University Press, 1977), p. 89.

22 Engels, 'Socialism: Utopian and Scientific', p. 137.

23 An obvious example is the creation of mass unemployment and the under-utilization of capital during economic depressions.

24 On Lenin's thought see N. Harding, *Lenin's Political Thought* (2 vols, Macmillan, 1982); P. Corrigan, R.R. Ramsay and D. Sayer, *Socialist Construction and Marxist Theory; Bolshevism and its Critique* (Macmillan, 1978); D. Lane, *Leninism* (Cambridge University Press, 1981); V.I. Lenin, 'What is to be Done?', 'Imperialism: The Highest Stage of Capitalism', and 'The State and Revolution', all in *Collected Works*, vols 5, 22, 25 respectively (1961, 1964, 1969).

25 Marx and Engels, 'Communist Manifesto', p. 38.

26 A modern version of this theory is to be found in the writings of Immanuel Wallerstein, see particularly his *The Modern World Economy* (Cambridge University

Press, 1970); also Theda Skocpol, 'Wallerstein's World Capitalist System: A Theoretical and Historical Critique', *American Journal of Sociology* 85 (1977), pp. 1075–90.

27 See particularly V.I. Lenin. 'The Development of Capitalism in Russia', in *Collected Works*, vol. 3 (1960).

28 P.I. Lyashchenko, *History of the National Economy of Russia* (Macmillan, 1949), pp. 669–70.

29 For details of the growth and distribution of the working class see David Lane, *Politics and Society in the USSR* (Martin Robertson, 1978), pp. 24–6

30 L. Trotsky, *History of the Russian Revolution* (University of Michigan Press, 1967).

31 V.I. Lenin, 'Two Tactics of Social Democracy in the Democratic Revolution', in *Selected Works* (Foreign Languages Publishing House, 1936), vol. 3, pp. 35–6.

32 Ibid., p. 73.

33 L. Trotsky, *Results and Perspectives* (1907; New Park, 1962), p. 34.

34 'Russia and Revolution', cited by B. Knei-Paz, *The Social and Political Thought of Leon Trotsky* (Clarendon Press, 1978), p. 18.

35 Lenin, 'Imperialism: The Highest Stage of Capitalism', ch. 7.

36 Then, they continued, the common ownership of land (preserved in the *obshchina*) 'may serve as the starting-point for communist development', Preface to the 1882 Russian edition of the 'Communist Manifesto', in Marx and Engels, *Selected Works*, vol. 1, p. 24.

37 V.I. Lenin, 'What is to be Done?', edition in *Selected Works*, vol 1 (Progress Publishers, 1977), p. 178.

38 Ibid.

39 Its full name was Russian Social-Democratic Labour Party (Bolsheviks).

40 This quotation may be found in Engels's preface to the 'Communist Manifesto' written in 1888, in Marx and Engels, *Selected Works*, vol. 1, p. 28.

41 V.I. Lenin, 'The Tasks of the Proletariat in the Present Revolution', in *Collected Works,* vol. 24 (1964).

42 Ibid., emphasis in the original.

43 Cited by E.H. Carr, *The Bolshevik Revolution* (Penguin, 1950), vol. 1, pp. 94–5.

44 This date is in the Julian calendar still used by the Orthodox Church; in the Gregorian calendar, in use in the rest of Europe, the date was 7 November.

45 Lenin, 'The Tasks of the Proletariat'.

46 Detailed accounts of the October Revolution may be found in M. Ferro, *October 1917: A Social History of the Russian Revolution* (Routledge, 1980); E. Acton, *Rethinking the Russian Revolution* (E. Arnold, 1990); I. Deutscher, *The Prophet Armed: Trotsky, 1879–1921* (Oxford University Press, 1954); S. Fitzpatrick, *The Russian Revolution 1917–1932* (Oxford University Press, 1983); E.H. Carr, *The Russian Revolution from Lenin to Stalin* (Macmillan, 1980).

Chapter 3   State Socialism: The Soviet Model

1 There are a vast number of histories and commentaries on the formation of the USSR. For a comprehensive history see the multivolumed work by E.H. Carr, *A History of Soviet Russia* (Macmillan, 1954–78). For a shorter economic history see

Alec Nove, *An Economic History of the USSR* (Penguin, 1969). Interpretations include Seweryn Bialer, *Stalin's Successors: Leadership, Stability and Change in the Soviet Union* (Cambridge University Press, 1980); C.E. Black (ed.), *The Transformation of Russian Society* (Harvard University Press, 1960); John Kautsky, *Political Change in Underdeveloped Countries: Nationalism and Communism* (John Wiley, 1962); C.K. Wilber, *The Soviet Model and Underdeveloped Countries* (University of North Carolina Press, 1969); Sheila Fitzpatrick (ed.), *Cultural Revolution in Russia, 1928–1931* (Indiana University Press, 1978); David Lane, 'Leninism as an Ideology of Soviet Development', in E. de Kadt and G. Williams (eds), *Sociology and Development* (Tavistock, 1974); Alexander Dallin and George W. Breslauer, *Political Terror in Communist Systems* (Stanford University Press, 1970); Alex Inkeles and R.A. Bauer, *The Soviet Citizen* (Harvard University Press, 1959).

2 See Roger Pethybridge, *The Social Prelude to Stalinism* (Macmillan, 1974).

3 Petr Nikitich Tkachev (1844–85) advocated a socialist revolution through seizure of the state machinery; he also had ideas about the conspiratorial nature of a centrally led political party. He is often characterized as a forerunner of Lenin. See M. Karpovich, 'A Forerunner of Lenin: P.N. Tkachev', *Review of Politics* (Notre Dame, Indiana), no. 6 (1944).

4 Pethybridge, *The Social Prelude to Stalinism*, ·p. 15.

5 Yu.A. Polyakov, V.B. Zhuromskaya and I.I. Kiselev, 'Polveka Molchaniya', *Sotsiologicheskie Issledovaniya*, no. 7 (1990), p. 69.

6 John Maynard Keynes, *A Short View of Russia* (Hogarth Press, 1925), p. 12.

7 Sidney and Beatrice Webb, *Soviet Communism: A New Civilisation*, vol. 2 (Scribners, 1938).

8 Keynes, *A Short View of Russia*, p. 13.

9 Ibid., p. 17.

10 For a more detailed account see Lane, 'Leninism as an Ideology of Soviet Development'.

11 Taylorism is the theory of scientific management, involving the study of the work process and its division into separate compartments. Employees are taught to economize on effort and are usually paid on a piecework basis. The organization of work is hierarchical.

12 Wilber, *The Soviet Model and Underdeveloped Countries*, p. 182.

13 Data cited in ibid., p. 192. G.W. Nutter and D.R. Hodgman were American economists who regularly reported to the American Joint Economic Committee of Congress. F. Seton is an English economist specializing in Soviet economics. Hodgman's index was 67 per cent of the official Soviet index, Nutter's only 40 per cent. Hence the data cited here are relatively conservative estimates. For full details see ibid., pp. 190–2.

14 A. Gerschenkron, 'The Rate of Growth in Russia', *Journal of Economic History* 7 (1947), supplement, p. 166.

15 *Narodnoe obrazovanie v SSSR* (Moscow: 1957), p. 733.

16 Calculated on census data published in Polyakov et al., 'Polveka Molchaniya', p. 67.

17 Data based on Soviet and Western sources, cited in Wilber, *The Soviet Model and Underdeveloped Countries*, p. 166.

18 See C. Lane, *The Rites of Rulers: Ritual in Industrial Society* (Cambridge University Press, 1981).

19 Bialer, *Stalin's Successors*, p. 12.
20 Blanka Vavakova, 'Social Differentiation and Collective Consciousness', in Pierre Kende and Zdenek Strmiska (eds), *Equality and Inequality in Eastern Europe* (Berg, 1987), p. 273. This source has other comparative data for Poland and Czechoslovakia.
21 Outside the USSR, once the system spread, the position of priests depended on the country: in Poland, they suffered a slight decline and in Czechoslovakia a considerable fall.
22 See details in David Lane, *The End of Social Inequality* (Allen and Unwin, 1982), ch. 3, and Kende and Strmiska, *Equality and Inequality in Eastern Europe*.
23 See findings in Inkeles and Bauer, *The Soviet Citizen*.
24 James R. Millar, 'History, Method and the Problem of Bias', in Frederic J. Fleron and Erik P. Hofmann, *Post-Communist Studies and Political Science* (Westview Press, 1993), p. 184.
25 Pethybridge, *The Social Prelude to Stalinism*, p. 219.
26 See, particularly, Robert Conquest, *The Great Terror* (Macmillan, 1968); S. Swianiewicz, *Forced Labor and Economic Development* (Oxford University Press, 1965). Alexander Solzhenitsyn's work is almost exclusively concerned with the system of camp repression.
27 Barrington Moore Jr, *Social Origins of Dictatorship and Democracy* (Allen Lane, 1967), p. 418.
28 Gabriel A. Almond and G. Bingham Powell Jr, *Comparative Politics* (Little, Brown, 1966).

Chapter 4   The Growth and Spread of Communism

1 For concise overviews of the world communist movement see Stephen White, J. Gardner, G. Schopflin and Tony Saich, *Communist and Post-Communist Political Systems* (Macmillan, 1990); B. Szajkowski (ed.), *Marxist Governments: A World Survey* (Macmillian, 1981–), a three-volumed survey of communist states, with chapters on each country; Gordon White, Robin Murray and Christine White (eds), *Revolutionary Socialist Development in the Third World* (Wheatsheaf, 1983).
2 For an excellent discussion of this topic see Leslie Holmes, *Politics in the Communist World* (Clarendon Press, 1986), ch. 2.
3 World Bank, *World Development Report, 1981* (New York, 1981), cited by S. White, J. Gardner and G. Schopflin, *Communist Political Systems* (Macmillan, 1982), table 1.1.
4 For brief descriptions of these states see Holmes, *Politics in the Communist World*, and Szajkowski, *Marxist Governments*.
5 For an overview see David and Marina Ottaway, *Afrocommunism* (Holmes and Meier, 1981); for an interesting interpretation of socialism and underdevelopment, see Ken Post and Phil Wright, *Socialism and Development* (Routledge, 1989); for other useful accounts see G. White et al., *Revolutionary Socialist Development*.
6 On Eastern Europe see S. White et al., *Communist and Post-Communist Political Systems*; G. Schopflin, *Politics in Eastern Europe* (Blackwell, 1993); T. Rakowska-

Harmstone (ed.), *Communism in Eastern Europe*, 2nd edn (Manchester University Press, 1984).

7 On communism in Poland see A. Korbonski, 'Poland', in T. Rakowska-Harmstone and A. Gyorgy (eds), *Communism in Eastern Europe*, 1st edn (Indiana University Press, 1971), pp. 50–85; Schopflin, *Politics in Eastern Europe*; B. Kaminski, *The Collapse of State Socialism* (Princeton University Press, 1991); D. Lane and G. Kolankiewicz (eds), *Social Groups in Polish Society* (Macmillan, 1973); A. Brumberg (ed.), *Poland: The Genesis of a Revolution* (Vintage, 1983); Timothy Garton-Ash, *The Polish Revolution: Solidarity* (Coronet, 1985); A. Touraine, *Solidarity: Poland 1980–1981* (Cambridge University Press, 1983); Roger East, *Revolutions in Eastern Europe* (Pinter, 1992), which has summaries of developments in all the other Eastern European countries too.

8 Oscar Halecki (ed.), *Poland* (New York, 1957), p. 101.

9 Richard F. Staar, *Poland 1944–1962* (Louisiana, 1962), p. 72.

10 Data cited in B. Kaminski, *The Collapse of State Socialism* (Princeton University Press, 1991), p. 96.

11 World Bank, *World Development Report, 1988* (Oxford University Press, 1988), p. 253.

12 Ibid., pp. 258–9.

13 On the early history of Solidarity see Touraine, *Solidarity*, and Garton-Ash, *The Polish Revolution*.

14 A. Pravda, 'Poland 1980: From "Premature Consumerism" to Labour Solidarity', *Soviet Studies* 34:2 (1982) pp. 167–99, this figure cited p. 179.

15 David S. Mason, *Revolution in East-Central Europe: The Rise and Fall of Communism* (Westview Press, 1992), p. 29. This figure includes membership of the affiliated 'rural solidarity'.

16 Roman Laba, 'Worker Roots of Solidarity', *Problems of Communism* 35 (July–Aug. 1986), pp. 47–67, these data p. 53.

17 See the discussion in Kaminski, *The Collapse of State Socialism*, p. 107.

18 On five crises of development (identity, legitimacy, penetration, participation and distribution), see Gabriel A. Almond and G.Bingham Powell Jr, *Comparative Politics* (Little, Brown, 1966).

19 Carl Bernstein, in *Time*, 24 Feb. 1992, p. 28.

20 The US Central Intelligence Agency, through the American trade union movement (AFL-CIO), priests and American agents, financed Solidarity and provided crucial media supplies. Walesa was also briefed on American policy – the kind of policy it would support. The Poles, in turn, through spies in the Polish government, provided the Americans with internal decisions and information about communications with Moscow. See ibid.; see also the view of Pipes, chapter 8 below.

21 On communism in China see R.C. Thornton, *China: A Political History, 1917–1980* (Westview, 1982); H. Hinton, *An Introduction to Chinese Politics* (Praeger, 1978); S.R. Schram, *The Political Thought of Mao Tse-tung* (Penguin, 1969); J.I. Watson, *Class and Stratification in Post-Revolutionary China* (Cambridge University Press, 1984); J. Domes, *The Government and Politics of the PRC* (Westview, 1985); G. Young, *China: Dilemmas of Modernisation* (Croom Helm, 1985); J. Wang, *Contemporary Chinese Politics* (Prentice-Hall, 1986); F. Schurmann, *Ideology and Organisation in Communist*

China (University of California Press, 1968); F.C. Teiwes, *Politics and Purges in China* (M.E. Sharpe, 1979).

22 T.J. Hughes and D.E.T. Luard, *The Economic Development of Communist China 1949–1960*, 2nd edn (Royal Institute of International Affairs, 1961), p. 16.

23 Schurmann, *Ideology and Organisation in Communist China*, pp. 239–50.

24 Hughes and Luard, *The Economic Development of Communist China*, p. 148.

25 G. White, 'Chinese Development Strategy after Mao', in G. White et al., *Revolutionary Socialist Development*, p. 157.

26 Schurmann, *Ideology and Organisation in Communist China*, p. 157.

27 Charles, Hoffmann, 'Work Incentives in Communist China', *Industrial Relations* 3:2 (1964), p. 93.

28 Stuart R. Schram (ed.), *Authority, Participation and Cultural Change in China* (Cambridge University Press, 1973), p. 85.

29 Schram, *The Political Thought of Mao Tse-tung*, p. 105.

30 J. Gardner and W. Idema, 'China's Educational Revolution', in Schram, *Authority, Participation and Cultural Change*, p. 259.

31 Nick Eberstadt, *The Poverty of Communism* (Transaction, 1988), pp. 267, 131, 281. In a detailed study Eberstadt documents the decline of health and conditions during the Great Leap Forward. He also points out that other similar countries also had improvements without the costs experienced by China.

32 Eberstadt gives the lower figure, ibid., p. 114, and Domes, *The Government and Politics of the PRC*, gives the latter. A figure of 40 million for the period 1959–61 was estimated by Cong Jin of the National Defence University: 'The Horrors of Mao', *Washington Post National Weekly*, 1–7 Aug. 1994, p. 7.

33 *Washington Post National Weekly*, 1–7 Aug. 1994, p. 6.

34 On communism in Third World states, see Szajkowski, *Marxist Governments*; G. White et al., *Revolutionary Socialist Development*; Holmes, *Politics in the Communist World*. On Cuba and Latin America see J. Dominquez, *Cuba* (Harvard University Press, 1978); J. Dominquez (ed.), *Cuba: Internal and International Affairs* (Sage, 1982); C. Mesa-Lago, *Cuba in the 1970s* (University of New Mexico Press, 1978); J. del Aguila, *Cuba: Dilemmas of a Revolution* (Westview Press, 1984); S.B. Liss, *Marxist Thought in Latin America* (University of California Press, 1984); R. Gott, *Guerrilla Movements in Latin America* (Doubleday, 1972); S. Eckstein, 'Cuba and the Capitalist World Economy', in C. Chase-Dunn (ed.), *Socialist States in the World System* (Sage, 1982); Francis Lambert, 'Cuba: Communist State or Personal Dictatorship?', in Archie Brown and Jack Gray, *Political Culture and Political Change in Communist States* (Macmillan, 1977); Lee Lockwood, *Castro's Cuba, Cuba's Fidel* (Westview Press, 1990).

35 Robert G. Wesson, *Communism and Communist Systems* (Prentice-Hall, 1978), p. 96.

36 Ibid.

37 Fidel Castro, *Granma Weekly Review*, 26 July 1968, cited in Lambert, 'Cuba', p. 241.

38 William M. LeoGrande, 'The Communist Party of Cuba since the First Congress', in Stephen White and Daniel Nelson (eds), *Communist Politics* (Macmillan, 1986), p. 191.

39 Ricardo Carciofi, 'Cuba in the Seventies', in White et al., *Revolutionary Socialist Development*, p. 207.

40 Lockwood, *Castro's Cuba, Cuba's Fidel*, p. 227.

41 From the time of Kennedy, subversion of left-wing governments was a major component of American foreign policy. Military and economic help was given to America's allies in Guatemala, the Dominican Republic and Nicaragua. The USA intervened directly to bring down the elected governments in Grenada and Chile. On US activity in Chile, see James F. Petras and Morris M. Morley, *How Allende Fell* (Spokesman, 1994), esp. ch. 8 on 'US Military Activity, the Coup and the Military Regime'.

42 Eberstadt, *The Poverty of Communism*, pp. 269, 281.

43 Douglas W. Payne, 'Fidel Castro versus Perestroika, Report on the USSR', 12 Jan. 1990, Radio Free Europe/Radio Liberty, Munich, p. 7.

44 Ibid., p. 9.

Chapter 5   Movements for Market and Political Reform

1 See particularly Minxin Pei, *From Reform to Revolution: The Demise of Communism in China and the Soviet Union* (Harvard University Press, 1994); Gilbert Rozman with Seizaburo Sato and Gerald Segal (eds), *Dismantling Communism: Common Causes and Regional Variations* (Johns Hopkins University Press, 1992); Victor Nee and David Stark, *Remaking the Economic Institutions of Socialism: China and Eastern Europe* (Stanford University Press, 1989); Judy Batt, *East Central Europe from Reform to Transformation* (Pinter, 1991).

2 A. Nove, *The Economics of Feasible Socialism Revisited* (Allen and Unwin, 1991); Pranab K. Bardhan and John E. Roemer, *Market Socialism: The Current Debate* (Oxford University Press, 1993); W. Brus and K. Laski, *From Marx to the Market* (Clarendon, 1989); Christopher Pierson, *Socialism after Communism: The New Market Socialism* (Polity Press, 1995); Anders Aslund (ed.), *Market Socialism or the Restoration of Capitalism?* (Cambridge University Press, 1992); Robert E. Lane, *The Market Experience* (Cambridge University Press, 1991). For a defence of planning and abolition of the market under socialism, see Ernest Mandel, 'In Defence of Socialist Planning', *New Left Review*, no. 159 (1986), and 'The Myth of the Socialist Market', *New Left Review*, no. 169 (1988); D.M. Nuti, 'Market Socialism: The Model That Might Have Been But Never Was', in Aslund, *Market Socialism*; David Miller, *Market, State and Community* (Clarendon, 1990).

3 P.A. Samuelson and W.D. Nordhaus, *Economics* (McGraw-Hill, 1985), p. 234.

4 Oskar Lange, 'Marxian Economics and Modern Economic Theory', *Review of Economic Studies* (June 1935), pp. 68–87, this quote at p. 72.

5 Ibid., p. 81.

6 Ibid., p. 72n.

7 See Pierson, *Socialism after Communism*.

8 Just how 'public' or 'collective' ownership is organized is a matter of debate, see ibid., ch. 4.

9 J. Kornai, *Economics of Shortage* (2 vols, North Holland Publishers, 1980).

10 For useful articles on Yugoslav socialism, see R. Remington, 'Yugoslavia', in T. Rakowska-Harmstone (ed.), *Communism in Eastern Europe*, 2nd edn (Manchester University Press, 1984); Fred Singleton, 'Yugoslavia', in B. Szajkowski (ed.), *Marxist*

Governments: A World Survey (Macmillan, 1981); Martin Schrenk et al., *Yugoslavia: Self-Management Socialism and the Challenges of Development* (Johns Hopkins University Press, 1979); Harold Lydall, *Yugoslav Socialism: Theory and Practice* (Clarendon, 1984); Ellen T. Comisso, *Workers' Control under Plan and Market* (Yale University Press, 1979).

11 See Jim Seroka, 'Yugoslavia and the Successor States', in Stephen White, Judy Batt and Paul G. Lewis (eds), *Developments in East European Politics* (Macmillan, 1993), pp. 103–4.

12 For background on Czechoslovakia see H.G. Skilling, *Czechoslovakia's Interrupted Revolution* (Princeton University Press, 1976), and 'Czechoslovak Political Culture: Pluralism in an International Context', in A. Brown (ed.), *Political Culture and Communist Studies* (Macmillan, 1984); D. Paul, *Czechoslovakia* (Westview, 1981); Z. Suda, *Zealots and Rebels: A History of the Communist Party of Czechoslovakia* (HIP, 1980); Otto Ulc, 'Czechoslovakia', in Rakowska-Harmstone, *Communism in Eastern Europe*, 2nd edn, pp. 115–36.

13 Otto Sik, *Market and Plan under Socialism* (International Arts and Sciences Press, 1967), p. 362.

14 Ibid., p. 355.

15 See G. White, 'Chinese Development Strategy after Mao', in G. White, Robin Murray and Christine White (eds), *Revolutionary Socialist Development in the Third World* (Wheatsheaf, 1983).

16 Gordon White and Paul Bowles, 'The Political Economy of Financial Reform in China', *Journal of Communist Studies and Transition Politics* 10:1 (Mar. 1994), p. 81.

17 Nicholas R. Lardy, 'China: Sustaining Development', in Rozman et al. (eds), *Dismantling Communism*, p. 208.

18 Ibid.

19 Ibid., p. 219.

20 Ibid., p. 214.

21 Ibid., p. 209.

22 Figures cited in Pei, *From Reform to Revolution*, p. 63.

23 Ibid., p. 21.

24 White and Bowles, 'The Political Economy of Financial Reform', p. 89.

25 See Nina P. Halpern, 'Economic Reform and Democratization in Communist Systems: The Case of China', *Studies in Comparative Communism* 22:2–3 (1989), pp. 144–5.

26 See David Bachman, 'Institutions, Factions, Conservatism, and Leadership Change in China: The Case of Hu Yaobang', in Raymond Taras (ed.), *Leadership Change in Communist States* (Unwin Hyman, 1989), p. 94.

27 Pei, *From Reform to Revolution*, pp. 71–2.

28 Ibid., p. 58.

29 On early reforms see J.S. Berliner, 'Managing the USSR Economy: Alternative Models', *Problems of Communism* 32:1 (Jan.–Feb. 1983); M. Ellman, *Socialist Planning* (Cambridge University Press, 1989); E.A. Hewett, *Reforming the Soviet Economy: Equality versus Efficiency* (Brookings Institution, 1988); A. Nove, *The Soviet Economic System* (Unwin Hyman, 1986); Nove, *The Economics of Feasible Socialism*.

30 See Peter Rutland, 'The Shchekino Method and the Struggle to Raise Labour Productivity', *Soviet Studies* 36:3 (July 1984), pp. 345–65. On labour and productiv-

ity see David Lane, *Soviet Labour and the Ethic of Communism: Full Employment and the Labour Process in the USSR* (Westview Press, 1987).

31 Data cited in Patrick Flaherty, 'Perestroika and the Neo-Liberal Project', in Ralph Miliband and Leo Panitch (eds), *The Socialist Register 1991* (Merlin Press, 1991), p. 130.

32 See the report by T. Zaslavskaya and the account by P. Hanson, 'The Novosibirsk Report: Comment', *Survey* 28:1 (1984), pp. 83–108.

33 More detailed discussions of the period of perestroika may be consulted in Mikhail Gorbachev, *Perestroika: New Thinking for Our Country and the World* (Collins, 1987); Rachel Walker, *Six Years that Shook the World* (Manchester University Press, 1993); Michael Urban, *More Power to the Soviets: The Democratic Revolution in Russia* (Edward Elgar, 1990); Stephen White, *Gorbachev and After* (Cambridge University Press, 1991); Robert T. Huber and Donald R. Kelley, *Perestroika-Era Politics: The New Soviet Legislature and Gorbachev's Political Reforms* (M.E. Sharpe, 1991).

34 T. Zaslavskaya, *The Second Socialist Revolution: An Alternative Soviet Strategy* (Taurus, 1990). For an overview of Soviet Marxist developments see James P. Scanlan, 'From Samizdat to Perestroika', in Raymond Taras, *The Road to Disillusion* (Sharpe, 1992), pp. 19–40.

35 See Stephen F. Cohen and Katrina van den Heuvel (eds), *Voices of Glasnost* (W.W. Norton, 1989).

36 Adam Smith, *The Wealth of Nations* (Penguin, 1974), p. 44.

37 Raymond L. Garthoff, *The Great Transition: American–Soviet Relations and the End of the Cold War* (Brookings Institution, 1994), p. 377.

38 Ibid., p. 377.

39 Zaslavskaya, *The Second Socialist Revolution*, p. 14.

40 Ibid.

41 M.S. Gorbachev's report to the Nineteenth Party Conference, 30 June 1988.

42 For a convincing demonstration of this point see Stephen Whitefield, *Industrial Power and the Soviet State* (Clarendon Press, 1993).

Chapter 6   Chronology and Precipitants of Regime Collapse

1 For detailed discussion see Karen Dawisha, *Eastern Europe, Gorbachev and Reform: The Great Challenge* (Cambridge University Press, 1988); George Schopflin, *Politics in Eastern Europe* (Blackwell, 1993). A number of accounts of various societies may be examined in Stephen White, Judy Batt and Paul G. Lewis, *Developments in East European Politics* (Macmillan, 1993); Stephen Whitefield (ed.), *The New Institutional Architecture of Eastern Europe* (Macmillan, 1993); Gale Stokes, *The Walls Came Tumbling Down: The Collapse of Communism in Eastern Europe* (Oxford University Press, 1993); Linda Cook, *The Soviet Social Contract and Why It Failed* (Harvard University Press, 1994); Timothy Garton Ash, *We, The People: The Revolutions of '89* (Penguin, 1990); Michael Waller, *The End of the Communist Power Monopoly* (Manchester University Press, 1993). For details on individual countries see Richard F. Staar (ed.), *1990 Yearbook on International Communist Affairs* (Hoover Institution Press, 1990); Roger East, *Revolutions in Eastern Europe* (Pinter, 1992).

2 In the lower house, the Sejm, the Communist Party won 173 seats, Solidarity Citizens' Committee 161 and the United Peasant Party 76; in the upper house, the Senate, Solidarity won 99 seats out of 100, and an independent was elected to the remaining seat.

3 Schopflin, *Politics in Eastern Europe*, p. 235.

4 See John Higley and Jan Pakulski, 'Elite Transformation in Central and Eastern Europe', *Australian Journal of Political Science* 30 (1995), p. 14.

5 East, *Revolutions*, p. 8.

6 George Schopflin, 'The End of Communism in Eastern Europe', *International Affairs* 66:1 (1990), p. 11.

7 See Michael Mccgwire, *Perestroika and Soviet National Security* (Brookings Institution, 1991), p. 361.

8 For an authoritative discussion see Dawisha, *Eastern Europe, Gorbachev and Reform*, esp. ch. 7.

9 I have conducted 116 interviews with members of the Gorbachev political elite (people at the level of government ministers, first secretaries and heads of departments of the CPSU) and leading advisers and journalists. In answer to a question as to which groups and individuals had influence over foreign policy, nearly half (50) of the respondents thought that Western political leaders had had 'a great deal of influence', and another 51 believed that they had had 'some influence'. As to the influence of individual politicians, when asked to name 'just one of those leaders who was specially important', after Alexandr Nikolaevich Iakovlev (77 responses) came Margaret Thatcher (31), Edward Shevardnadze (26), then Ronald Reagan (18), George Bush (7) and Helmut Kohl (7). See David Lane, 'The Gorbachev Revolution: The Role of the Political Elite in Regime Disintegration', *Political Studies* 44 (1996), pp. 4–23.

10 Dawisha, *Eastern Europe, Gorbachev and Reform*, p. 224.

11 Mccgwire, *Perestroika and Soviet National Security*, p. 360. See also, Dawisha, *Eastern Europe, Gorbachev and Reform*, p. 220.

12 For an excellent overview of the Gorbachev era see Stephen White, *Gorbachev and After* (Cambridge University Press, 1993).

13 On the fall in living standards and the failure of perestroika see William Moskoff, *Hard Times: Impoverishment and Protest in the Perestroika Years* (M.E. Sharpe, 1993).

14 On the growth of a wealthy class see O. Kryshtanovskaya, 'The New Business Elite', in David Lane (ed.), *Russia in Flux* (Elgar, 1992), and on poverty and income distribution see A. McAuley, 'Poverty and Underprivileged Groups', in ibid.

15 Michael Ellman and Vladimir Kontorovich, 'The End of the Soviet System: What We Learn from the Insiders', Fifth World Congress, International Council for Central and East European Studies, Warsaw, 1995, pp. 27–8.

16 Adam Smith, *The Wealth of Nations* (Penguin, 1986), p. 39.

17 Ellman and Kontorovich, *The End of the Soviet System*, pp. 34–5.

18 Data cited by Mark R. Beissinger, 'Demise of an Empire-State: Identity, Legitimacy, and the Deconstruction of Soviet Politics', in Crawford Young (ed.), *The Rising Tide of Cultural Nationalism: The Nation-State at Bay?* (University of Wisconsin Press, 1993), p. 106.

19 Lane, 'The Gorbachev Revolution'.

20 *The Independent* (London), 17 May 1994 (p. 1). The US intervention, it is claimed

here, was crucial in defeating the coup. The information was derived from Seymour Hersh writing for the *Atlantic Monthly* (no date given). The role of *spetssluzhby* (special forces) was emphasized by other Russian respondents with links to the KGB interviewed in Moscow as part of my own research on political leadership.

21 See Lane, 'The Gorbachev Revolution'.

22 Valerie Bunce, *Do New Leaders Make a Difference? Executive Succession and Public Policy under Capitalism* (Yale University Press, 1981).

23 Higley and Pakulski, 'Elite Transformation in Central and Eastern Europe', p. 7.

Chapter 7 Explaining State Socialism

1 See particularly their influential book, C.J. Friedrich and Z. Brzezinski, *Totalitarian Dictatorship and Autocracy* (Praeger, 1966).

2 C.J. Friedrich, M. Curtis and B.R. Barber, *Totalitarianism in Perspective: Three Views* (Praeger, 1969), p. 136. Friedrich and Brzezinski's descriptive definition stressed the following features of a totalitarian society: an official ideology; a single mass party; terroristic police control of the population; a party monopoly of control over effective mass communications and the armed forces; and central direction and control of the entire economy and corporate entities.

3 Hannah Arendt, *The Origins of Totalitarianism* (Harcourt, Brace, 1966), p. 326.

4 Herbert J. Spiro, 'Totalitarianism', in *International Encyclopedia of the Social Sciences*, vol. 19 (Macmillan, 1968), p. 112.

5 Adam Westoby, *The Evolution of Communism* (Polity Press, 1989); Claude Lefort, *The Political Forms of Modern Society: Bureaucracy, Democracy, Totalitarianism* (Polity Press, 1986).

6 Westoby, *The Evolution of Communism*, p. 2.

7 Ibid., pp. 7, 8.

8 Jeffrey C. Goldfarb, *Beyond Glasnost: The Post-Totalitarian Mind* (University of Chicago Press, 1989), p. 4.

9 Ibid., p. 48.

10 Ibid., p. 39.

11 Ibid.

12 Ibid., pp. 215–16.

13 Ibid., p. 107.

14 Z, 'To the Stalin Mausoleum', *Daedalus* 119:1 (1990), pp. 300–1. This leaves the societal form undefined.

15 William Kornhauser, *The Politics of Mass Society* (Routledge, 1960), p. 123.

16 David Lane, *Politics and Society in the USSR* (Martin Robertson, 1978), pp. 323–4.

17 Richard Pipes, *Communism: The Vanished Specter* (Oxford University Press, 1994), p. 31.

18 Friedrich and Brzezinski, *Totalitarian Dictatorship and Autocracy*, p. 375.

19 Ibid., p. 282.

20 Tony Cliff, *Russia: A Marxist Analysis* (International Socialism, 1964), p. 106.

21 Ibid.

22 A. Callinicos, *The Revenge of History* (Polity Press, 1991), p. 16.

23 Cliff, *Russia*, pp. 110, 113.

24 Ibid.: the quote is on p. 159 and the above is based on pp. 155–61.

25 Callinicos, *The Revenge of History*.

26 Chris Harman, 'The Storm Breaks', *International Socialism*, no. 46 (Spring 1990), p. 35.

27 V.I. Lenin, 'The State and Revolution', in *Selected Works*, vol. 2 (Progress Publishers, 1977), p. 155.

28 Harman, 'The Storm Breaks', p. 82.

29 L. Trotsky, *The Revolution Betrayed* (New Park, 1945), p. 248.

30 Ibid., pp. 248–9.

31 E. Mandel, 'Once Again on the Trotskyist Definition of the Social Nature of the Soviet Union', *Critique*, no. 12 (1980).

32 Ibid., p. 20.

33 S. Meikle, 'Has Marxism a Future?' *Critique*, no. 13 (1981), p. 109. A good account of Ticktin's position may be gleaned from H. Ticktin, 'Socialism, the Market and the State', *Critique*, no. 3 (1974).

34 Hillel Ticktin, *Origins of the Crisis in the USSR* (M.E. Sharpe, 1992), p. 14.

35 Ibid., p. 10.

36 H. Ticktin, 'Towards a Political Economy of the USSR', *Critique*, no. 1 (1973), p. 22.

37 Ibid., p. 12.

38 Ticktin, *Origins of the Crisis*, p. 87.

39 I exclude here the work of J.K. Galbraith, *The New Industrial State* (Hamish Hamilton, 1967), who considered a dual convergence: for the efficient operation of the industrial system, he claimed, 'planning must replace the market' (p. 389).

40 P.A. Sorokin, *Russia and the United States* (Dutton, 1944), p. 26.

41 Talcott Parsons, 'Social Classes and Class Conflict in the Light of Recent Sociological Theory', in Parsons, *Essays in Sociological Theory* (Collier Macmillan, 1964), p. 333.

42 Talcott Parsons, *The System of Modern Societies* (Prentice-Hall, 1971), see ch. 7.

43 See Clark Kerr, *Industrialism and Industrial Man* (Penguin, 1962). The common features of industrial societies are discussed in Parsons's 'Characteristics of Industrial Societies', reprinted in C.E. Black, *The Transformation of Russian Society* (Cambridge University Press, 1960).

44 Parsons, *The System of Modern Societies*, p. 114.

45 Talcott Parsons, 'Communism and the West: The Sociology of the Conflict', in A. and E. Etzioni, *Social Change: Sources, Patterns and Consequences* (Basic Books, 1964), pp. 397–8.

46 D. Lane, *The Socialist Industrial State* (Allen and Unwin, 1976), p. 70.

47 Talcott Parsons, 'Evolutionary Universals', *American Sociological Review* 39:3 (June 1964), p. 356.

48 D. Bell, *The End of Ideology: On the Exhaustion of Political Ideas in the '50s* (Collier, 1961).

49 D. Bell, 'The "End of Ideology in the Soviet Union"', in M. Drachkovich, *The Appeals and Paradoxes of Contemporary Communism* (Praeger, 1966).

50 Galbraith, *The New Industrial State*, p. 390.

51 A. Inkeles and R.A. Bauer, *The Soviet Citizen* (Harvard University Press, 1959), p. 390. See also his 'industrial society' model: A. Inkeles, 'Models and Issues in the

Analysis of Soviet Society', in Inkeles (ed.), *Social Change in Soviet Russia* (Simon and Schuster, 1969), p. 431.
52 John H. Goldthorpe, 'Social Stratification in Industrial Society', in R. Bendix and S.M. Lipset, *Class, Status and Power* (Routledge, 1966).
53 Ibid., pp. 657–8.
54 See his 'Theories of Industrial Society', a paper given at the International Sociological Association's Seventh World Congress of Sociology, 1970, pp. 11–13.
55 A. Giddens, *The Class Structure of the Advanced Societies* (Hutchinson, 1973), p. 294.
56 Ibid.
57 Frank Parkin, 'System Contradiction and Political Transformation', *European Journal of Sociology* 13 (1972).

Chapter 8   The Fall

1 There are many books and articles 'explaining' the collapse; among the more important are the following: Z. Brzezinski, *The Grand Failure: The Birth and Death of Communism in the Twentieth Century* (Macdonald, 1989); Z, 'To the Stalin Mausoleum', *Daedalus* 119:1 (1990), pp. 195–344; Samuel P. Huntington, *The Third Wave* (University of Oklahoma Press, 1991); G. Schopflin, 'The End of Communism in Eastern Europe', *International Affairs* 66:1 (1990), pp. 3–16; Leslie Holmes, *The End of Communist Power* (Polity Press, 1993); Michael Waller, *The End of the Communist Power Monopoly* (Manchester University Press, 1993); Robin Blackburn (ed.), *After the Fall* (Verso, 1991); Ralph Miliband and Leon Panitch (eds), *Communist Regimes: The Aftermath* (*Socialist Register 1991*) (Merlin Press, 1991); D. Deudney and G.J. Ikenberry, 'Soviet Reform and the End of Cold War', in Frederic J. Fleron and Erik P. Hoffmann (eds), *Post-Communist Studies and Political Science: Methodology and Empirical Theory in Sovietology* (Westview Press, 1993), pp. 205–37; Daniel Chirot (ed.), *The Crisis of Leninism and the Decline of the Left: The Revolutions of 1989* (University of Washington Press, 1991); Alexander Dallin, 'Causes of the Collapse of the USSR', *Post-Soviet Affairs* 8:4 (1992), pp. 279–302; A.C. Janos, 'Social Science, Communism and the Dynamics of Political Change', *World Politics* (Oct. 1991), pp. 81–112; Ken Jowitt, *New World Disorder: The Leninist Extinction* (University of California Press, 1992); Richard Pipes, *Communism: The Vanished Specter* (Oxford University Press, 1994).
2 Here I follow a Parsonian approach; for a concise introduction see G. Rocher, *Talcott Parsons and American Sociology* (Nelson, 1974), pp. 63–7; T. Parsons, 'General Theory in Sociology', in R.K. Merton et al., *Sociology Today*, vol. 1 (Free Press, 1959).
3 Figure 8.1 is based on data from *Statisticheski ezhegodnik stran – chlenov soveta ekonomicheskoi vzaimopomoshchi 1988* (Moscow: 1988), pp. 25–35, and also the 1971 edition. See also the economic data collected by Central Intelligence Agency, *Handbook of Economic Statistics* (Washington D.C.: 1991). For a detailed study of economic decline during perestroika, see William Moskoff, *Hard Times* (M.E. Sharpe, 1993).
4 Minxin Pei, *From Reform to Revolution* (Harvard University Press, 1994), p. 21.
5 On the rise of corruption see Holmes, *The End of Communist Power*.

6 Nick Eberstadt documents the inadequacy of the Marxist-Leninist states in alleviating poverty: *The Poverty of Communism* (Transaction, 1988).
7 On the interdependence of motivational commitments and other subsystems, see David Lane, *Soviet Labour and the Ethic of Communism* (Wheatsheaf, 1987), p. 231.
8 Michael Ellman and Vladimir Kontorovich, 'Overview', in Ellman and Kontorovich (eds), *The Disintegration of the Soviet Economic System* (Routledge, 1992), p. 13.
9 A more detailed account is given in David Lane, 'The Roots of Political Reform: The Changing Social Structure of the USSR', in C. Merridale and C. Ward, *Perestroika: The Historical Perspective* (Edward Arnold, 1991), pp. 95–114. See also M.G. Field (ed.), *The Social Consequences of Modernisation in Communist Societies* (Johns Hopkins University Press, 1974); M. Lewin, *The Gorbachev Phenomenon* (University of California Press, 1988).
10 'Non-productive' refers to activity which does not lead to the production of any kind of physical commodity.
11 *Statisticheski ezhegodnik stran – chlenov soveta ekonomicheskoi vzaimopomoshchi* (Moscow: 1988), pp. 418–19.
12 *Narodnoe obrazovanie v SSSR* (Moscow: 1957), p. 733.
13 Of these, 15.5 million had higher education. Data from *Narkhoz v 1987g* (Moscow: 1988), p. 370.
14 The index of professional ('scientific') personnel per 10,000 nationals in 1989 was Russians 71, Armenians 70, Georgians 67, Estonians 61, Latvians 51, Lithuanians 44, Ukrainians 39, Belorussians 38, Azeri 29, Kazakh 23, Tadzhik 18, Moldavian 16, Uzbek 14, Turkmen 13, Tadzhik 12. (The Jewish people had an index of 424.)
15 For details of national/ethnic levels of education, occupation and language, see David Lane, *Soviet Society Under Perestroika* (Routledge, 1992), ch. 6.
16 Pei, *From Revolution to Reform*, p. 59.
17 Studies of émigrés, for example, showed a consistent pattern of changing support: in the 1980s, the young were much more critical of state socialism, whereas in the early post-war generation, youth had been more supportive; see J.R. Berliner, 'The Harvard Project and the Soviet Interview Project', in Fleron and Hoffmann, *Post-Communist Studies and Political Science*, pp. 177–82.
18 J.R. Millar, 'History, Method and the Problem of Bias', in Fleron and Hoffmann, *Post-Communist Studies and Political Science*, p. 187.
19 David S. Mason, 'Attitudes toward the Market and Political Participation in the Postcommunist States', *Slavic Review* 54:2 (Summer 1995), pp. 393–5. Mason points out that 'in many of these countries the new governments are dominated by the highly educated, because the revolutions swept into power intellectuals who had previously opposed the communist system.'
20 Jean-Charles Asselain, 'The Distribution of Incomes in East-Central Europe', in Pierre Kende and Zdenek Strmiska, *Equality and Inequality in Eastern Europe* (Berg, 1987). Taking the average workers wage as 1, in Poland the average salary of managers and white-collar workers dropped from 2.5 in 1938 to 1.2 in 1949, and in Hungary the differential of engineers and technicians fell from 3 to 1.99 and administrative personnel from 2.4 to 1.41 (ibid., p. 26). In Poland between 1931–2 and 1969, meat consumption fell from 47.5 kg (per capita per annum) to 44.9 kg for managerial and white-collar households, and rose from 33.8 kg to 49.5 kg for working-class households (ibid., p. 30 n12).

21 'KPSS v tsifrakh', *Partiinaia zhizn'*, no. 4 (1986), p. 8.
22 *Izvestiia Ts.K. KPSS*, no. 7 (Moscow: 1990), p. 140.
23 'KPSS v tsifrakh', pp. 23, 20.
24 *Vestnik statistiki* (Moscow: 1983), p. 61.
25 *Izvestiia*, 5 May 1989.
26 *Izvestiia*, 6 May 1989.
27 Ottorino Cappelli, 'Comparative Communism's Fall. The First Phase: "The Intelligentsia Revolution" of 1989–1990', *Harriman Institute Forum* 3:6 (June 1990), p. 2.
28 Cited in ibid., p. 3.
29 Ibid., p. 4.
30 On the loss of support of intellectuals in relation to the fall of the communist system, see G. Schopflin, *Politics in Eastern Europe* (Blackwell, 1993), pp. 227–30.
31 See John E. Roemer, *A General Theory of Exploitation and Class* (Harvard University Press, 1982), p. 238.
32 Ibid.
33 Anthony Giddens, *The Class Structure of the Advanced Societies* (Hutchinson, 1973), p. 294.
34 F. Feher, A. Heller and G. Markus, *Dictatorship over Needs* (Blackwell, 1983), pp. 18, 19, 31.
35 E.O. Wright, 'A General Framework for the Analysis of Class Structure', *Politics and Society* 13 (1984), p. 393. Here he uses the economists' concept of administration as being a factor of production and gives exploitation a different meaning from the Marxist notion. Exploitation in Marxism is the process in which surplus must be capable of use in the process of accumulation. The necessity to extract surplus labour and its use for accumulation is a dynamic of capitalism and it not only defines the boundaries of the capitalist class, but also explains the capitalist form of antagonism between ruling class and proletariat, and the tendency for absorption of all strata into one or other of these classes, necessitating the revolutionary transformation to socialism.
36 Furedi argues that the concepts developed in *Capital* are not appropriate to analyse Soviet society: F. Furedi, *The Soviet Union Demystified: A Materialist Analysis* (Junius, 1986), p. 83.
37 Rudolf Bahro, *The Alternative in Eastern Europe* (New Left Books, 1978). Political class has also been grasped by Zygmunt Bauman, 'Officialdom and Class', in Frank Parkin (ed.), *The Social Analysis of Class Structure* (Tavistock, 1974), pp. 129–48. However, he (like Bahro) emphasizes the top members of such groups, and does not consider, as here, the vertical stratification of the bureaucratic class. They also do not consider the crucial position of persons in ambiguous class positions. Bauman, for example, categorically denies that officialdom and class 'do not overlap' (p. 143).
38 Such exploitation is not illegitimate: it is 'socially necessary because it improves welfare'. Differentials of earnings (or levels of consumption) provide incentives and reward for the use of certain skills: the elimination of such inequality would lead to a 'retardation' in development; Roemer, *A General Theory of Exploitation and Class*, pp. 148, 240–2.
39 Haller and Mach, for instance, show that divergences between Austria and Poland may be caused both by different systemic features rooted in the political and economic orders, and by common factors such as level of economic development:

M. Haller, and B.W. Mach, 'Structural Changes in Mobility in a Capitalist and a Socialist Society: Comparison of Them in Austria and Poland', in M. Niessen and J. Peschar (eds), *International Comparative Research* (Pergamon, 1984), p. 53. Western comparative sociologists have endorsed similarities between capitalist and state socialist societies. Social mobility, for instance, has been held to have a 'basic' similarity in all industrial societies determined by the occupational division of labour; see for example, D.B. Grusky and R.M. Hauser, 'Comparative Social Mobility Revisited', *American Sociological Review* 49 (1984), and R. Erikson and J.H. Goldthorpe, 'Commonality and Variation in Social Fluidity in Industrial Nations', *European Sociological Review* 3:1 (May 1987), pp. 55–6.

40 For a discussion of the attitudes of the political elite, see David Lane, 'The Gorbachev Revolution: The Role of the Political Elite in Regime Disintegration', *Political Studies* 44 (Jan. 1996), pp. 4–23.

41 George Konrad and Ivan Szelenyi conflate the intelligentsia into the bureaucratic class. In their view, the state socialist system represented the rule of the intelligentsia: 'the transformation of the intelligentsia into a class, principally in the rational-redistributive economies, has indeed meant that in the industrially backward agrarian societies of Eastern Europe the intelligentsia, organized into a government-bureaucratic ruling class, has taken the lead in modernization, replacing a weak bourgeoisie incapable of breaking with feudalism' (*The Intellectuals on the Road to Class Power* (Harvester, 1979), p. 10). This position, it is argued here, ignores the conflict between the two class groups. Also, like the state capitalist theory, it does not show why a move to capitalism and the privatization of assets is necessary. In Wright's analysis, the intelligentsia is located in a contradictory class position and 'experts' and 'state bureaucrats' are seen as different groups vying for power; see Wright, 'A General Framework', pp. 402, 422 n46.

42 For details of the divisions within the government bureaucracy and their resistance to reform, see David Lane and Cameron Ross, 'Limitations of Party Control: The Government Bureaucracy in the USSR', *Communist and Post-Communist Studies* 27:1 (1994), pp. 19–38.

43 Millar, 'History, Method, and the Problem of Bias', pp. 186, 187.

44 See Mason, 'Attitudes toward the Market', esp. pp. 388–90. These conclusions are based on comprehensive interviews in the post-communist societies. His findings are discussed below, chapter 9.

45 David Lane and Cameron Ross, 'The Social Background and Political Allegiance of the Political Elite of the USSR', *Europe-Asia Studies* 46:3 (1994), pp. 452, 453–4. See also the discussion of the Russian parliament (RSFSR) under Yeltsin: David Lane and Cameron Ross, 'The Changing Composition and Structure of the Political Elites', in David Lane (ed.), *Russia in Transition* (Longman, 1995).

46 T.F. Remington, 'Regime Transition in Communist Systems', in Fleron and Hoffmann, *Post-Communist Studies and Political Science*, p. 278.

47 Ibid.

48 A political movement strongly in favour of radical reform and a move to the market, and hostile to the Communist Party.

49 Marc Garcelon, 'The Estate of Change: The Specialist Rebellion and the Democratic Movement in Moscow, 1989–1991', Kennan Institute, Washington, D.C., 1995, p. 13.

50 Ellman and Kontorovich, 'Overview', p. 26.

51 David Lane, 'Gorbachev's Political Elite', *Journal of Communist Studies and Transition Politics* 10:1 (Mar. 1994), p. 113.

52 J.J. Rousseau, *The Social Contract and Discourses* (Dutton, 1950), p. 6.

53 For a useful discussion see Agnes Heller, 'Phases of Legitimation in Soviet-type Societies', in T.H. Rigby and Ferenc Feher (eds), *Political Legitimation in Communist States* (Macmillan, 1982), pp. 45–63.

54 'Yakovlev on "Abyss" of Marxism', BBC World Broadcasts SU1197 B4, 8 Oct. 1991.

55 Quoted in Pei, *From Reform to Revolution*, p. 67, and Letter to Gorbachev from Ligachev, 17 Mar. 1990, reprinted in Yegor Ligachev, *Inside Gorbachev's Kremlin* (Pantheon, 1993).

56 Heller, 'Phases of Legitimation', p. 46.

57 See George Schopflin, 'Conservatism in Central and Eastern Europe', in J.M. Kovacs (ed.), *Transition to Capitalism?* (Transaction, 1994), pp. 187–204.

58 Mark R. Beissinger, 'The Rising Tide of Cultural Pluralism', in Crawford Young (ed.), *The Rising Tide of Cultural Pluralism: The Nation-State at Bay* (University of Wisconsin Press, 1993), p. 99. See also Mark Beissinger and Lubomyr Hajda, 'Nationalism and Reform in Soviet Politics', in Lubomyr Hajda and Mark Beissinger, *The Nationalities Factor in Soviet Politics and Society* (Westview Press, 1990), pp. 305–22.

59 Michael Walzer, *The Company of Critics: Social Criticism and Political Commitment in the Twentieth Century* (Basic Books, 1988), p. 88.

60 Andrew Walder, 'Career Mobility and the Communist Political Order', *American Sociological Review* 60:3 (June 1995), p. 324.

61 E. Gellner, *Culture, Identity, and Politics* (Cambridge University Press, 1987), p. 6.

62 Peter Dicken, *Global Shift* (Paul Chapman, 1992), p. 30.

63 Ibid., p. 22.

64 See Timothy W. Luke, 'Technology and Soviet Foreign Trade: On the Political Economy of an Underdeveloped Superpower', *International Studies Quarterly* 29:3 (Sept. 1985), p. 328.

65 Luke, 'Technology and Soviet Trade'.

66 These results include multiple answers.

67 Marc Garcelon, 'The Estate of Change', p. 30.

68 In practice, to achieve this democratic facade, hundreds of thousands of people with the complicity of the CIA were killed in countries such as Nicaragua, Chile and Indonesia, let alone in the civil wars in Korea, Malaya and Vietnam. Noam Chomsky, for example, points out that prior to the change in emphasis in American foreign policy, in Central America alone 200,000 people had been killed under regimes supported by the USA. By 1990, the association with such traditional coercive regimes had been renounced and the *Washington Post's* correspondent could write from Guatemala, 'For the first time, all five of the countries are led by presidents who were elected in contests widely considered free and fair'; Noam Chomsky, *Deterring Democracy* (Hill and Wang, 1992), pp. 216–17.

69 Concurrently, the West also pursued a policy of subversion. American policy involved CIA intervention in support of anti-communist insurgents in Chile, Guatemala, Indonesia, Cambodia, Angola and Nicaragua, and the invasion of Grenada.

70 In spite of the negative aspects of capitalist states, associated with enormous abuses of civil rights, the international media portrayed them in a more positive light and, as noted above, the development of these states was in the direction of civil rights, the market and democracy.

71 This policy was spelled out in National Security Decision 75 (Dec. 1982), which is still a classified document.

72 Cited in Raymond L. Garthoff, *The Great Transition: American–Soviet Relations and the End of the Cold War* (Brookings Institution, 1994), p. 11.

73 Huntington, *The Third Wave*, pp. 93–5.

74 Michael MccGwire, *Perestroika and Soviet National Security* (Brookings Institution, 1991), pp. 117–18.

75 In the United Kingdom, the Romanian autocratic leader and his wife were given a state welcome by the Queen of England.

76 See MccGwire, *Perestroika*, pp. 110–13.

77 Ibid., p. 118.

78 Richard Pipes, 'Misinterpreting the Cold War: The Hardliners Had It Right', *Foreign Affairs* 74:1 (1995), pp. 154–60, esp. p. 159. Pipes was an adviser to Reagan and probably knew the content of National Security Decision no. 75, though he relies on the evidence of Peter Schweizer, *Victory* (Atlantic Monthly Press, 1994).

79 He also reiterates CIA support for Solidarity in Poland.

80 Evidence is contained in a letter of Yazov, the Soviet Defence Minister, see Garthoff, *The Great Transition*, p. 395 n39. A secret Politburo document, referring to contacts between Soviet citizens and émigrés in the UK from the Baltic States, Radio Free Europe and others, expressed concern at activities of an anti-Soviet and anti-communist character; ibid., p. 396.

81 The communist states, of course, also engaged in ideological, economic and political subversion, with manifestly little success, in the stable Western democratic countries.

82 Fred Halliday, 'The Ends of Cold War', in R. Blackburn, *After the Fall* (Verso, 1991), p. 87.

83 State socialism had previously emphasized group and class rights rather than individual ones, which were (under the conditions of state socialism) claims against the state.

84 Schopflin, 'The End of Communism in Eastern Europe', p. 16.

85 Huntington, *The Third Wave*, p. 90.

86 Barrington Moore Jr, *Social Origins of Dictatorship and Democracy* (Allen Lane, 1967), p. 418.

87 Charles Lindblom, *Politics and Markets* (Basic Books, 1977), p. 162.

88 See Lane, 'The Gorbachev Revolution'.

89 See for example, Janos, 'Social Science, Communism and the Dynamics of Political Change', pp. 81–112; Russell Bova, 'Political Dynamics of the Post-Communist Transition', *World Politics* (Oct. 1991), pp. 113–39. Pei, *From Reform to Revolution.*

90 G. O'Donnell and P.C. Schmitter, *Transitions from Authoritarian Rule: Tentative Conclusions about Uncertain Democracies* (Johns Hopkins University Press, 1986), pp. ix, 18.

91 Ibid., p. 19.

92 Andrei Grachev, 'Russia in the World', paper delivered at annual conference of British National Association for Slavic and East European Studies, Cambridge 1995. p. 3.

93 See discussion in Richard Rose, 'Comparing Forms of Comparative Analysis', *Political Studies* 39:3 (1991), p. 462.
94 Higley and Burton's seminal article is concerned with *national elites* and ignores the international dimension; see John Higley and Michael G. Burton, 'The Elite Variable in Democratic Transitions and Breakdowns', *American Sociological Review* 54 (1989). On the role of US foreign policy as a catalyst of collapse in Eastern Europe, see Pipes, 'Misinterpreting the Cold War', pp. 154–60. Pipes is concerned more with economic and military collapse; the evidence here would point to ideological and elite dissension as well as policy formation.
95 MccGwire argues, for example, that 'the assumption that it was the confrontational policies of the Reagan administration that led to the Gorbachev revolution is not only wrong, it is dangerous' (*Perestroika*, p. 381). This line of argument is correct in pointing to the dangers of these policies.
96 For instance, international congresses of communist and workers' parties, organized by the USSR, had been boycotted by major ruling communist parties (Chinese, Vietnamese, North Korean and Albanian), and the resulting declarations had only been signed by 61 out of the 75 attending; see Stephen White, *Gorbachev and After* (Cambridge University Press, 1992), p. 192.
97 Andrei Grachev, *Dal'she bez menia: ukhod prezidenta* (Moscow: Kultura, 1994), p. 100; my thanks to Archie Brown for drawing my attention to this source.
98 *The Economist*, 11 Feb. 1989, p. 43, cited by S.M. Lipset, 'No Third Way', in Chirot, *The Crisis of Leninism*, p. 187.
99 Richard Pipes (Director of East European and Security Affairs for the US National Security Council in 1981–2), writing in 1984, expected this to be the most likely outcome; Pipes, *Communism*, p. 37.
100 National Security Review 3 (Feb. 1989), discussed by Garthoff, *The Great Transition*, p. 377.
101 Cited by Garthoff, *The Great Transition*, p. 407.
102 Ibid., p. 415.
103 Cited in ibid., p. 470.
104 Brzezinski, *The Grand Failure*.
105 See Z, 'To the Stalin Mausoleum', and Schopflin, 'The End of Communism in Eastern Europe'.

Chapter 9   The World of the Comrades: An Appraisal

1 S. and B. Webb, *Soviet Communism* (Scribner, 1938), vol. 2, see Epilogue.
2 Richard Pipes, *Communism: The Vanished Specter* (Oxford University Press, 1994), p. 53.
3 C.B. Macpherson, *The Real World of Democracy* (Clarendon, 1966), pp. 44–5.
4 John E. Roemer, *A General Theory of Exploitation and Class* (Harvard University Press, 1982), see pp. 238–42.
5 Cited by F. Feher, A. Heller and G. Markus, *Dictatorship Over Needs* (Blackwell, 1983), p. 299.
6 Harry Braverman, 'The Successes, the Failures and the Prospects', in L. Huberman and P.M. Sweezy (eds), *Fifty Years of Soviet Power* (M. R. Press, 1967), p. 24.

7 Anthony Giddens, *The Class Structure of the Advanced Societies* (Hutchinson, 1973), p. 294.
8 Feher et al., *Dictatorship Over Needs*, p. 299.
9 Tom Bottomore, *The Socialist Economy: Theory and Practice* (Harvester, 1990), p. 21.
10 Chris Harman, 'The Storm Breaks', *International Socialism*, no. 46 (Spring 1990), p. 82; Alex Callinicos, *The Revenge of History: Marxism and the East European Revolutions* (Polity, 1991), pp. 50–66.
11 George Schopflin, 'The End of Communism in Eastern Europe', *International Affairs* 66:1 (1990), p. 3.
12 Fred Halliday, 'The Ends of Cold War', in Robin Blackburn (ed.), *After the Fall* (Verso, 1991), p. 86.
13 John Saville, 'The Communist Experience: A Personal Appraisal', in Ralph Miliband and Leo Panitch (eds), *Communist Regimes: The Aftermath* (*The Socialist Register 1991*) (Merlin, 1991), p. 7.
14 See Alistair McAuley, 'Poverty and Inequality', in David Lane (ed.), *Russia in Transition* (Longman, 1995).
15 The privatization of property gives rise not only to an entrepreneurial bourgeoisie, but also to a state capitalist one. The move from state socialism is as much to state capitalism as to private capitalism.
16 Pipes, *Communism*, p. 61. By private property, socialists have in mind, not the nationalization of 'all wealth', but the public ownership of the means of production – physical assets which are utilized for the extraction of surplus value. Private possessions are not under threat from socialist forms of nationalization.
17 F. Fukuyama, *The End of History and the Last Man* (Avon, 1992), p. 65.
18 Pipes, *Communism*, p. 62.
19 Ibid.
20 Ownership may take the form not only of private ownership but also of state capitalist ownership.
21 Zbigniew Brzezinski, *The Grand Failure* (Macdonald, 1990).
22 Fukuyama, *The End of History*.
23 Pipes, *Communism*, pp. 56–64.
24 R. Dahrendorf, *Reflections on the Revolution in Europe* (Chatto and Windus, 1990), p. 38.
25 See Brzezinski, *The Grand Failure*, ch. 22.
26 Cited in S. Bialer, 'Gorbachev's Program of Change: Sources, Significance, Prospects', *Political Science Quarterly*, no. 103 (Autumn 1988), p. 410.
27 S. Huntington, *Political Order in Changing Societies* (Yale University Press, 1968), p. 369.
28 For a useful comparative analysis see Christopher Pierson, *Socialism after Communism: The New Market Socialism* (Polity Press, 1995), part I.
29 See David S. Mason, 'Attitudes toward the Market and Political Participation in the Postcommunist States', *Slavic Review* 54:2 (Summer 1995), esp. pp. 388–90. These conclusions are based on comprehensive interviews in the post-communist societies.
30 See for details John T. Ishiyama, 'Communist Parties in Transition', *Comparative Politics* 27:2 (Jan. 1995), p. 157; 'Electing to Turn Back the Clock', *Transition* 1:4, 29 March 1995; '1994 Overview', *Transition* 1:1, 30 Jan. 1995. Most of these parties,

including the Russian ones, are more social democratic in orientation, supporting competitive elections and different forms of property.

31 Numerous surveys of popular opinion have shown these trends, for example, in December 1993 a majority of people polled in Russia, Ukraine and Belarus claimed they had been 'better off' under socialism. RFE/RL Research Report, vol. 2, no. 24, Munich, 11 June 1993.

32 Mason, 'Attitudes toward the Market', p. 393.

33 'Communist Manifesto', in K. Marx and F. Engels, *Selected Works in Two Volumes*, vol. 1 (Lawrence and Wishart, 1958), p. 38.

34 On political culture see Stephen White, *Political Culture and Soviet Politics* (Macmillan, 1979), esp. ch. 2. On the role of the ministries see Stephen Whitefield, *Industrial Power and the Soviet State* (Clarendon Press, 1993).

35 These are known in Melanesia where it is thought that ancestors will return bringing with them cargoes of precious goods (including Western consumer ones); they will also liberate the people from their oppressors and ensure an era of happiness and plenty.

36 Brzezinski notes this possibility but ends his book triumphantly predicting that 'democracy . . . will dominate the twenty-first century'; *The Grand Failure*, p. 258.

37 Ralph Miliband, *Socialism for a Sceptical Age* (Polity Press, 1994), p. 188. See also Saville, 'The Communist Experience'; S.M. Lipset, 'No Third Way', in Daniel Chirot (ed.), *The Crisis of Leninism and the Decline of the Left* (University of Washington Press, 1991). Even a positive evaluation of 'market socialism' leads Christopher Pierson to conclude: 'I doubt that market socialism offers in itself a convincing solution', see *Socialism After Communism*, p. 221.

38 For a useful discussion of factors in its decline see Pierson, *Socialism After Communism*, part I.

39 Cited by Lipset, 'No Third Way', p. 208.

40 See discussion in Huntington, *Political Order in Changing Societies*, p. 365.

41 Vaclav Havel, address to World Economic Forum, Davos 1992, cited by Pipes, *Communism*, pp. 75–6.

42 J. Habermas, 'What Does Socialism Mean Today?', in Robin Blackburn, *After the Fall* (Verso, 1991), p. 45.

43 Ernesto Laclau and C. Mouffe, *Hegemony and Socialist Strategy* (Verso, 1995), p. 176.

44 Otherwise, pursuit of policies, such as whether women should be able to join the US marines, deflects attention from the major forces of political power.

Index

Index by Judith Lavender